高职高专国际商务应用系列教材

外贸单证操作与实训指导

WAIMAO DANZHENG CAOZUO YU SHIXUN ZHIDAO

周文苑　编著

清华大学出版社
北　京

内容简介

本书依据高职高专教育的特点和培养目标，强调理论的实用性并立足专业技能的培养，按照《外贸单证实务与操作》的章目编排，共分为三大部分：第一部分是跟学做单项能力训练，共14个项目；第二部分是独立完成综合制单实训，共8个项目，涵盖了目前国际贸易中的主要结汇方式和贸易术语；第三部分是基础理论与知识综合训练，提供5套综合训练试题。

本书特别适用于外贸单证实务等课程的课堂教学与实训，可作为全国国际商务单证员考试用书，也可作为外贸从业人员的参考用书。

图书在版编目(CIP)数据

外贸单证操作与实训指导/周文苑编著．—北京：清华大学出版社，2019(2022.1重印)
(高职高专国际商务应用系列教材)
ISBN 978-7-302-52240-9

Ⅰ.①外… Ⅱ.①周… Ⅲ.①进出口贸易—原始凭证—高等职业教育—教材 Ⅳ.①F740.44

中国版本图书馆CIP数据核字(2019)第018398号

责任编辑：陈凌云
封面设计：刘艳芝
责任校对：刘　静
责任印制：沈　露

出版发行：清华大学出版社
网　　址：http://www.tup.com.cn，http://www.wqbook.com
地　　址：北京清华大学学研大厦A座　　**邮　　编：**100084
社 总 机：010-62770175　　**邮　　购：**010-62786544
投稿与读者服务：010-62776969，c-service@tup.tsinghua.edu.cn
质量反馈：010-62772015，zhiliang@tup.tsinghua.edu.cn
印 装 者：三河市少明印务有限公司
经　　销：全国新华书店
开　　本：185mm×260mm　　**印　　张：**15.75　　**字　　数：**378千字
版　　次：2019年7月第1版　　**印　　次：**2022年1月第2次印刷
定　　价：48.00元

产品编号：069405-02

前　　言

外贸单证实务是一门实践性很强的课程。虽然近年来国际商务单证员等相关培训认证已广泛推行，但有针对性的实训材料较少。本书作为《外贸单证实务与操作》的配套实训用书，力求使学生在学好教材的同时有针对性地进行训练，达到巩固、强化的目的。

本书的编写具有如下特点。

1. 时效性强

本书是作者在《外贸单证实务与操作》的基础上，依据国际商务单证员的业务规格和要求，结合最新的国际惯例如《跟单信用证统一惯例——2007 修订本》(国际商会第 600 号出版物，简称 UCP 600)、《2010 国际贸易术语解释通则》(*International Rules for the Interpretation of Trade Terms 2010*，Incoterms® 2010)以及我国最新政策编写而成。本书采用的单证材料和案例是外贸公司最新的实际业务资料，力求贴近实际。

2. 单证真

书中所有单证都是来自外贸公司的实例，力求让读者接触到最新、最真实的外贸单证业务。除了对客户名等内容进行了改编外，其他内容全部保留。

3. 题型全

书中既有常用术语中英文互译的基础训练，又有大量选择题、判断题等与历年单证考试真题形式与内容一致的理论习题训练，还有针对单证缮制的单项技能训练和单证操作综合技能训练，方便学员根据自身需求选择。

4. 针对性强

本书一方面按照主教材《外贸单证实务与操作》的框架编排习题，另外也考虑国际商务单证员、国际商务操作员、跟单员等各类职业资格考试的需求，以各类考试的内容和题型为基础，并有所侧重。本书可作为全国国际商务单证员资格认证考试的参考教材，帮助学生取得相应的资格证书。目前，各高等职业院校都非常重视培养学生获取职业资格证书的能力，本书对于准备参加各类国际商务单证员考试的人员来说是一本很好的参考书。如果能结合主教材《外贸单证实务与操作》进行学习，效果更佳。

本书为 2015 年苏州市优秀新课程研究项目(项目名称：外贸单证实务)的成果。

在本书的编写和出版过程中，得到了很多同事、朋友以及有关外贸公司领导的大力支持与帮助。同时，本书也汲取了许多同行专家的教研思路与经验成果，在此一一表示感谢。由于编者学识水平、实践经验有限，书中难免存在纰漏与错误，恳请读者与专家批评指正。

周文苑

2019 年 1 月

目　　录

第一部分　跟学做项目单项能力训练

第二部分　独立完成综合制单实训

第三部分　基础理论与知识综合训练

第一部分

跟学做项目单项能力训练

项目一　单证员工作任务分析

一、常用术语中英文互译

1. 单证____________　　2. 正本____________

3. 副本____________　　4. 签字单据____________

5. FOB ____________　　6. CIF ____________

7. CFR ____________　　8. Documents ____________

9. In duplicate ____________　　10. Original ____________

二、单项选择题

1. 狭义的单证是指(　　)。
   A. 文件和凭证　　B. 单据和文件
   C. 单据和信用证　　D. 信用证和凭证
2. 在信用证业务中,有关当事方处理的是(　　)。
   A. 服务　　B. 货物　　C. 单据　　D. 其他行为
3. 信用证项下,受益人向客户收取货款的凭据是(　　)。
   A. 实际货物　　B. 与信用证规定相符的全套单据
   C. 买卖合同　　D. 客户保函
4. 在国际商务单证缮制的基本要求中,(　　)是单证工作的前提。
   A. 正确　　B. 整洁　　C. 及时　　D. 简明
5. 关于各种单据的出单日期,下列表述正确的是(　　)。
   A. 保险单的出单期可以晚于已装船提单的出单期
   B. 提单签发日可迟于信用证或合同规定的最迟装运时间
   C. 通常汇票是议付单据中出单时间最晚的单据
   D. 议付单据中,发票日期一般比其他单据晚
6. 按照贸易双方涉及的单证划分,出口单证不包括(　　)。
   A. 商业发票　　B. 汇票　　C. 信用证　　D. 产地证
7. 金融单据又称资金单据,是指(　　)。
   A. 汇票、发票、付款收据　　B. 汇票、支票、本票
   C. 发票、提单、保险单　　D. 汇票、发票、提单
8. UN/EDIFACT 标准将国际贸易单证分为(　　)大类。
   A. 九　　B. 四　　C. 两　　D. 五
9. 根据联合国设计推荐使用的货币代码,下列表述不正确的是(　　)。
   A. CNY90.00　　B. GBP90.00　　C. USD90.00　　D. RMB90.00

10. 信用证支付方式下，银行处理单据时不负责审核(　　)。
A. 单据与有关国际惯例是否相符　　B. 单据与信用证是否相符
C. 单据与国际贸易合同是否相符　　D. 单据与单据是否相符

三、多项选择题

1. 单证工作主要有(　　)等方面的内容，它贯穿于进出口合同履行的全过程。
A. 归档　　B. 制单　　C. 审单　　D. 交单
2. 国际商务单证的工作意义包括(　　)。
A. 它是国际结算的工具　　B. 它是经营管理的重要环节
C. 它代表了一笔交易的本质　　D. 它是政策性很强的涉外工作
3. 外贸单证工作具有(　　)等特点，必须仔细、认真、及时地做好这项工作。
A. 工作量大　　B. 涉及面广　　C. 实践性强　　D. 要求高
4. 下列关于单证"整洁"的表述，正确的有(　　)。
A. 单证的表面清洁、美观、大方
B. 单证内容清楚、易认
C. 单证格式的设计和缮制标准规范
D. 更改处加盖校对章或简签
5. 出现(　　)情况，开证行有权拒付票款。
A. 单据内容与信用证条款不符　　B. 实际货物未装运
C. 单据与货物有出入　　D. 单据与单据之间不符
E. 单据内容与合同条款规定不符
6. 按单证的用途划分，下列选项中，(　　)是商业单据。
A. 发票　　B. 装箱单　　C. 报关单　　D. 汇票
7. 货运单据即各种方式运输单据的统称，包括(　　)。
A. 装运通知　　B. 海运提单　　C. 报关单　　D. 船舱证明
E. 空运单
8. 对单证管理提出的两大基本要求是(　　)。
A. 应该依据贸易合同对信用证的条款进行逐项审核
B. 建立完备的单证管理制度
C. 对不利于受益人的条款，应该及时联系申请人通过开证行修改
D. 通过分析，提高单证工作的质量和效率
9. 在国际贸易中使用 EDI 的现实意义有(　　)。
A. 降低经营成本及费用　　B. 速度快，时效性强
C. 准确率高，差错率少　　D. 节省时间，提高企业管理水平
10. 多套单据的审单方法包括(　　)。
A. 按装运日期审单法　　B. 纵横审单法
C. 按地区客户审单法　　D. 先数字后文字审单法

四、判断题

1. 在国际结算中，货物是贸易双方进行结算的基础和依据。　　(　　)

2. 从商业观点看，CIF 合同的目的不是货物本身，而是与货物有关单据的买卖。（　　）

3. 单证的处理必须符合国家相关外贸法规和制度。（　　）

4. 单证“三相符”中，最主要的是“单货相符”。（　　）

5. 制单原则中所说的“及时”不仅指按适当日期及时出单，还包括及时向银行交单。（　　）

6. 信用证、贸易合同、商业发票、产地证都属于出口单证。（　　）

7. 按单证的用途，可将单证划分为商业单据和银行单据。（　　）

8. 标准化唛头由发货人的简称、参考号、目的地和件号构成，不得使用几何或其他图形。（　　）

9. 使用国际标准或代码时，货币代号由三个英文字母组成，前两个代表国名，后一个代表货币。（　　）

10. 使用国际标准或代码时，地名代码 CNSH 表示中国上海，USNY 表示美国纽约，GBLON 表示英国伦敦。（　　）

五、简答题

1. 国际商务单证工作的基本要求有哪些？

2. 简述国际商务单证的分类。

3. 制作和审核出口单据的主要依据是什么？

六、技能操作题

1. 苏州恒润贸易有限公司向法国新城贸易有限公司出口某产品 500 箱，已知收货人代号为 JQL，目的地为 Osaka Japan，参考号为 01-368-98。请根据以上条件制作标准化唛头。

2. 请用联合国设计推荐使用的国际标准化地名代码表示“伦敦”“上海”“纽约”。

项目二　国际贸易合同签订与条款分析

一、常用术语中英文互译

1. 合同____________________　　2. 进出口________________________

3. 销售确认书______________　　4. 价格__________________________

5. Amount _________________　　6. Article ________________________

7. Destination ______________　　8. Time of delivery ________________

9. Time of payment __________　　10. Time of shipment _______________

二、单项选择题

1. 根据《联合国国际货物销售合同公约》(以下简称《公约》)规定,合同成立的时间是(　　)。

A. 接受生效时　　B. 交易双方签订书面合同时

C. 在合同获得国家批准时　　D. 当发盘到达受盘人时

2. 下列条件中,(　　)不是构成发盘的必备条件。

A. 发盘的内容必须十分确定　　B. 主要交易条件必须十分完整、齐全

C. 向一个或一个以上特定的人发出　　D. 表明发盘人承受约束的意旨

3. 议付就是(　　)。

A. 贴现　　B. 出口押汇　　C. 交单　　D. 托收

4. 某公司向欧洲某客户出口一批食品,于3月16日发盘,限3月20日复到有效。3月18日接对方来电:"你方16日电接受,希望在5月装船。"该公司未提出异议,于是(　　)。

A. 这笔交易达成　　B. 须经该公司确认后交易才达成

C. 属于还盘,交易未达成　　D. 属于有条件地接受,交易未达成

5. 下列函电表述中,构成一项有效发盘的是(　　)。

A. 请改报装运期10日复到有效

B. 你15日电每公吨30英镑20日复到

C. 你15日电可供100件参考价为每件8美元

D. 你15日电接受,但以D/P替代L/C

6. 按照《公约》规定,发盘(　　)。

A. 可以撤销但不能撤回　　B. 可以撤回但不能撤销

C. 既不能撤销也不能撤回　　D. 既可以撤回也可以撤销

7. 一般而言,制单的程序是(　　)。

A. 先缮制汇票,然后按汇票内容分别缮制其他单证

B. 先缮制发票,然后按发票内容分别缮制其他单证

C. 先缮制装箱单,然后按装箱单内容分别缮制其他单证

D. 先缮制提单,然后按提单内容分别缮制其他单证

8. 我国进口货物运输保险可分为预约保险和逐笔保险两种方式。买方采用逐笔保险方式一般是在(　　)。

A. 进口数量较大时　　B. 进口数量不大时

C. 进口产品贵重时　　D. 进口产品廉价时

9. 按一般情况,在交易磋商过程中,如果受盘人对发盘表示有条件的接受,则意味着(　　)。

A. 接受有效　　B. 合同成立

C. 合同生效　　D. 构成还盘

10. 我国有权签订对外贸易合同的主体是(　　)。

A. 自然人　　B. 法人

C. 法人与自然人　　D. 自然人或法人且须取得外贸经营权

三、多项选择题

1. 根据《公约》规定,一项已生效的发盘不能撤销的条件是(　　)。

A. 发盘规定了有效期

B. 发盘未规定有效期

C. 发盘中明确规定该发盘是不可撤销的

D. 发盘中未表明可否撤销

E. 受盘人有理由相信该发盘不可撤销,并采取了行动

2. 促使发盘终止的原因主要有(　　)。

A. 发盘的有效期届满

B. 发盘被发盘人依法撤回或撤销

C. 受盘人对发盘的拒绝或还盘

D. 发盘人发盘后发生了不可抗力事故或当事人丧失行为能力

3. 进出口贸易合同有口头合同和书面合同两种形式。为了更好地明确买卖双方的权利、责任与义务,我国对外贸易中采用的合同形式主要有(　　)。

A. 销售合同　　B. 口头约定　　C. 售货确认书　　D. 订单

4. 以下关于议付的表述,正确的有(　　)。

A. 出口商方面的银行在审单后购买出口商在信用证项下出具的汇票和全套货运单据,扣除手续费和买单日至开证行付款日之间的利息,将余下货款交付给出口商

B. 开证行在审单后购买出口商在信用证项下出具的汇票和全套货运单据扣除手续费和买单日至开证银行付款日之间的利息,将余下货款交付给出口商

C. 开证行委托付款行对汇票及/或单据进行付款

D. 被授权议付的银行对汇票及/或单据做出对价,仅审核单据未做出对价并不是议付

E. 开证行直接对汇票及/或单据进行付款

5. 我国出口结汇的做法有(　　)。

A. 收妥结汇　　B. 出口押汇　　C. T/T 付款　　D. 托收

6. 关于还盘的法律效力,下列说法正确的是(　　)。

A. 对发盘的拒绝和否定　　B. 构成一项新的发盘

C. 原发盘因还盘而失效　　D. 有条件地接受构成一项还盘

E. 对发盘实质性的变更即构成一项还盘

7. 构成一项有效接受,应具备的条件有(　　)。

A. 接受由特定的受盘人做出

B. 接受的内容必须与发盘相符

C. 必须在有效期内表示接受

D. 接受必须在发盘规定的有效期内送达发盘人

8. 对非实质性变更的接受,下列条件中,使合同成立的有(　　)。

A. 只要发盘人立即表示确认　　B. 只要发盘人不表示反对

C. 发盘人表示沉默　　D. 发盘人口头表示反对

E. 发盘人口头表示接受

9. 万先生于 2018 年 5 月 13 日收到电文“你 10 日电我方接受,但支付条件由 D/P 改为 L/C 即期”,该电文是(　　)。

A. 有效接受　　B. 还盘

C. 对原发盘的拒绝　　D. 对发盘表示有条件地接受

E. 实质性变更发盘条件

10. 一般来说,履行出口合同的各个环节中,最为重要的工作环节是(　　)。

A. 备货　　B. 催证、审证、改证

C. 租船订舱　　D. 制单结汇

四、判断题

1. A 公司于 16 日向欧洲 B 客户发盘,注明 5/6 月装船,19 日复到有效。18 日接到对方来电:“16 日电接受,希望尽量在 5 月装船。”这笔交易须经该公司确认后才能达成。(　　)

2. 根据联合国贸发会 1996 年通过的《电子商务示范法》的解释,通过以数据电文交换而订立的合同,符合法律要求的书面合同的性质。(　　)

3. 如发盘未规定有效期,受盘人可在任何时间表示接受。(　　)

4. 发盘的约束力是指对受盘人的约束力。(　　)

5. 还盘在形式上不同于拒绝,但还盘和拒绝都可导致原发盘的失效。(　　)

6. 在进出口业务中,进口人收到货物后,发现货物与合同规定不符时,在任何时候都可以向供货方提出索赔。(　　)

7. 在国际货物买卖合同中,在货物的风险转移至买方之后,卖方对货物与合同不符概不承担责任。(　　)

8. 出口押汇是指出口地银行在收到货款贷记其账户的通知时,向受益人付款的一种结汇方式。(　　)

9. 在交易磋商过程中,对发盘的逾期接受一律无效。(　　)

10. 根据 UCP 600 的规定,议付是指由议付行对汇票和(或)单据做出对价。只审单而不做出对价,不能构成议付。(　　)

五、简答题

1. 信用证项下结汇的方式有哪几种？哪种结汇方式对出口人有利？为什么？

2. 简述合同有效成立的条件。

3. 简述我国外贸进出口合同履行的一般程序。

4. 我国出口企业对意大利某商发盘限10日复到有效。9日，意商用电报通知我方接受该发盘，由于电报局传递延误，我方于11日上午才收到对方的接受通知。而我方在收到接受通知前已获悉市场价格上涨。对此，我方应如何处理？

5. 某年5月3日，A公司向国外B公司发盘，报谷物300公吨，250.00美元/公吨，发盘有效期为10天。5月6日，B公司复电，称对该批谷物感兴趣，但要进一步考虑。5月8日，B公司来电，要求将谷物数量增加到500公吨，价格降低至225.00美元/公吨。5月9日，B公司又来电，重复5月8日来电的内容。5月11日，我方将货物卖给了C商，并于5月13日复电B商，货已售出。但B商坚持要我A公司交货，否则以我方毁约为由，要求赔偿。试问我方应否赔偿？为什么？

六、技能操作题

1. 请填写CIF合同履行中出口商涉及的部分单据的出单机构(见表1-2-1)。

表1-2-1 CIF合同履行中的单据名称及出单机构

合同履行阶段	单据名称	出单机构
1. 办理运输	海运货物委托书	
	海运出口托运单	
	海运提单	
2. 办理保险	投保单	
	保险单	
3. 办理商检	出境货物报检单	
	商检证书/通关单	
4. 办理报关	出口报关单	
	商业发票	
	装箱单	

2. 阅读理解。

(1) 仔细阅读销售合同(表1-2-2)，回答问题。

表1-2-2 销售合同

SUZHOU BAOLING TEXTILE PRODUCTS CO.,LTD. SALES CONFIRMATION	
NO.:BL20180929	DATE:SEP. 20,2018
THE SELLERS: SUZHOU BAOLING TEXTILE PRODUCTS CO.,LTD.	THE BUYERS: BTSC CO.,LTD.

续表

<table>
<tr><td colspan="4">THE UNDERSIGNED SELLERS AND BUYERS HAVE AGREED TO CLOSE THE FOLLOWING TRANSACTION ACCORDING IN THE TERMS AND CONDITIONS STIPULATED BELOW:</td></tr>
<tr><td>1. Name of commodity and specification</td><td>2. Quantity</td><td>3. Unit Price</td><td>4. Amount</td></tr>
<tr><td></td><td></td><td colspan="2">FOB SHANGHAI,CHINA</td></tr>
<tr><td>POCKETING</td><td>213YDS</td><td>USD0.6/YD</td><td>USD127.8</td></tr>
<tr><td>TAPE</td><td>38,118YDS</td><td>USD0.02/YD</td><td>USD762.36</td></tr>
<tr><td>TAPE</td><td>11,460YDS</td><td>USD0.01/YD</td><td>USD114.6</td></tr>
<tr><td>TAPE</td><td>29,102YDS</td><td>USD0.009/YD</td><td>USD261.92</td></tr>
<tr><td>TOTAL:</td><td>78,893YDS</td><td></td><td>USD1,266.68</td></tr>
<tr><td colspan="4">5. TOTAL AMOUNT:SAY U. S. DOLLAR ONE THOUSAND TWO HUNDRED AND SIXTY SIX POINT SIX EIGHT CENTS ONLY.</td></tr>
<tr><td colspan="4">6. TIME OF SHIPMENT:BEFORE:SEP. 28,2018</td></tr>
<tr><td colspan="4">7. PORT OF LOADING:SHANGHAI PORT,CHINA</td></tr>
<tr><td colspan="4">8. PORT OF DESTINATION:DANANG,VIETNAM</td></tr>
<tr><td colspan="4">9. TERMS OF PAYMENT:BY T/T AFTER SHIPMENT</td></tr>
<tr><td colspan="4">10. PACKING:STANDARD EXPORT PACKING</td></tr>
<tr><td colspan="4">11. SHIPPING MARKS.
ONEWOO VIETNAM CO. ,LTD.
PO#:
DANANG
PACKING#:</td></tr>
<tr><td colspan="2">THE SELLERS: MARRY</td><td colspan="2">THE BUYERS: 张琪</td></tr>
</table>

请从上述合同中找出以下内容。

① 买方：____________________________；

② 卖方：____________________________；

③ 合同日期：____________________________；

④ 合同编号：____________________________；

⑤ 价格术语：____________________________；

⑥ 总金额：____________________________；

⑦ 交货期限：____________________________；

⑧ 运输路线：____________________________；

⑨ 付款方式：____________________________；

⑩ 包装要求：____________________________。

(2) 仔细阅读销售合同(见表 1-2-3)，回答问题。

表 1-2-3 销售合同

青岛经贸有限公司

QINGDAO TRADING CO.,LTD.

SALES CONTRACT

CONTRACT NO.:ICD180908

DATE: SEP.08,2018

BUYER:UNITED(ASIA)HOLDINGS GROUP LIMITED

SELLER:QINGDAO TRADING CO.,LTD.

The buyer agrees to buy and the seller agrees to sell the following goods on terms and conditions as set forth below:

唛头及编号 Marks & Numbers	货物描述 Description of Goods	数量 Quantity (SET)	单价 U/P	总值 Amount
			FOB SHANGHAI,CHINA	
N/M	ROTARY TABLET PRESS MACHINE ZP18	3SETS	USD4,005/SET	USD12,015.00
	ROTARY TABLET PRESS MACHINE ZP21	2SETS	USD4,005/SET	USD8,010.00
	ROTARY TABLET PRESS MACHINE ZP23	2SETS	USD4,005/SET	USD8,010.00
	SUGAR COATING MACHINE	1SETS	USD1,550/SET	USD1,550.00
	THERMOFORMING MACHINE FSC-350	1SETS	USD12,780/SET	USD12,780.00
	FLUID BED DRYER FL-B-120	1SETS	USD16,350/SET	USD16,350.00
TOTAL:		10SETS		USD58,715.00

Times of Shipment:WITHIN OCT.,2018

Port of Loading:SHANGHAI,CHINA

Port of Destination:KARACHI PORT,PAKISTAN

Shipping Marks:N/M

Mode of Transport:BY SEA FREIGHT

Terms of Payment:D/P AT SIGHT

THE BUYER THE SELLER:

UNITED(ASIA)HOLDINGS GROUP LIMITED **青岛经贸有限公司**

请从上述合同中找出以下内容。

① 买方:________________________;

② 卖方:________________________;

③ 合同日期:________________________;

④ 合同编号：________________________________；

⑤ 价格术语：________________________________；

⑥ 总金额：__________________________________；

⑦ 交货期限：________________________________；

⑧ 运输路线：________________________________；

⑨ 付款方式：________________________________；

⑩ 商品品名：________________________________。

（3）仔细阅读形式发票（见表 1-2-4），回答问题。

表 1-2-4　形式发票

WuJang Guangfa Ventilation Facilities Co. ,Ltd.

Proforma Invoice

No. PITC20180903FH
Date：16th. May,2018

Contact：Elsa Zhou	Contact：Dmitry Yudina Nicolaevich
Tel：0512-186 1234 5678	Tel：+790 3137 7180
Email：elsa@guangfafengji. com	Email：yudina@mail. ru
Add：GaoXin Industrial Park，Wujang，Jangsu Province，China	Add：Maryinskiy bul. 2-567，Moscow，123456，Russia

MODEL	Item Description	Quantity(pc)	FOB SHANGHAI(USD)	Amount(USD)
S60×100	Cross flow fan	300	3. 80	$ 1,140. 00
S60×120	Cross flow fan	1,000	4. 45	$ 4,450. 00
S60×160	Cross flow fan	1,200	4. 50	$ 5,400. 00
S60×180	Cross flow fan	800	4. 60	$ 3,680. 00
S60×240	Cross flow fan	700	6. 50	$ 4,550. 00
TOTAL		4,000		$ 19,220. 00

Total Value：U. S. DOLLAR Nineteen thousand two hundred and twenty ONLY

Delivery Time：30 work days after payment

Payment Terms：30% T/T in advance and 70% against B/L COPY

Additional information：
Beneficiary：WuJang Guangfa Ventilation Facilities Co，. Ltd.
Bank name：China Huaxia Bank Suzhou Wujiang Branch
Account No. ：6226 3029 1227 1234
Address：No. 12，Gaoxin Road，Songlin Town，Wujiang City，Jiangsu
Post Code：215200

吴江广发通风设备有限公司
WuJang Guangfa Ventilation Facilities Co. ,Ltd.

请从上述发票中找出以下内容。

① 买方：________________________；

② 卖方：________________________；

③ 日期：________________________；

④ 编号：________________________；

⑤ 价格术语：________________________；

⑥ 总金额：________________________；

⑦ 交货期限：________________________；

⑧ 交易数量：________________________；

⑨ 付款方式：________________________；

⑩ 商品品名：________________________。

项目三　信用证条款分析

一、常用术语中英文互译

1. 不可撤销信用证________
2. 付款行________
3. 跟单信用证________
4. 开证申请人________
5. 开证行________
6. 受益人________
7. 通知行________
8. 议付行________
9. 保兑行________
10. 承兑________
11. Irrevocable ________
12. Date of issue ________
13. Currency code,amount ________
14. Expiry date ________
15. Applicable rules ________
16. Available with...by...________
17. Drawee ________
18. Documents required ________
19. Charges ________
20. Period for presentation ________

二、单项选择题

1. 汇付的三种汇款方法中,以(　　)方式付款最为快捷。

A. 电汇　　B. 信汇　　C. 票汇　　D. 信用证

2. 通过汇出行开立的银行汇票的转移而实现款项支付的汇款方式是(　　)。

A. 电汇　　B. 信汇　　C. 票汇　　D. 银行转账

3. 下列关于汇付的表述,正确的是(　　)。

A. 汇款人通过银行将款项交付给收款人的方式

B. 属于银行信用

C. 一种保证收款人收到款项的方式

D. 一种逆汇方式

4. 在托收和汇付支付条件下,单据的缮制必须以(　　)为依据,如有特殊要求,应参照相应文件或资料。

A. 信用证　　B. 发票　　C. 合同　　D. 提单

5. 信用证的汇票条款注明"Drawn on us",则汇票的付款人应是(　　)。

A. 开证申请人　　B. 开证行　　C. 通知行　　D. 议付行

6. 信用证体现了(　　)。

A. 信用证的开证申请人与开证行之间的契约关系

B. 开证行与信用证受益人之间的契约关系

C. 信用证开证申请人与开证行之间的契约关系,也体现了开证行与信用证受益人之间的契约关系

D. 开证行与通知行之间的契约关系

7. 一般而言，对于出口商来说，采用信用证结算方式与采用即期付款交单结算方式相比，前者承担的风险(　　)。

A. 更小　　B. 更大　　C. 一样　　D. 无法比较

8. 托收是出口人委托并通过银行收取货款的一种支付方式。在托收方式下，使用的汇票是(　　)。

A. 商业汇票，属于商业信用　　B. 银行汇票，属于银行信用

C. 商业汇票，属于银行信用　　D. 银行汇票，属于商业信用

9. 托收的优点不包括(　　)。

A. 进口人可免去申请开立信用证的手续，不必预付银行押金

B. 属于银行信用，出口人能安全、及时收汇

C. 有利于资金融通和周转，增强出口商品的竞争力

D. 减少费用支出

10. L/C 与托收方式相结合的支付方式，其全套货运单据应(　　)。

A. 随信用证项下的汇票

B. 随托收项下的汇票

C. 50%随信用证项下的汇票，50%随托收项下的汇票

D. 单据与单据分列在信用证和托收汇票项下

三、多项选择题

1. 支付条款要明确结算方式，如果采用汇付方式，应在合同中规定(　　)等内容。

A. 具体的汇付方法　　B. 汇付的当事人

C. 金额　　D. 汇付的时间

2. 选择结算方式时，应考虑的因素有(　　)。

A. 客户信用　　B. 货源情况　　C. 经营意图　　D. 运输单据

E. 贸易术语

3. 根据 UCP 600 的规定，信用证支付方式的特点有(　　)。

A. 信用证属于银行信用，开证行负有第一性付款责任

B. 信用证一经开证行开立，即是独立于买卖合同之外的自主性文件

C. 信用证条件下由申请人直接向卖方付款

D. 信用证业务是一种单纯的单据业务，银行只处理单据，不涉及货物和合同行为

4. 托收业务的主要当事人有(　　)。

A. 委托人　　B. 汇出行　　C. 提示行　　D. 托收行

E. 代收行

5. 付款交单业务的主要特征有(　　)。

A. 付款交单属于商业信用

B. 付款交单业务中为融资目的也可使用远期汇票

C. 付款交单的安全性高于承兑交单

D. 付款交单属于银行信用

6. 信用证项下的汇票出票日期是议付日期，汇票的出票日期(　　)。

A. 不得晚于信用证有效期　　B. 不得晚于提单签发日后第 21 日

C. 不得早于其他单据日期　　D. 可以早于其他单据日期

7. 属于商业信用的结算方式有(　　)。

A. 电汇　　B. 信用证　　C. 付款交单　　D. 承兑交单

8. 国际货款结算票据主要包括(　　)。

A. 外币现钞　　B. 汇票　　C. 支票　　D. 本票

9. 根据我国《票据法》,汇票上必须记载的事项包括(　　)。

A. 确定的金额　　B. 汇票日期　　C. 付款人名称　　D. 合同编号

10. 下列关于信用证与合同关系的表述,正确的有(　　)。

A. 信用证的开立以买卖合同为依据　　B. 信用证业务受买卖合同的约束

C. 合同是审核信用证的依据　　D. 银行按信用证规定处理信用证业务

四、判断题

1. 出口人开具的汇票,如开证行付款后向开证人提示遭拒付时,开证行有权行使追索权。　(　　)

2. 跟单信用证是一种银行信用,开证行负第一性的付款责任,开立银行保函的担保行通常负第二性的付款责任。　(　　)

3. 可转让信用证和对背信用证一样,都有两个受益人和两家开证行。　(　　)

4. 根据我国《票据法》,承兑附有条件的,视为拒付。　(　　)

5. 在D/P条件下,银行交单是以进口人付款为条件的,如进口人不付款,货物所有权仍在出口人手里,所以D/P对出口人没有什么风险。　(　　)

6. 托收方式下,银行只是作为受托人替出口人收款,没有检查单据的义务。因此,如果出口人出具伪造单据,造成进口人损失,银行不承担责任。　(　　)

7. 在见索即偿保函业务中,担保银行的付款责任既可以是第一性,也可以是第二性,这视保函中的索偿条件而定。　(　　)

8. 备用信用证条件下,如果开证申请人按期履行了合同的义务,则该信用证必须被使用。　(　　)

9. 信用证的性质是银行信用,因此,信用证项下使用的汇票必定是银行汇票。　(　　)

10. 一张可撤销的信用证,无论在什么情况下,都可以撤销。　(　　)

五、简答题

1. 简述跟单托收的定义及其种类。

2. 选择结算方式时应考虑哪些因素?

3. 简述银行保函与信用证的区别。

4. 简述跟单信用证的特点。

5. 简述背书的定义及其种类。

6. 国内A公司以D/P即期付款交单方式出口一批商品,并委托国内甲银行将单证寄至第三国乙银行,由第三国乙银行转给进口国丙银行托收。后来得知丙银行破产收不到货款,该公司要求退回有关单证,但毫无结果。请问托收银行应承担什么责任?

7. 我国ABC公司与日本公司签订进口合同,从加拿大进口木材到中国,使用信用证方式结算货款,信用证中规定"Available with issuing bank by acceptance,Drafts at 90 days

after sight drawn on the issuing bank"。开证行收到单据日为2018年3月17日。2018年3月31日，开证行收到法院发出的针对该信用证业务项下的将付款项的止付令，理由是ABC公司存在欺诈行为。请问，法院签发的止付令是否恰当？在此种情况下，开证行是否可以免除其付款责任？试分析其原因。

六、技能操作题

1. 请根据表1-3-1提供的信息，按进出口贸易的一般原理和实际经验，在表中填入相应的结算方式（从信用证、托收、汇付三种方式中选取一种）。

表1-3-1 结算方式选择

序号	有关业务情况	结算方式
1	出口的货物是库存的一批电器，国内没有市场； 进口商是我方的长期客户，有良好的商业信誉	
2	出口的货物为农副产品，在该国有一定的市场占有率； 进口商是我方新客户，商业信誉不详	
3	出口的货物是紧缺的原材料产品，市场销路很好； 产品在该国有一定的市场占有率； 进口商是我方长期的客户，商业信誉很好	
4	出口的货物为家用电器，长期出口该国，有一定的市场占有率； 进口商是我方的长期客户，有良好的商业信誉； 该国最近经济状况不好，政局动荡，可能会实行外汇管制	

2. 技能训练：仔细阅读信用证（见表1-3-2），回答问题。

表1-3-2 信用证

BASIC HEADER　　F 01 BKCHCNBJA5XX 9828 707873

APPL. HEADER　　0 700 1630000731 CATHUS6LAXXX 1809 042841 0308010730 N
+CATHAY BANK，LOS ANGELES，U. S. A
(BANK NO. 2504307)+LOS ANGELES，U. S. A.

MT：700 ________ ISSUE OF A DOCUMENTARY CREDIT ________

SEQUENCE OF TOTAL：	27：1/1
FORM OF DOCUMENTARY CREDIT：	40A：IRREVOCABLE
DOCUMENTARY CREDIT NUMBER：	20：031M01413
DATE OF ISSUE：	31C：180731
DATE AND PLACE OF EXPIRY：	31D：180915CHINA
APPLICANT：	50：NEW WORLD INTERNATIONAL INC. 129 HAYWARD WAY ST. MONTE，CA 91513
BENEFICIARY：	59：QINGDAO YUANDA INDUSTRY AND COMMERCE CO.，LTD. PINGDU BRANCH QINGDAO，CHINA
CURRENCY CODE AMOUNT：	32B：USD30，940.00
AVAILABLY WITH...BY...	41D：ANY BANK BY NEGOTIATION

续表

DRAFT AT:	42C:30 DAYS AFTER SIGHT
DRAWEE:	42D:CATHAY BANK LOS ANGELES,CA.
PARTIAL SHIPMENTS:	43P:NOT ALLOWED
TRANSHIPMENT:	43T:NOT ALLOWED
LOADING ON BOARD/DISP/TAKING IN CHARGE AT/FROM:	44A:QINGDAO PORT,CHINA
FOR TRANSPORTATION TO:	44B:LOS ANGELES PORT,CA,U. S. A.
LATEST DATE OF SHIPMENT:	44C:180831
DESCRIPT. GOODS AND/OR SERVICE:	45A:LADIES SLIPPERS FOB QINGDAO,CHINA
DOCUMENTS REQUIRED:	46A: +SIGNED COMMERCIAL INVOICE IN 1 ORIGINAL AND 3 COPIES +PACKING LIST IN 1 ORIGINAL AND 3 COPIES +FULL SET OF CLEAN ON BOARD OCEAN BILLS OF LADING CONSIGNED TO ORDER OF NEW WORLD INTERNATIONAL INC. ,MARKED FREIGHT COLLECT NOTIFY: NEW WORLD INTERNATIONAL INC. 129 HAYWARD WAY ST. MONTE,CA 91513
ADDITIONAL CONDITIONS:	47A: +INSURANCE TO BE COVERED BY BUYER. + A DISCREPANCY FEE OF USD50. 00 WILL BE DEDUCTED FROM PROCEEDS ON EACH SET OF DISCREPANT DOCUMENTS PRESENTED. +THE REQUIRED DOCUMENTS MUST BE SENT TO CATHAY BANK, 772 NORTH BROADWAY, LOS ANGELES, CALIFORNIA 9072, USA ATTN. INTERNATIONAL DEPT. IN ONE LOT BY EXPRESS AIRMAIL.
CHARGES:	71B: ALL BANKING CHARGES OUTSIDEOF OUR COUN-TER ARE FOR ACCOUNT OF THE BENEFICIARY.
CONFIRMATION INSTRUCTIONS:	49:WITHOUT
"ADVICE THROUGH" BANK:	57D:YOUR PINGDU SUB-BRANCH 198 ZHENGYANG ROAD PINGDU DISTRICT QINGDAO,CHINA
SENDER TO RECEIVER INFO	72: THIS CREDIT IS SUBJECT TO THE UNIFORM CUSTOMS AND PRACTICE FOR DOCUMENTARY CREDITS, 1993 REVISION, ICC PUBLICATION NO. 500.

仔细阅读上述信用证,找出以下内容。

(1) 信用证种类:________________________________;

(2) 信用证号码:________________________________;

(3) 开证日期:________________________________;

(4) 信用证的有效期、到期地点：________________;
(5) 开证申请人：________________;
(6) 受益人：________________;
(7) 付款行：________________;
(8) 开证行：________________;
(9) 通知行：________________;
(10) 信用证金额及币种：________________;
(11) 分批装运、转运：________________;
(12) 装运港(地)、目的港(地)：________________;
(13) 最迟装运期：________________;
(14) 货名及规格：________________;
(15) 货物数量：________________;
(16) 价格术语：________________;
(17) 海运提单种类：________________;
(18) 交单期限：________________;
(19) 信用证要求的单据：________________;
(20) 信用证特别条款：________________。

3. 技能训练：仔细阅读信用证(见表 1-3-3)，填写信用证分析单(见表 1-3-4)。

表 1-3-3 信用证

2018 MAR. 07 03:45:34 LOGICAL TERMINAL SZEX

MT S700 ISSUE OF A DOCUMENTARY CREDIT

PAGE 00001
FUNC MSG700
UMR 29641915

MSGACK DWS765I AUTH OK, KEY DIGEST, BKCHCNBJ BOTKJPJT RECORD
BASIC HEADER F 01 BKCHCNBJA950 1917 337220
APPLICATION HEADER 0 700 1514 180507 BREXPLPWAXXX 2568 717704 180507
* BRE BANK S. A. (FORMERLY BANK
* ROZWOJU EKSPORT U. S. A.)
* WARSZAWA
* (HEAD OFFICE)

USER HEADER SERVICE CODE 103:
BANK PRIORITY 113:
MSG USER REF. 108: 759424
INFO FROM CI 115:

==

27: Sequence of Total: 1/1
20: Documentary Credit Number: Z0LINT04672-DK00
40A: Form of Documentary Credit: IRREVOCABLE
31C: Date of Issue: 20180507
40E: Applicable Rules: UCP LATEST VERSION
31D: Date and Place of Expiry: DATE 180527 Place CHINA
50: Applicant: ZELMER PRO SPOLKA ZO U. L. WOFMANOWEJ 29 RIESZOW
59: Beneficiary: SuZhou bluebird IMP. and EXP.

续表

Co.,Ltd. WenYuan Road,NiKou Industrial Zone SuZhou,CHINA. 32B: Currency Code and Amount: USD213,280.00 41D: Available with... by...: BKCHCNBJ95B * BANK OF CHINA * SUZHOU * (SUZHOU BRANCH) By DEF Payment 42P: Deferred Payment Details:60 Days After Shipment Date 43P: Partial Shipments:ALLOWED 43T:Transhipment:ALLOWED 44E: Port of Loading/Airport of Departure:Shanghai in China 44F: Port of Discharge/Airport of Destination:Any Port in Europe 44C: Latest Date of Shipment:20180516 45A: Description of Goods: Brush Type NO.540.0000 GREY —4,100PCS Brush Type NO.540.0000 BLACK —800PCS Brush Type NO.550.0000 GREY —3,900PCS Brush Type NO.550.0000 BLACK —600PCS Brush Type NO.560.0000 GREY —2,500PCS Brush Type NO.560.0000 BLACK —500PCS AT USD 17.2/PC as per Proforma Invoice 11578822-26 Delivery Terms:FOB SHANGHAI IN CHINA 46A: Documents Required: 1. SIGNED COMMERCIAL INVOICE,1 ORIGINAL,1 COPY. 2. PACKING LIST,1 ORIGINAL,1 COPY. 3. CERTIFICATE OF ORIGIN,1 ORIGINAL. 4. SGS INSPECTION CERTIFICATE 1 ORIGINAL. 5. FULL SET 3/3 ORIGINAL PLUS 1 NON-NEGOTIABLE COPY OF SHIPPED ON BOARD MARINE/OCEAN BILLS OF LADING ISSUED TO ORDER AND BLANK ENDORSED NOTIFY APPLICANT,MARKED “FREIGHT COLLECT”. 47A: Additional Conditions: 1. FOC SPARE PARTS AND GIFT BOXES ACCEPTABLE. 2. SGS INSPECTION CERTIFICATE NOT INDICATED QUANTITY OF SPARE PARTS AND GIFT BOXES ACCEPTABLE. 3. PAYMENT UNDER RESERVE OR AGAINST AN INDEMNITY PROHIBIT DOCS SHOWING ANY ALTERATIONS/CORRECTIONS WITHOUT AUTHENTICATE OF THE ISSUER ARE NOT ACCEPTABLE. 4. A DISCREPANCY FEE USD140.00 WILL BE DEDUCTED FROM PROCEED UNDER EACH PRESENTATION OF INCORRECT DOCUMENTS. 5. IN CASE DISCREPANT DOCUMENTS ARE REJECTED WE WILL ACT ACCORDING TO ARTICLE 16 POINT C Ⅲ B OF UCP 600. 6. DOCUMENTS TO BE SENT TO BRE BANK SA P. O. BOX 123, UL, SENAT, 00-950 WARSZAWA. 7. DOCUMENTS TO BE ISSUED IN DOCUMENTARY CREDIT LANGUAGE. 71B: Details of charges: ALL BANKING CHARGES OUTSIDE POLAND ARE FOR ACCOUNT OF THE BENEFICIARY.

续表

48: Presentation Period:

DOCUMENTS TO BE PRESENTED NOT LATER THAN 21 DAYS AFTER THE DATE OF DOCUMENT OF SHIPMENT HOWEVER WITHIN CREDIT VALIDITY.

49: Confirmation: WITHOUT

78: Bank Instructions: AGAINST DOCUMENTS STRICTLY COMPLYING WITH L/C TERMS, WE SHALL REMIT COVER AT MATURITY IN ACCORDANCE WITH INSTRUCTIONS RECEIVED.

Trailer: ORDER IS<MAC:><PAC:><ENC:><CHK:><TNG:><PDE:>

MAC: 213C79GA

CHK: DC472A32D926

表 1-3-4 信用证分析单

<table>
<tr><td colspan="10">(1) 编号:
(2) 本证　　年　　月　　日收到</td></tr>
<tr><td colspan="2">开证行(3)</td><td colspan="2"></td><td colspan="2">开证日(4)</td><td colspan="4"></td></tr>
<tr><td colspan="2">申请人(5)</td><td colspan="2"></td><td colspan="2">受益人(6)</td><td colspan="4"></td></tr>
<tr><td colspan="2">信用证金额(7)</td><td colspan="2"></td><td colspan="2">信用证号码(8)</td><td colspan="4"></td></tr>
<tr><td colspan="2">汇票付款人(9)</td><td colspan="2"></td><td colspan="2">汇票期限(10)</td><td colspan="4"></td></tr>
<tr><td colspan="2">可否转运(11)</td><td colspan="2"></td><td colspan="2">可否分批(12)</td><td colspan="4"></td></tr>
<tr><td colspan="2">装运期限(13)</td><td></td><td>信用证有效期(14)</td><td colspan="2"></td><td colspan="2">到期地点(15)</td><td colspan="2"></td></tr>
<tr><td colspan="2">运输标志(16)</td><td colspan="2"></td><td colspan="2">交单日(17)</td><td colspan="4"></td></tr>
<tr><td>单据名称</td><td>提单(18)</td><td>发票(19)</td><td>装箱单(20)</td><td>保险单(21)</td><td>检验证(22)</td><td></td><td></td><td></td><td></td></tr>
<tr><td>银行</td><td></td><td></td><td></td><td></td><td></td><td></td><td></td><td></td><td></td></tr>
<tr><td>客户</td><td></td><td></td><td></td><td></td><td></td><td></td><td></td><td></td><td></td></tr>
<tr><td colspan="2" rowspan="3">提单或承运单据</td><td colspan="2">抬头(23)</td><td colspan="6"></td></tr>
<tr><td colspan="2">通知(24)</td><td colspan="6"></td></tr>
<tr><td colspan="2">注意事项</td><td colspan="6"></td></tr>
<tr><td colspan="2" rowspan="2">保险</td><td colspan="2">险别(25)</td><td colspan="6"></td></tr>
<tr><td colspan="2">加成(26)</td><td colspan="6"></td></tr>
<tr><td colspan="10">其他注意事项:</td></tr>
</table>

4. 技能训练:仔细阅读信用证(见表 1-3-5),回答问题。

表 1-3-5 信用证

Eximbills Enterprise Incoming Swift

==

Message Type: 710
Send Bank: BKNZNZ3XXXX
BANK OF NEW ZEALAND
WELLINGTON
Recv Bank: SPDBCNSH123
SHANGHAI PUDONG DEVELOPMENT BANK
215005 SUZHOU
User Name: 11008164 Print Times: 1
Print Date: 2018-02-21 09:23:43 MIR: 180221BKNZNZ3XXXX8816668164

==

27: Sequence of Total: 1/1
40A: Form of Documentary Credit: IRREVOCABLE
20: Documentary Credit Number: 226121301122
31C: Date of Issue: 20180221
40E: Applicable Rules: UCP LATEST VERSION
31D: Date and Place of Expiry: DATE 180514 Place CHINA
50: Applicant: ELSA TRADING COMPANY LTD.
PO BOX 11450
OTAHUHU
AUCKLAND NZ
59: Beneficiary: SuZhou AIKE ELECTRICS Co., LTD.
1599 TONGDA ROAD, SuZhou JIANGSU, CHINA.
32B: Currency Code and Amount: USD 63,907.78
39A: Percentage Credit Amount Tolerance: 10/10
41D: Available with ...by ...: ANY BANK BY NEGOTIATION
42C: Drafts at...: AT SIGHT
42A: Drawee: BKNZNZ3X
43P: Partial Shipments: ALLOWED
43T: Transhipment: ALLOWED
44E: Port of Loading/Airport of Departure: SHANGHAI CHINA
44F: Port of Discharge/Airport of Destination: AUCKLAND, NEW ZEALAND
44D: Shipment Period: NOT EARLIER THAN 180414 AND NOT LATER THAN 180430
45A: Description of Goods and/or Services:
AS PER VARIOUS BRISCOES ORDER:
P O 2500020164
ZIP123 SLOW COOKERS ROUND 3.5L 3,226PCS
ZIP456 SLOW COOKERS OVAL 3.5L 3,226PCS
GIFT BOX 24PCS
SPARE PARTS 48PCS
FOB SHANGHAI, CHINA
46A: Documents Required:
+SIGNED COMMERCIAL INVOICE(S) IN 1 ORIGINAL(S) +1 COPY(IES)
+PACKING LIST(S) IN 1 ORIGINAL(S) +1 COPY(IES)
+FULL SET, CLEAN ON BOARD, MARINE/OCEAN BILLS OF LADING ISSUED TO ORDER, BLANK ENDORSED, AND MARKED FREIGHT COLLECT

续表

+CERTIFICATE OF ORIGIN, 1 ORIGINAL IN 1 ORIGINAL(S) +1 COPY(IES), FOR EACH PRODUCTION BY AN INDEPENDENT ASSESSOR.

47A: Additional Conditions:

+INSURANCE BUYERS CARE.

+WE SHALL DUDUCT A FEE OF NZD140.00 OR ITS EQUIVALENT FOR EACH SET OF DOCUMENTS CONTAINING DISCREPANCIES.

+WE SHALL DEDUCT OUR REIMBURSEMENT FEE AND COMMUNICATION COSTS FROM EACH DRAWING PRESENTED.

+ONLY BILL OF LADING ISSUED BY COMPREHENSIVE INTERNATIONAL FREIGHT FORWARDERS LTD. SHOWING MONDIALE FREIGHT SERVICES LTD. AS THEIR NEW ZEALAND AGENT ACCEPTED.

+APPROXIMATE 0.5 PERCENT SPARE PARTS FOR EACH 40′ HQ CONTAINER SHIPMENT.

+INVOICE MAY SHOW SPARE PARTS FREE OF CHARGE.

+TRADE AND ECONOMIC SANCTIONS('SANCTIONS') IMPOSED BY GOVERNMENTS, GOVERNMENT AGENCIES OR DEPARTMENTS(INCLUDING THE UNITED NATIONS AND EUPOPEAN UNION) IMPACT UPON TRANSACTIONS INVOLVING VARIOUS COUNTRIES, OR PERSONS RESIDENT WITHIN THOSE COUNTRIES. BANK OF NEW ZEALAND('BNZ') MIGHT BE SUBJECT TO AND AFFECTED BY, SANCTIONS, WITH WHICH IT WILL COMPLY. PLEASE CONTACT BNZ FOR CLARIFICATION BEFORE PRESENTING DOCUMENTS TO BNZ FOR NEGOTIATION OR UNDERTAKING ANY DEALINGS REGARDING THIS CREDIT. BNZ IS NOT AND WILL NOT BE LIABLE FOR ANY LOSS OR DAMAGE WHATSOEVER ASSOCIATED DIRECTLY OR INDIRECTLY WITH THE APPLICATION OF SANCTIONS TO A TRANSACTION OR FINANCIAL, SERVICE INVOLVING BNZ.

BNZ IS NOT REQUIRED TO PERFORM ANY OBLIGATION UNDER THIS CREDIT WHICH IT DETERMINES IN ITS DISCRETION WILL, OR WOULD BE LIKELY TO, CONTRAVENE OR BREACH ANY SANCTION. THIS CLAUSE APPLIES NOTWITHSTANDING ANY INCONSISTENCY WITH THE CURRENT EDITION OF THE INTERNATIONAL CHAMBER OF COMMERCE CUSTOMS AND PRACTICES FOR DOCUMENTARY CREDITS.

71B: charges: ALL CHARGES EXCEPT OPENING BANK ESTABLISHMENT AND AMENDMENT FEES ARE FOR ACCOUNT OF BENEFICIARY.

48: Period for Presentation: 14 DAYS

49: Confirmation Instructions: WITHOUT

78: Instructions to the Paying Bank:

+PAYMENT WILL BE MADE IN ACCORDANCE WITH YOUR INSTRUCTIONS UPON RECEIPT OF DOCUMENTS COMPLYING WITH TERMS OF THIS CREDIT.

+THE NEGOTIATING BANK IS TO FORWARD DOCUMENTS IS ONE LOT BY COURIER TO Bank of New Zealand INTL BANKING CENTRE LEVEL 1, 80 QUEEN ST, AUCKLAND, NEW ZEALAND.

57D: "Advise through" Bank: SPDBCNSH123

仔细阅读上述信用证，找出下列内容。

(1) 信用证种类：______________________________；

(2) 信用证号码：______________________________；

(3) 开证日期：______________________________；

(4) 信用证的有效期、到期地点：______________________________；

(5) 开证申请人：________________________；

(6) 受益人：________________________；

(7) 付款行：________________________；

(8) 开证行：________________________；

(9) 通知行：________________________；

(10) 信用证金额及币种：________________________；

(11) 分批装运、转运：________________________；

(12) 装运港(地)、目的港(地)：________________________；

(13) 最迟装运期：________________________；

(14) 货名及规格：________________________；

(15) 货物数量：________________________；

(16) 价格术语：________________________；

(17) 海运提单种类：________________________；

(18) 交单期限：________________________；

(19) 信用证要求的单据：________________________；

(20) 信用证特别条款：________________________。

项目四　信用证审核与修改

一、常用术语中英文互译

1. 商业发票____________________　　2. 提单____________________

3. 转运____________________　　4. 修改____________________

5. Certificate of origin ____________　　6. Issue ____________________

7. Partial shipments ______________　　8. Deduct __________________

9. Sequence ____________________　　10. Discrepancy ______________

二、单项选择题

1. 信用证修改通知书的内容在两项以上者，受益人(　　)。

A. 要么全部接受，要么全部拒绝　　B. 可选择接受

C. 必须全部接受　　D. 只能部分接受

2. 根据 UCP 600 的解释，若信用证条款未明确规定是否"允许分期发运""允许转运"，则应理解为(　　)。

A. 允许分期发运，但不允许转运　　B. 允许分期发运，允许转运

C. 允许转运，但不允许分期发运　　D. 不允许分期发运，不允许转运

3. 我公司按 CIF London USD80 Per m/t 向英国出口数量为 10 000m/t 的散装货，国外开立信用证金额为 80 万美元，则卖方发货时应注意(　　)。

A. 数量和金额不能增减

B. 数量和金额可在 5%以内增减

C. 数量和金额可在 10%以内增减

D. 数量在 9 500～10 000 公吨，金额不得超过 80 万美元

4. 在假远期信用证业务中，银行贴现的利息由(　　)负担。

A. 开证申请人　　B. 受益人　　C. 议付行　　D. 开证行

5. 根据 UCP 600 的规定，若信用证没有特别说明，则信用证(　　)。

A. 未注明"Transferable"字样或条款，即为可转让信用证

B. 未注明"Transferable"字样，即为可撤销信用证

C. 未注明"Confirmed"字样，即为不保兑信用证

D. 未注明是否即期付款，即为远期付款信用证

6. 国外进口商来证规定，散装货物数量为 1 000 公吨，总金额为 90 万美元，未表明金额及数量可否伸缩，不准分批装运。根据 UCP 600 的规定，我方出口商发货时应掌握(　　)。

A. 数量和总金额均不能增减

B. 数量和总金额幅度可在 10%以内增减

C. 数量和总金额幅度可在 5%以内增减

D. 数量可有5%的伸缩，金额不得超过90万美元

7. 下列关于信用证修改的表述，错误的是（　　）。

A. 修改应由开证人办理

B. 经开证行、受益人同意，才能生效

C. 受益人可对一份修改通知书中的内容有选择地接受

D. 原证的条款，在受益人向通知行发出接受修改前仍对受益人有效

8. 不可撤销信用证开出后，对其中条款的修改，下列表述正确的是（　　）。

A. 不容许任何形式的修改

B. 只能在一定范围内修改

C. 在信用证有效期内，任何一方的任何修改，都必须经买卖双方协商一致同意后，由开证申请人通过开证行办理修改

D. 买卖双方都可直接要求开证行修改

9. 信用证装运期规定为ABOUT 18TH APR. 2018，装运日期（　　）。

A. 可含当日提前或延后10天　　B. 可含当日提前或延后5天

C. 可不含当日提前或延后10天　　D. 可不含当日提前或延后5天

10. 以下不属于出口商审证内容的是（　　）。

A. 信用证与合同的一致性　　B. 信用证条款的可接受性

C. 价格条件的完整性　　D. 开证银行的资信

三、多项选择题

1. 信用证审核的要点包括（　　）。

A. 是否与开证申请书一致　　B. 信用证条款与买卖合同是否一致

C. 是否加列了对卖方不利的条款　　D. 是否有境外有效期

E. 是否存在软条款

2. 对于保兑信用证，承担第一性付款责任的银行有（　　）。

A. 通知行　　B. 开证行　　C. 议付行　　D. 保兑行

3. 以下条款中，（　　）条款应被视为信用证的"软条款"。

A. 检验人在检验证书上的签名必须与开证行所保留的签名样本相符

B. 受益人出具的报关单、合同及商业发票必须进行使馆认证

C. 必须得到开证申请人对样品的确认后，信用证方可生效

D. 货物必须经有关人员检验合格后方可装船

4. 根据UCP 600的规定，下列关于通知行责任的叙述，正确的有（　　）。

A. 决定通知时要检验信用证的表面真实性

B. 决定不通知时必须告知开证行以免误事

C. 对内容不全、条款不清的信用证或修改书，可以预先通知受益人仅供参考而不承担责任

D. 如果开证行授权通知行对信用证加具保兑，通知行必须根据开证行指示行事

5. 审核进口商开来信用证的主要依据是买卖双方签订的贸易合同和UCP 600的有关规定，分别由（　　）审核。

A. 通知行　　B. 开证人　　C. 受益人　　D. 保兑行

6. 以下关于信用证与合同关系的表述，正确的有（　　）。

A. 信用证的开立以买卖合同为依据

B. 信用证的履行不受买卖合同的约束

C. 有关银行只根据信用证的规定办理信用证业务

D. 合同是审核信用证的依据

7. 在审核信用证金额与货币时，需要审核的内容包括（　　）。

A. 信用证总金额的大小写必须一致

B. 来证采用的货币与合同规定的货币必须一致

C. 发票或汇票金额不能超过信用证规定的总金额

D. 若合同中订有溢短装条款，信用证金额应有相应规定

E. 信用证金额中必须注明折扣率

8. 下列信用证条款中，属于软条款的是（　　）。

A. 三份正本已装船海运提单，做成"凭指定"抬头，通知买方

B. 一份开证申请人手签的质量检验证书，字迹须和开证行预留签字样本相符

C. 待进口商取得进口许可证后，开证行以信用证修改形式通知信用证生效

D. 所装船名和船期由进口商通知开证行，开证行以信用证修改形式通知受益人

E. 货物运抵目的港后，待进口地商检机构检验合格并出具书面证书后开证行才付款

9. 根据 UCP 600 的规定，可转让信用证中可变更的内容有（　　）。

A. 有效期和装运日期　　B. 信用证金额和单价

C. 货物描述　　D. 申请人名称

10. 在审核信用证各相关日期是否合理时，需要注意的是（　　）。

A. 未规定有效期的信用证无效

B. 未规定装运期，则信用证有效期为最迟装运期

C. 未规定交单期，受益人应在装运日期后的 21 天内交单，且在信用证有效期内

D. 未规定交单期，按惯例受益人应在装运日期后的 15 天内交单

四、判断题

1. 信用证可以不规定装运期，但必须明示有效期。（　　）

2. 根据 UCP 600 的解释，除非信用证另有规定，否则银行可以接受出具日期早于信用证开立日期的单据。（　　）

3. 可撤销信用证对出口人安全收汇没有保证，因为开证行可在任何情况下单方面撤销和修改信用证。（　　）

4. 对不可撤销信用证中任何条款的修改，都必须经有关当事人全部同意后才能生效，对同一修改通知书中的内容允许部分接受。（　　）

5. 信用证受益人收到来证后，经审核，如发现来证内容与成交合同不符，受益人可经过通知行转告开证行，要求开证行对不符点进行修改。（　　）

6. 按 UCP 600 的规定，如信用证规定"在或大概在某月某日内装运"，则为前后 10 天内装运，起讫日期包括在内。（　　）

7. 信用证修改通知书的内容，受益人可根据实际情况，接受其中第一部分，拒绝其中的

另一部分。 （ ）

8. 信用证修改通知书必须由原通知行转递或通知。 （ ）

9. 信用证可以不规定有效期，但必须规定装运期。 （ ）

10. 在审核信用证时，对信用证中的附加条款一般可以不审核。 （ ）

五、简答题

1. 简述审核信用证的依据及主要步骤。

2. 简述信用证受益人审核信用证的要点。

3. 简述修改信用证的原则和步骤。

4. 中方 A 公司与加拿大 B 公司在 2018 年 1 月 3 日按 CIF 条件签订一出口 10 万码法兰绒的合同，支付方式为不可撤销即期信用证。加拿大 B 公司于 2018 年 3 月通过银行开来信用证，经审核与合同相符，其中保险金额为发票金额加 10%。中方 A 公司正在备货期间，加拿大 B 公司通过银行传递给中方 A 公司一份信用证修改书，内容为将投保金额改为按发票金额加 15%。中方 A 公司按原证规定投保、发货，并于货物装运后在信用证有效期内，向议付行提交全套装运单据。议付行议付后将全套单据寄开证行，开证行以保险单与信用证修改书不符为由拒付。请问：开证行拒付的理由是否合理？

5. 国外一家贸易公司与我国某进出口公司订立合同，购买小麦 500 吨。合同规定：2018 年 1 月 30 日前开出信用证，2 月 5 日前装船。1 月 25 日买方开来信用证，有效期至 2 月 10 日。由于卖方按期装船发生困难，故来电请买方将装船期延至 2 月 17 日并将信用证有效期延长至 2 月 20 日，买方回电表示同意，但未通知开证银行。2 月 17 日货物装船后，卖方到银行议付时，遭到拒绝。

请问：

（1）银行是否有权拒绝付货款？为什么？

（2）作为卖方，应当如何处理此事？

六、技能操作题

1. 根据销售合同（见表 1-4-1）和补充资料审核进口国开来的信用证（见表 1-4-2）。

表 1-4-1 销售合同

明基贸易有限公司

MJ TRADE CO.,LTD.

12F 7 BLDG SHATOUJIAO FREE TRADE ZONE,YANTIAN,SHENZHEN,CHINA 416061

销售合同

SALE CONTRACT

To:
COMPANHIA BRASILEIRA DE
DISTRIBUICAO ROD. ANHANGUERA,KM 17,8
OSASCO-SP-BRASIL

Contract No.:TR100566
Date:16 JULY,2018

This sales contract is made between the sellers and buyers whereby the seller agree to sell and the buyers agree to buy the undermentioned goods according to the terms and conditions stipulated below:

续表

Descriptions of Goods	Quantity	Unit Price	Amount
PENGUIM HUMIDIFIER (BLACK BODY - WHITE DETAIL)- 127V	1,280PCS	@USD13.70/PC	CIF SANTOS USD17,536.00
PENGUIM HUMIDIFIER (BLACK BODY - WHITE DETAIL)- 220V	600PCS	@USD13.70/PC	USD8,220.00
TOTAL:	1,880PCS		USD25.756.00
5% MORE OR LESS AMOUNT AND QUANTITY ARE ALLOWED.			

Total amount in words SAY U. S. DOLLARS Twenty Five Thousand Seven Hundred And Fifty Six ONLY.

Packing 4PC in one Ctn, total packed in 470Ctns.

Delivery Sea freight from Shanghai to SanTos allowing partial shipments and transhipment

Shipping Mark MJ HONGKONG/100566/SANTOS. 1-470

Time of Shipment On or before 12 SEP. ,2018

Terms of Payment By 100pct irrevocable letter of credit in favour of the Seller to be available by darfts at sight to open and to reach the seller before July 25, 2018 and to remain valid for negotiation in China until the 15th days after the foresaid time of the shipment. The L/C must mention this contract number. All banking charges outside BRAZIL are for of the beneficiary.

Insurance To be effected by the sellers for 110 pct of the invoice value covering all risks and war risk of Institute Cargo Clause (A)

Documents required

1. Signed invoice in 3 originals plus 1 copy.
2. Full set clean on board Bill of Lading made out to order blank endorsed notify the buyer.
3. Insurance policy in duplicate.
4. Packing list in 3 originals plus 1 copy.
5. Certificate of Origin in duplicate.

The Seller

MJ Trade Co. ,Ltd.

张三

签署

The Buyer

COMPANHIA BRASILEIRA

HARK

Signature

补充资料如下。

最迟开证日期：2018 年 7 月 21 日

开户行及账号：BANK OF BRAZIL RIO DE JANEIRO,2357924680

法人代表：HARK

开证方式：电开

表 1-4-2 信用证

FROM:BANK OF BRAZIL RIO DE JANEIRO
TO:SHANGHAI PUDONG DEVELOPMENT BANK
27:SEQUENCE OF TOTAL: 1/1
40A:FORM OF DOCUMENTARY CREDIT: IRREVOCABLE
20:DOCUMENTARY CREDIT NUMBER: HJQ234

续表

31C:DATE OF ISSUE: 180723
40E:APPLICABLE RULES:UCP LATEST VERSION
31D:DATE AND PLACE OF EXPIRY:180906 CHINA
50: APPLICANT:
COMPANHIA BRASILEIRA DE
DISTRIBUICAO
ROD. ANHANGUERA,KM 17,8
OSASCO-SP-BRASIL
59:BENEFICIARY:
N. J TRADE CO. ,LTD.
12F 7 BLDG SHATOUJIAO FREE
TRADE ZONE,YANTIAN,SHENZHEN,CHINA 416061
32B:CURRENCY CODE,AMOUNT:USD25,136
41D:AVAILABLE WITH ...BY ...:ANY BANK BY NEGOTIATION
42C:DRAFTS AT ...:30 DAYS AFTER SIGHT
42D:DRAWEE:OURSELVES
43P:PARTIAL SHIPMENTS:PARTIAL SHIPMENTS ARE PROHIBITED
43T:TRANSSHIPMENT:TRANSSHIPMENT ARE PROHIBITED
44E:PORT OF LOADING/AIRPORT OF DEPARTURE:YANTIAN
44F:PORT OF DISCHARGE/AIRPORT OF DESTINATION:ANY PORT IN BRASIL
44C:LATEST DATE OF SHIPMENT:180901
45A:DESCRIPTION OF GOODS AND/OR SERVICES:
PENGUIM HUMIDIFIER (BLACK BODY - WHITE DETAIL) - 127V
PENGUIM HUMIDIFIER (BLACK BODY - WHITE DETAIL) - 220V
AS PER DESCRIBED ON S/C NO. 100566 DATED JULY 16,2018.
CIF SANTOS
AS PER INCOTERMS 2010 OF ICC PARIS.
46A:DOCUMENTS REQUIRED:

1. 3 ORIGINALS PLUS 1 COPY OF SIGNED BY HAND AND STAMPED COMMERCIAL INVOICE WITH COMPLETE DESCRIPTION OF GOODS,SHOWING CIF AMOUNT IN FIGURES.

2. 3/3 ORIGINALS PLUS 3 COPIES OF CLEAN ON BOARD BILL OF LADIN CONSIGNED TO COMPANHIA BRASILEIRA DE DISTRIBUICAO, CNPJ 47. 508. 411/0078-35 ROD. ANHANGUERA, KM 17, 8 - OSASCO - BRAZIL, NOTIFY PARTY SAME AS CONSIGNEE, FREIGHT PREPAID COVERING SHIPMENT FROM SHANGHAI TO SANTOS - BRAZIL. BILL OF LADING MUST SHOW:PO NUMBER,NUMBER OF CARTONS.

3. 3 ORIGINALS PLUS 1 COPY OF SIGNED BY HAND AND STAMPED PACKING LIST WITH FULL DESCRIPTION OF GOODS.

4. 1 ORIGINAL PLUS 1 COPY OF CERTIFICATE OF ORIGIN.

5. FULL SET OF NEGOTIABLE INSURANCE POLICY OR CERTIFICATE BLANK ENDORSED FOR 110% OF INVOICE VALUE COVERING ALL RISKS AND WAR RISK OF Institute Cargo Clause (A).

47A:ADDITIONAL CONDITIONS:

1. ALL DISCREPANCIES DUE TO TYPOGRAPHICAL MISTAKES ARE WAIVED.

2. NUMBER OF THIS LETTER OF CREDIT AND THE REFERENC TR100566 MUST BE STATED ON ALL DOCUMENTS.

3. WILL BE REFUSED SHIPPING DOCUMENTS SHOWING SHIPMENT DATE PRIOR OF ISSUANCE OF THIS LETTER OF CREDIT.

续表

DRAFT
71B:DETAILS CHARGES: BANKING CHARGES OUTSIDE OF BRASIL ARE FOR BENEFICIARY'S ACCOUNT. 48:PRESENTATION PERIOD: DOCUMENTS MUST BE PRESENTED WITHIN 14 DAYS AFTER ISSUANCE OF THE TRANSPORT DOCUMENT BUT WITHIN THE VALIDITY OF THIS CREDIT. 49:CONFIRMA INSTRUCTIONS: WITHOUT 53A:REIMBURSEMENT BANK:SCBLUS33 78:INSTRUCTIONS: 1. WHETHER ALL TERMS AND CONDITIONS ARE COMPLIED WITH,PLEASE CLAIM REIMBURSE,ON THE 5TH WORKING DAY AFTER YOUR IMMEDIATE TESTED MESSAGE TO US INFORMING AMOUNT OF DOCS., SHIPMENT AND NEGOTIATION DATES, AWB AND COMM. INVOICE NRS, DEPATURE PLACE, DESTINATION AND CONFIRMING THAT SHIPPING DOCUMENTS ARE BEING REMITTED TO OUR OFFICE. 2. PLEASE ADVISE BENEFICIARY URGENTLY UNDER ADVISE TO US.

补充资料如下。

INV. NO.:S2000307　　INV. DATE:AUG. 14,2018

B/L. NO.:ZHY20110　　B/L. DATE:SEP. 01,2018

REFERENCE NO.:G114303101620078　　S/C NO.:MLI-11895/10

NAME OF STEAMER:FANYA W. 102　　CONTAINER & SEAL NO.:TEXU47683001/WG9006

SHIPPING MARKS:MJ HONGKONG.
100566
SANTOS
1-470

H. S. NO.: 5802. 4060

POLICY NO.:SH089921

FREIGHT FEE:USD1,100　　INSURANCE FEE:USD1,000

报检单编号:985614322　　报检单位登记号:347698580

GOODS:

PENGUIM HUMIDIFIER (BLACK BODY - WHITE DETAIL) - 127V:
@USD13. 70/PCS 1,280PCS

PENGUIM HUMIDIFIER (BLACK BODY - WHITE DETAIL) - 220V:
@USD13. 70/PCS 600PCS

PACKED IN 470 CARTONS,TOTAL QUANTITY:1,880PCS

TOTAL WEIGHT:N/W:3,525.00KGS G/W: 3,995.00KGS MEAS:59.40CBM

该货物是完全自产品。

经审核,该信用证存在以下问题:

(1) ______________________________;

(2) ______________________________;

(3) ______________________________;

(4) ______________________________;

(5) ______________________________;

(6) ______________________________;

(7) ______________________________;

(8) ______________________________;

(9) ______________________________;

(10) ______________________________;

(11) ______________________________;

(12) ______________________________。

2. 根据合同审核信用证。

以下是受益人根据合同规定审核来证的实务操作,先看合同(见表 1-4-3),然后根据合同内容审核信用证(见表 1-4-4)与合同不相符的地方。

表 1-4-3 销售合同

上海茂林贸易有限公司

SHANGHAI MAOLIN TRADE CO.,LTD.

No. 97 Maoming Nan Road,Shanghai,P. R. of China

销售合同

SALE CONTRACT

To:
EASTERN TRADING COMPANY
81 WORDFORD STREET,
LONDON
UNITED KINGDOM

Contract No.:SH2018X826
Date:26 AUG.,2018

This sales contract is made between the sellers and buyers whereby the seller agree to sell and the buyers agree to buy the undermentioned goods according to the terms and conditions stipulated below:

Description of Goods	Quantity	Unit Price	Amount
WOOLLEN BLANKETS			CIF LONDON
ART. NO. H666	600PCS	@USD15.50/PC	USD9,300.00
ART. NO. HX88	600PCS	@USD16.30/PC	USD9,780.00
ART. NO. HE21	720PCS	@USD18.50/PC	USD13,320.00
TOTAL:	1,920PCS		USD32,400.00
5% MORE OR LESS AMOUNT AND QUANTITY ARE ALLOWED.			

Total amount in words SAY U. S. DOLLARS THIRTY TWO THOUSAND FOUR HUNSRED ONLY.

Packing 24Pc in one Ctn,total packed in 80Ctns.

Delivery Sea freight from Shanghai to London allowing partial shipments and transshipment

Shipping Mark EASTERN/2018X826/LONDON/NO. 1-80

Time of Shipment On or before Oct. 15,2018

Terms of Payment By 100pct irrevocable letter of credit in favour of the Seller to be available by darfts at sight to open and to reach the seller before Sep. 05,2018 and to remain valid for negotiation in China until the 15th days after the foresaid time of the shipment. The L/C must mention this contract number. All banking charges outside U. K. are for A/C of the beneficiary.

Insurance To be effected by the sellers for 110 pct of the invoice value covering all risks and war risk of Institute Cargo Clause (A)

续表

Documents required

1. Signed invoice in triplicate
2. Full set clean on board Bill of Lading made out to order blank endorsed notify the buyer
3. Insurance policy in duplicate
4. Packing list in triplicate
5. Certificate of Origin in duplicate issued by a relevant authority

The Seller	**The Buyer**
Shanghai Maolin Trade Co.,Ltd.	Eastern Trading Company
张三	Whuit Brown
签署	Signature

表 1-4-4 信用证

ISSUING BANK:UNITED GREAT KINGDOM BANK LTD.,LONDON
CREDIT NUMBER:LOD88095
DATE OF ISSUE:2018.09.01
EXPIRYDATE AND PLACE: DATE 2018.10.20 PLACE U.K.
APPLICANT:EASTERN TRADING COMPANY
81 WORDFORD STREET,LONDON UNITED KINGDOM
BENEFICIARY:SHANGHAI MAOLIN TRADE CORP.
NO.97 MAOMING NAN ROAD SHANGHAI P.R.OF CHINA
AMOUNT:USD32,040.00 (SAY U.S.DOLLARS THIRTY TWO THOUSAND AND FORTY ONLY)
THE CREDIT IS AVAILABLE WITH ANY BANK BY NEGOTIATION DRAFTS AT 30 DAYS AFTER SIGHT FOR FULL INVOICE VALUE DRAWN ON US
PARTIAL SHIPMENT:NOT ALLOWED
TRANSHIPMENT:ALLOWED
PORT OF LOADING:SHANGHAI
PORT OF DISCHARGE:LONDON
LATEST SHIPMENT DATE:2018.10.15
DESCRIPTION OF GOODS:WOOLLEN BLANKETS,CIF LONDON

ART. NO. H666	600PCS	@USD15.50/PC	USD9,300.00
ART. NO. HX88	600PCS	@USD16.30/PC	USD9,780.00
ART. NO. HE21	720PCS	@USD18.00/PC	USD12,960.00
TOTAL:	1,920PCS		USD32,040.00

AS PER CONTRACT NO.:SH2018X806
DOCUMENTS REQUIRED:
* SIGNED COMMERCIAL INVOICE IN TRIPLICATE
* PACKING LIST IN TRIPLICATE
* FULL SET OF CLEAN ON BOARD MARINE BILLS OF LADING MADE OUT TO ORDER MARKED FREIGHT PREPAID NOTIFY APPLICANT
* GSP FORM A CERTIFYING THAT THE GOODS ARE OF CHINESE ORIGIN ISSUED BY COMPETENT AUTHORITIES
* INSURANCE POLICY/CERTIFICATE COVERING ALL RISKS INCLUDING WAREHOUSE TO WAREHOUSE CLAUSE UP TO FINAL DESTINATION AT LONDON FOR AT LEAST 110 PCT OF CIF VALUE AS PER INSTITUTE CARGO CLAUSE (A)

续表

* SHIPPING ADVICES MUST BE SENT TO APPLICANT WITHIN IMMEDIATELY AFTER SHIPMENT ADVISING THE INVOICE VALUE, NUMBER OF PACKAGES, GROSS AND NET WEIGHT, VESSEL NAME, BILL OF LADING NO. AND DATE, CONTRACT NO. SHOWING SHIPPING MARK AS: EASTERN 2018X826 LONDON NO. 1-80 PRESENTATION PERIOD: 10 DAYS AFTER ISSUANCE DATE OF SHIPPING DOCUMENTS BUT WITHIN THE VALIDITY OF THE CREDIT CONFIRMATION: WITHOUT INSTRUCTIONS: THIS CREDIT IS SUBJECT TO UNIFORM CUSTOMS A PRACTICE FOR DOCUMENTARY CREDIT ICC NO. 600. THE NEGOTIATION BANK MUST FORWARD THE DRAFTS AND ALL DOCUMENTS BY REGISTERED AIRMAIL DIRECT TO US IN TWO CONSECUTIVE LOTS. UPON RECEIPT OF THE DRAFTS AND DOCUMENTS IN ORDER, WE WILL REMIT THE PROCEEDS AS INSTRUCTED BY THE NEGOTIATING BANK.

经审核，该信用证存在以下问题：

(1) ________________________________;

(2) ________________________________;

(3) ________________________________;

(4) ________________________________;

(5) ________________________________;

(6) ________________________________;

(7) ________________________________;

(8) ________________________________;

(9) ________________________________;

(10) ________________________________;

(11) ________________________________;

(12) ________________________________。

项目五　缮制商业发票

一、常用术语中英文互译

1. 商业发票＿＿＿＿＿＿＿＿　　2. 一式三份＿＿＿＿＿＿＿＿

3. 保险费＿＿＿＿＿＿＿＿　　4. 佣金＿＿＿＿＿＿＿＿

5. 付款方式＿＿＿＿＿＿＿＿　　6. Invoice no. ＿＿＿＿＿＿＿＿

7. Unit price ＿＿＿＿＿＿＿＿　　8. Amount total ＿＿＿＿＿＿＿＿

9. Marks & nos. ＿＿＿＿＿＿＿＿　　10. Description of goods ＿＿＿＿＿＿＿＿

二、单项选择题

1. 发票的日期在结汇单据中应(　　)。

A. 早于汇票的签发日期　　B. 早于提单的签发日期

C. 早于保险单的签发日期　　D. 早于其他所有单据

2. 如来证没有申请人(或付款人)一栏,而是直接指明汇票付款人时,如“WE OPEN CREDIT NO. PS8803 AVAILABLE BY DRAFTS DRAWN ON EEC CO.,LTD.”,发票的抬头人应做成(　　)。

A. 空白抬头　　B. 开证行

C. DRAWN ON EEC CO.,LTD.　　D. EEC CO.,LTD.

3. 某进出口公司工作人员在缮制信用证时,在货物名称一栏错把 BLACK TEA(红茶)写作 BLACK TEE,审证时没留意到这个问题,制作发票时应(　　)。

A. 改作“BLACK TEA”

B. 按原文写作“BLACK TEE”

C. 按原文写作“BLACK TEE”,然后在后面加上(BLACK TEA)

D. 把“信用证”改成“托收”收款

4. 根据 UCP 600 的规定,商业发票中货物的描述(　　)。

A. 可以使用统称,不得与信用证中有关货物的描述有抵触

B. 可以使用统称,并可与信用证中有关货物的描述有所不同

C. 必须完全符合信用证中的描述

D. 必须与合同的描述完全一致

5. 在下面的发票中,属于进口国海关估价、核税以及征收反倾销税依据的是(　　)。

A. 商业发票　　B. 领事发票　　C. 海关发票　　D. 厂商发票

6. 出口企业审单时,要做到单证一致、单单一致。在单据中处于中心地位的是(　　)。

A. 汇票　　B. 提单　　C. 保险单　　D. 商业发票

7. 卖方应买方的要求,可以将报价出售货物的名称、规格、单价等开立一种非正式的发票,以供买方作为申请许可证或申请批给外汇的证件,这种发票称作(　　)。

A. 海关发票　B. 形式发票　C. 银行发票　D. 联合发票

8. 假如信用证的价格条款规定，商品的价格为USD4.00，CIFC5 London，且商品数量为6,145PCS，信用证的金额为扣除佣金的净值，在发票总值栏中的金额应填写(　　)。

A. CIFC5 London　USD24,580.00
—C5　USD1,229.00
———————————
CIF London　USD23,351.00

B. CIFC5 London　USD24,580.00
—C5　USD2,229.00
———————————
CIF London　USD22,351.00

C. CIFC5 London　USD24,580.00
—C5　USD1,299.00
———————————
CIF London　USD23,281.00

D. CIFC5 London　USD24,580.00
—C5　USD1,339.00
———————————
CIF London　USD23,241.00

9. 信用证中规定"Commercial Invoice In Triplicate Certifying that the Goods Herein Are In Accordance With Those Specified In the S/C NO. 9857"，制作发票时应(　　)。

A. 商业发票一式两份，然后在发票上注明"Commercial Invoice In Triplicate Certifying that the Goods Herein Are In Accordance With Those Specified In the S/C NO. 9857"

B. 商业发票一式三份，然后在发票上注明"Commercial Invoice In Triplicate Certifying that the Goods Herein Are In Accordance With Those Specified In the S/C NO. 9857"

C. 商业发票一式三份，然后在发票上注明"We Certify that the Goods Herein Are In Accordance With Those Specified In the S/C NO. 9857"

D. 商业发票一式两份，然后在发票上注明"We Certify that the Goods Herein Are In Accordance With Those Specified In the S/C NO. 9857"

10. 货物外包装上印有火的标志，这是(　　)。

A. 运输标志　B. 唛头　C. 指示性标志　D. 警告性标志

三、多项选择题

1. 商业发票由出口企业自行拟制，无统一格式，但基本栏目大致相同，包括(　　)。

A. 信用证介绍部分

B. 首文部分包括发票名称、号码、出票日期地点、抬头人、合同号、运输路线等

C. 本文部分包括货物描述、单价、总金额、唛头等

D. 结文部分包括有关货物产地、包装材料等各种证明句、发票制作人签章等

2. 在显示发票抬头人时，必须注意的事项有(　　)。

A. 抬头可以是空白的

B. 如果信用证有指定其他抬头人的，按来证规定制单

C. 如果信用证已被转让，则银行也可接受由第二受益人提交的以第一受益人为抬头的发票

D. 必须做成信用证的申请人名称、地址

3. 国外来证有时要求在发票上加注各种费用金额、特定号码、有关证明句，可将这些内容打在发票商品栏以下空白处的有(　　)。

A. 唛头

B. 运费、保险费等

C. 缮打证明句，如澳大利亚来证要求加注原料来源证明句，有些国家来证要求加注非以色列证明句等

D. 注明特定号码，如进口证号、配额许可证号码等

4. 下面关于海关发票的表述中，正确的有(　　)。

A. 由出口商填写

B. 由进口商填写

C. 是出口商向出口地海关报关时提供的单据

D. 是进口商向进口地海关报关时提供的单据

E. 是进口地海关进行估价定税、征收差别关税或反倾销税的依据

5. 某来证规定"ABOUT 20 MT CITRIC ACID MONO BP80 AT USD1,180.00/MT CFR HAIFA PORT"，"PCT credit amount tolerance：10/10"，"CURRENCY CODE AMOUNT：USD23,600.00"，以下发票的数量和金额，符合规定的有(　　)。

A. 20MT，USD23,600.00　　　　B. 25MT，USD29,500.00

C. 22MT，USD25,960.00　　　　D. 18MT，USD21,240.00

6. 商业发票是货主在准备全套出口文件时首先编制的文件，在出口货物装运前的(　　)环节要使用商业发票。

A. 托运订舱　　B. 商品报检　　C. 出口报关　　D. 海关查验

E. 办理投保

7. 形式发票也称预开发票或估价发票，通常在未成交前，为进口商向其本国当局申请进口许可证或请求核批外汇之用。下列说法中，正确的有(　　)。

A. 形式发票不是一种正式发票

B. 能用于托收和议付，正式成交后不要另外重新缮制商业发票

C. 假如来证附有形式发票，则形式发票构成信用证的组成部分，制单时要按形式发票内容全部打上

D. 形式发票与商业发票的关系密切，信用证在货物描述后面常有"按照某月某日之形式发票"等条款

8. 厂商发票是厂方出具给出口商的销售货物的凭证。以下关于来证要求提供厂商发票的目的，说法错误的有(　　)。

A. 检查是否有削价倾销行为，以便确定是否征收"反倾销税"

B. 按某些国家法令规定，出口商对其国家输入货物时必须取得进口国在出口国或其邻近地区的领事签证的、作为装运单据一部分和货物进口报关的前提条件之一的特殊发票

C. 为进口商向其本国当局申请进口许可证或请求核批外汇之用

D. 作为国际商务单据中的基础单据，是缮制报关单、产地证、报检单、投保单等其他单据的依据

9. 海关发票的主要作用是（　　）。

A. 作为进口货物估价完税的依据　　B. 买卖双方收付货款的依据

C. 核定货物原产地的依据　　D. 进出口海关统计资料的依据

10. 唛头的主要内容包括（　　）。

A. 目的港（地）名称　　B. 收货人名称

C. 件号　　D. 信用证号或合同号

四、判断题

1. 商业发票的名称通常以“COMMERCIAL INVOICE”或“INVOICE”或“PROFORMA INVOICE”等字样表示，应与信用证规定的一致。（　　）

2. 根据 UCP 600 的规定，商业发票的总值一定不能高于信用证金额。（　　）

3. 有的来证要求在发票上加注“证明所列内容真实无误”，我国出口商为避免麻烦应一律拒绝。（　　）

4. 信用证规定：FROM CHINA PORT TO LONDON，发票上应严格按照信用证要求填上“FROM CHINA PORT TO LONDON”。（　　）

5. 根据 UCP 600 的规定，除商业发票外，其他单据中对货物的表述均可使用统称。（　　）

6. 根据 UCP 600 的规定，无论信用证有无规定，商业发票必须签章才能生效。（　　）

7. 海关发票是根据某些进口国海关特定的格式，由出口人填制，供进口人凭以向进口海关报关时用的一种特别的发票。各国的海关发票可以相互替代。（　　）

8. 如果合同和信用证中均未规定具体唛头，货物为大宗散装货物，则发票的唛头栏可以留空不填。（　　）

9. 信用证中的数量和金额可以冠以“大约”（about）或类似文字，但是在缮制单证时，发票中的数量和金额不能冠以“大约”（about）或类似的文字。（　　）

10. 信用证关于货物的描述为“blue cotton wears”，发票显示为“colored cotton wears”是可以接受的。（　　）

五、简答题

1. 简述商业发票的含义和作用。

2. 简述海关发票的概念和作用。

3. 有一份信用证对货物的描述如下：7,000PCS OF 100% COTTON SHIRTS AT USD8.60 PER PCS AS PER CONTRACT NO.02AB120 FOB SHANGHAI。开证行收到单据后，经过审核发现商业发票未注明 FOB SHANGHAI，认为单证不符拒绝付款。而受益人认为价格术语不是货物描述的一部分，而且其已经在提单中注明了“FREIGHT

COLLECT”,表明价格术语就是 FOB 价,因此单证是相符的。请问哪一方有理?

六、技能操作题

1. 根据项目三表 1-3-5 所示的信用证以及下述补充资料制作商业发票(见表 1-5-1)。补充资料如下。

合同号:2500020184　　日期:2018-01-10

商业发票号:HMC18-107　　日期:2018-04-11

货物描述:

货名	件数	包装	毛重	净重	体积
SLOW COOKER ZIP123	3,226PCS	@2PCS/CTN	@4KGS/PCS	@3.5KGS/PCS	67.75M3
SLOW COOKER ZIP456	3,226PCS	@2PCS/CTN	@4.8KGS/PCS	@4.15KGS/PCS	83.88M3
GIFT BOX	24PCS	4CTNS	@0.42KGS/PCS	@0.33KGS/PCS	0.62M3
SPARE PARTS	48PCS	30CTNS	@1.5KGS/PCS	@1.2KGS/PCS	1.06M3

B/L DATE:2018-4-25

唛头:SPIL
2500020184
AUCKLAND
3,260CTNS

表 1-5-1　商业发票

<table>
<tr><td colspan="5">苏州艾可电器有限公司
SUZHOU AIKE ELECTRICS CO.,LTD.</td></tr>
<tr><td colspan="3">SOLD TO:</td><td colspan="2">INVOICE NO.:
INVOICE DATE:
ORDER NO.:</td></tr>
<tr><td colspan="5">COMMERCIAL INVOICE</td></tr>
<tr><td colspan="2">FROM:</td><td>TO:</td><td colspan="2">VESSEL:</td></tr>
<tr><td colspan="3">ON BOARD DATE:</td><td colspan="2"></td></tr>
<tr><td>Marks & Nos.</td><td>Description of Goods</td><td>Quantity</td><td>Unit Price</td><td>Amount</td></tr>
<tr><td></td><td></td><td></td><td></td><td></td></tr>
<tr><td></td><td></td><td></td><td></td><td></td></tr>
<tr><td></td><td></td><td></td><td></td><td></td></tr>
<tr><td></td><td></td><td></td><td></td><td></td></tr>
<tr><td colspan="5"></td></tr>
<tr><td colspan="5">苏州艾可电器有限公司(章)
SUZHOU AIKE ELECTRICS CO.,LTD.
张大虞(章)</td></tr>
</table>

2. 根据相关资料缮制商业发票(见表 1-5-2)。

相关资料如下。

合同号：TY20180610　　日期：2018-06-10

商业发票号：IY20120710　　日期：2018-07-10

客户名称及地址：TS MAPLE COMPANY 19 VTRA ORCHARD ROAD,SINGAPORE

价格条款：CIF SINGAPORE　　付款方式：D/P AT SIGHT

装运港：TIANJIN

货物描述：

SILK BLOUSES SIZE 7(160cm)　5,000SETS@　USD35.00/SET　USD175,000.00

SILK BLOUSES SIZE 9(170cm)　6,000SETS@　USD38.00/SET　USD228,000.00

装箱情况：PACKED IN 1 CARTON OF 20PCS EACH

项目	CTNS	G. W. (KGS)	N. W. (KGS)	MEAS(CBM)
SILK BLOUSES SIZE 7(160cm)	250	1.0KG/250	0.8KG/200	$0.02M^3/5$
SILK BLOUSES SIZE 9(170cm)	300	1.5KG/450	1.3KG/390	$0.03M^3/9$

唛头：N/M

表 1-5-2　商业发票

BEIJING TIANYE CLOTHING MANUFACTURE CO. ,LTD.

HAIDIAN DISTRICT,BEIJING,CHINA

TEL:0086-010-6238 7997　　INV. NO. : ________

FAX:0086-010-6238 7996　　DATE: ________

S/C NO. : ________

COMMERCIAL INVOICE

TO:

FROM: ________　　TO: ________

L/C NO. : ________　　ISSUED BY: ________

MARKS & NO.	DESCRIPTION OF GOODS	QTY(PCS)	UNIT PRICE(USD)	AMOUNT(USD)
TOTAL				

TOTAL AMOUNT:

WE HEREBY CERTIFY THAT THE ABOVE MENTIONED GOODS ARE OF CHINESE ORIGIN.

3. 根据信用证(见表 1-5-3)及相关资料填写完整商业发票(见表 1-5-4)。

表 1-5-3 信用证

FROM:REPUBLIC NATIONAL BANK OF MIAMI,MIAMI,
TO:BANK OF CHINA,SUZHOU BRANCH

Form of Doc. Credit	*40 A:IRREVOCABLE
Doc. Credit Number	*20:NBM-08007678
Date of Issue	31C:18/02/08
Expiry	*31D:Date 18/04/30 Place CHINA
Applicant	*50:JAMES BROWN AND SONS 2116 N. W. 21 STREET MIAMI FL. 33142, U. S. A.
Beneficiary	*59:JIANGSU HAO YUE TRADING CO. 12 HONGQI ROAD SUZHOU,CHINA
Amount	*32B:Currency USD Amount 82,800.00
Pos./Neg. Tol. (%)	39A:5/5
Available with/by	*41D:ANY BANK BY NEGOTIATION
Draft at...	42C:DRAFTS AT SIGHT FOR FULL INVOICE VALUE
Drawee	42A:REPUBLIC NATIONAL BANK OF MIAMI NEW YORK
Partial Shipments	43P:NOT ALLOWED
Port of loading	44E:SHANGHAI
Port of discharge	44F:MIAMI U. S. A.
Latest Date of Shipment	44C:18/04/15
Description of Goods	45A: FISHING BOOTS ART. NO. JB702,2,640PAIRS USD15.00 PER PAIR ART. NO. JB703,3,600PAIRS USD12.00 PER PAIR PACKING: 12PAIRS PER CARTON TRADE TERMS: CFR MIAMI FL. ALL DETAILS ARE AS PER S/C NO. 18JB558
Documents required	46A: +FULL SET OF CLEAN ON BOARD OCEAN BILLS OF LADING MADE OUT TO ORDER, BLANK ENDORSED, MARKED "FREIGHT PREPAID" AND NOTIFY APPLICANT. +SIGNED COMMERCIAL INVOICE IN ONE ORIGINAL AND THREECOPIES. +PACKING LIST IN ONE ORIGINAL AND THREE COPIES. +MANUALLY SIGNED CERTIFICATE OF ORIGIN IN ONEORIGINAL AND ONE COPY. +CERTIFICATE OF QUALITY ISSUED BY THE MANUFACTURER OR THE PRODUCER IN ONE ORIGINAL AND ONE COPY.
Additional Cond.	47A: 1. A HANDING FEE OF USD80.00 WILL BE DEDUCTED IF DISCREPANCY DOCUMENTS PRESENTED. 2. INSURANCE TO BE EFFECTED BY BUYER. 3. ALL DOCUMENTS MUST BE IN ENGLISH. 4. ALL DOCUMENTS INDICATING THIS L/C NUMBER.

续表

Details of Charges 71B:	ALL BANKING CHARGES AND EXPENSES OUTSIDE THE ISSUING BANK IS FOR BENEFICIARY'S ACCOUNT.
Presentation Period 48:	DOCUMENTS TO BE PRESENTED WITHIN 15 DAYS AFTER THEDATE OF SHIPMENT, BUT WITHIN THE VALIDITY OF THE CREDIT.

相关资料如下。

发票号码：18HY34-95　　发票日期：2018年3月31日

提单号码：COS180410SHM　　提单日期：2018年4月10日

船名：DONG FENG V. 5615W　　装箱：1×40′ FCL CY/CY

集装箱号：TRIU3568032　　封号：199345-0

产地证号：JS/18/18HY8765　　产地证日期：2018年4月7日

商品编号：4823.2900　　海运费：USD3 500.00

生产厂家：吴江制靴厂　　净重：22.00KGS/CTN

毛重：24.50KGS/CTN　　尺码：58CM×46CM×40CM/CTN

议付银行：中国银行苏州分行

唛头：

J B A S
08JB558
MIAMI, FL
NO. 1-520
MADE IN CHINA

表 1-5-4 商业发票

<table>
<tr><td colspan="5" align="center">江 苏 好 跃 贸 易 公 司
JIANGSU HAO YUE TRADING CO.
12 HONGQI ROAD SUZHOU CHINA</td></tr>
<tr><td colspan="5" align="center">商业发票
COMMERCIAL INVOICE</td></tr>
<tr><td colspan="5">Messrs: (1)</td></tr>
<tr><td colspan="2" rowspan="4"></td><td colspan="3">Invoice No. : 08HY34-95</td></tr>
<tr><td colspan="3">Invoice Date: MAR. 31, 2018</td></tr>
<tr><td colspan="3">Credit No. : NBM-08007678</td></tr>
<tr><td colspan="3">Credit Date: FEB. 08, 2018</td></tr>
<tr><td colspan="2"></td><td colspan="2">Terms of Payment:</td><td>(3)</td></tr>
<tr><td colspan="5">Exporter: (2)</td></tr>
<tr><td colspan="2"></td><td colspan="2">Transport details:</td><td>(4)</td></tr>
<tr><td>Marks & Nos.</td><td>Description of Goods</td><td>Quantity</td><td>Unit Price</td><td>Amount</td></tr>
<tr><td>(5)</td><td>FISHING BOOTS</td><td></td><td>(6)</td><td></td></tr>
<tr><td></td><td>ART. NO.</td><td>(7)</td><td>(8)</td><td>(9)</td></tr>
<tr><td></td><td>JB702</td><td></td><td></td><td></td></tr>
<tr><td></td><td>JB703</td><td></td><td></td><td></td></tr>
<tr><td></td><td>TOTAL:</td><td>6,240PAIRS</td><td></td><td>USD82,800.00</td></tr>
</table>

续表

SAY U. S. DOLLARS EIGHTY TWO THOUSAND EIGHT HUNDRED ONLY. (10) TOTAL PACKED IN 520CARTONS. TOTAL GROSS WEIGHT：12,740.00KGS. PACKING：12PAIRS PER CARTON.
江苏好跃贸易公司(章) JIANGSU HAO YUE TRADING CO. 张大虞(章)

4．阅读理解。

(1) 请根据商业发票(见表 1-5-5)找出相关内容。

表 1-5-5 商业发票

<table>
<tr><td colspan="5">Changshu Sun Machinery Co. ,Ltd.
Yushan town changshu city,JiangSu Province,China
Tel:86-512-5281 2450</td></tr>
<tr><td colspan="5">COMMERCIAL INVOICE</td></tr>
<tr><td colspan="2">Exporter：
Changshu Sun Machinery Co. ,Ltd.
YUSHAN TOWN,CHANGSHU CITY,JIANGSU PROVINCE,CHINA
TEL:86-512-5281 2450</td><td colspan="3" rowspan="2"></td></tr>
<tr><td colspan="2">To：
AG PLASTIC FACTORY ALKHARJ INDUSTRIAL CITY
ROAD1399 SAUDI ARABIA
MOBILE:00 966 555 666 789</td></tr>
<tr><td colspan="2" rowspan="2">Issuing Bank</td><td>Invoice No.
2018E-N829</td><td colspan="2">2018-08-29</td></tr>
<tr><td colspan="3">CFR RIYADH DRY PORT</td></tr>
<tr><td>Shipping Marks</td><td>Item</td><td>Quantity</td><td colspan="2">Amount(USD)</td></tr>
<tr><td rowspan="3">N/M</td><td></td><td>2SET/14PKGS</td><td colspan="2">13,3300USD</td></tr>
<tr><td>DESCRIPTION OF GOODS:
BLOW MOULDING MACHINE ABLB75-1</td><td>1SET/7PKGS
1SET/7PKGS</td><td colspan="2">71,500USD
61,800USD</td></tr>
<tr><td>BLOW MOULDING MACHINE ABLB75-2</td><td></td><td colspan="2"></td></tr>
<tr><td colspan="2">TOTAL</td><td>2SETS/14PKGS</td><td colspan="2">133,300</td></tr>
<tr><td colspan="5">THE COUNTRY OF ORIGIN HAS BEEN MENTIONED/PRINTED ON EACH AND EVERY PACKAGE.
常熟市阳光机械有限公司(signature)
周 慧</td></tr>
</table>

根据上述发票找出下列内容。

① 出口商名称：________________________；

② 发票抬头人：________________________；

③ 发票号码：________________________；

④ 发票日期：________________________；

⑤ 目的港：________________________；

⑥ 运输方式：________________________；

⑦ 货物描述：________________________；

⑧ 价格术语：________________________；

⑨ 商品总价：________________________；

⑩ 唛头：________________________。

(2) 根据商业发票(见表 1-5-6)找出相关内容。

表 1-5-6 商业发票

<table>
<tr><td colspan="3">苏州乐家对外贸易公司
SUZHOU LEJIA FOREIGN TRADE CORPORATION
NO. 1299 SHUSHAN VILLAGE, GAOXIN ZONE, SUZHOU 215011 CHINA
TEL: 0512-4386 2243 FAX: 0512-6388 2254</td></tr>
<tr><td colspan="3">发票
INVOICE</td></tr>
<tr><td colspan="2">致
To:
SOUTHERN EXCHANGE L. P.
DBA TEXSPORT, ATTN DORIE PETER
P. O. BOX 55889, HOUSTON, TX 77255-5889, USA</td><td>发票编号
Invoice No.: SP-5002
销售编号
S/C No.: 21FKS-118-5002
日期
Date: SEP. 10, 2018</td></tr>
<tr><td>装船口岸
From: SHANGHAI, CHINA</td><td>目的港
To: LONG BEACH, CA, USA</td><td rowspan="3">装运工具
By: SEA</td></tr>
<tr><td>支付方式
Payment by: T/T</td><td>支付银行
Issued by: AMEGY BANK N. A., USA</td></tr>
<tr><td>提单号
B/L No.: ______</td><td>集装箱号/封号
Container No. /Seal No.: ______</td></tr>
<tr><td>唛头及包/箱号
MARKS & Nos.</td><td>数量与货品名称
DESCRIPTION AND QUANTITY</td><td>金额
AMOUNT</td></tr>
<tr><td>16041
Quantity: 4 ea.
Case No.: 1-UP
Made in China</td><td>CAMPING EQUIPMENT AS PER PO NO. 5001
1) ITEM # 16041: 752 PCS @USD18.85</td><td>FOB SHANGHAI
USD14, 175.20</td></tr>
</table>

续表

16046 Quantity：2 ea. Case No.：1-UP Made in China	2）ITEM＃16046：280 PCS @USD25.30	USD7,084.00
16048 Quantity：1 ea. Case No.：1-UP Made in China	3）ITEM＃16048：800 PCS @USD28.35	USD22,680.00

TOTAL：　　1,832 PCS　　USD43,939.20

SAY TOTAL AMOUNT U. S. DOLLARS FORTY-THREE THOUSAND AND NINE HUNDRED AND THIRTH NINE AND CENTS TWENTY ONLY.

WE HEREBY CERTIFY THAT THE ABOVE SHIPMENT CONTAINS NO SOLID WOOD PACKING MATERIALS.

兹证明上列商品确系中华人民共和国出产或制造

This is to certify that the above mentioned commodities were produced or manufactured in The People's Republic of China

苏州乐家对外贸易公司

SUZHOU LEJIA FOREIGN TRADE CORPORATION

陈乐家

根据上述发票找出下列内容。

① 出口商名称：________________；

② 发票抬头人：________________；

③ 发票号码：________________；

④ 发票日期：________________；

⑤ 合同号码：________________；

⑥ 运输方式：________________；

⑦ 货物描述：________________；

⑧ 价格术语：________________；

⑨ 商品总价：________________；

⑩ 付款方式：________________；

⑪ 目的港：________________；

⑫ 装运港：________________；

⑬ 商品单价：________________；

⑭ 证明文句：________________；

⑮ 唛头：________________。

项目六　缮制装箱单

一、常用术语中英文互译

1. 装箱单________________　　2. 包装________________

3. 重量单________________　　4. 数量________________

5. 毛重________________　　6. Net weight ________________

7. Carton no. ________________　　8. Bundle ________________

9. Roll ________________　　10. Each carton cotains 2 sets ________

二、单项选择题

1. 对于价值较低的农产品,买卖双方往往采用(　　)计算其重量。

A. 法定重量　　B. 理论重量　　C. 净重　　D. 以毛作净

2. 买卖双方以 CIF 条件达成 10 万吨散装小麦的交易合同,卖方如不希望在交货时因数量产生纠纷,最好在合同中订立(　　)。

A. 品质机动幅度　　B. 仓至仓条款

C. 溢短装条款　　D. 禁止转运条款

3. 某贸易公司向英国客商出口平纹印花纯棉坯布,信用证中规定"数量约为 100 000 码",根据 UCP 600 的规定,卖方可以理解为交货数量有不超过(　　)的增减幅度。

A. 3%　　B. 5%　　C. 10%　　D. 15%

4. 信用证中规定"PACKING LIST IN FOUR COPIES",则受益人提交的装箱单的份数为(　　)。

A. 4 份副本　　B. 1 份正本 3 份副本

C. 不需提交正本　　D. 4 份正本 4 份副本

5. 某公司出口货物,从黄埔港发运,运往汉堡,在香港转船,在装箱单"TRANSPORT DETAILS"一栏填写错误的是(　　)。

A. FROM HUANGPU TO HAMBURG W/T HONGKONG

B. FROM HUANGPU TO HAMBURG VIA HONGKONG

C. FROM HUANGPU TO HONGKONG AND THENCE TOHAMBURG

D. FROM HUANGPU TO HAMBURG WITH TRANSSHIPMENT AT HONGKONG

6. 在商品和包装上不注明生产国的包装是(　　)。

A. 中性包装　　B. 无牌包装　　C. 非使用包装　　D. 使用包装

7. 运输标志是(　　)。

A. Shipping Mark　　B. Customary Tare

C. Bulk Cargo　　D. Sale by Seller's Band

8. 缮制装箱单据时，一般不应显示货物的(　　)。

A. 品名、总金额　　B. 单价、总金额
C. 包装件数、品名　　D. 品名、单价

9. 货物的外包装上有一只酒杯的图案，这种标志属于(　　)。

A. 危险性标志　　B. 指示性标志
C. 警告性标志　　D. 易燃性标志

10. 进口生丝毛，一般采用(　　)计算重量。

A. 净重　　B. 毛重　　C. 公量　　D. 理论重量

三、多项选择题

1. 印刷在运输包装上的唛头，其作用是在运输过程中使有关人员易于辨认货物，便于核对单证。按习惯做法，唛头由(　　)提供。

A. 卖方　　B. 买方　　C. 船方　　D. 货代公司

2. 根据在流通过程中所起的不同作用，商品包装可分为(　　)。

A. 运输包装　　B. 装卸包装　　C. 储存包装　　D. 销售包装

3. 买卖双方在合同中对交货数量规定了溢短装条款，溢短装的选择权可以在合同中规定由(　　)行使。

A. 卖方　　B. 买方　　C. 拖车公司　　D. 船公司

4. 当合同中规定采用净重计算商品重量时，国际上通常采用(　　)计算包装的重量。

A. 按实际皮重　　B. 按约定皮重
C. 按平均皮重　　D. 按习惯皮重

5. 运输包装分为单件运输包装和集合运输包装，以下属于集合运输包装的有(　　)。

A. 卖方　　B. 买方　　C. 拖车公司　　D. 船公司

6. 中性包装单据上不能出现(　　)。

A. 出口方名称　　B. 提单号码　　C. 合同号码　　D. 保险单号码

7. 以下单据中，对发票起补充说明作用的有(　　)。

A. 装箱单　　B. 提单　　C. 尺码单　　D. 重量单
E. 品质证书

8. 装箱单主要是补充发票内容的不足，通过包装件数、唛头、规格等明确产品的包装情况，(　　)。

A. 便于进口商了解产品的数量与包装
B. 便于进口国海关检查与核对产品
C. 是出口商必须向进口商提交的单据
D. 是出口商必须向银行提交的单据

9. 装箱单的编号一栏一般填写(　　)。

A. 发票号码　　B. 提单号码　　C. 合同号码　　D. 保险单号码

10. 当信用证要求同时出具(　　)，但未列明具体内容时，出口商可以将这几种单据合并缮制，分别冠以相应的单据名称，并满足信用证对各类单据的份数要求。

A. 发票　　B. 装箱单　　C. 重量单　　D. 尺码单

四、判断题

1. 装箱单的主要作用是补充商业发票内容的不足，便于买方掌握商品的包装、数量及供进口国海关检查和核对货物。（ ）

2. 某工厂出口货物一批，合同中规定使用纸箱包装。为了更好地保护商品，卖方在交货时没有经过买方的同意就采用了木箱包装，这种替客户着想的做法是对的。（ ）

3. 信用证中规定包装采用"SEAWORTHY PACKING"，UCP 600 规定，受益人在出口时根据货物情况采用了纸箱作为运输包装，在制作装箱单时，包装材料一栏应填写"SEAWORTHY PACKING"。（ ）

4. 国际贸易的习惯做法是将包装费包括在货价内，不另计收。（ ）

5. 装箱单的出单日期可以早于发票日期，也可晚于发票日期 1～2 天。（ ）

6. 受益人在制作相关单据时，必须将运输包装上的标志都注明在单据上。（ ）

7. 在国际货物买卖合同中，约定包装时，"习惯包装""适合海运包装"等都是常用的、比较好的规定方法。（ ）

8. 除非信用证特别要求，否则银行可以接受装箱单表面无抬头的表示。（ ）

9. 装箱单表明的货物应为发票描述的货物，单据必须完全一致。（ ）

10. 装箱单需要显示货物的单价和总价等信息。（ ）

五、简答题

1. 在外贸业务中，包装单据有什么作用？

2. 我国某外贸公司从日本进口鱼粉 5 000 公吨，合同条款如下：价格为 CIF 广州 100 美元/公吨，单层新麻袋包装，50 千克/袋，以即期信用证方式付款。货到广州港后，我方发现货物扣除麻袋重量后不足 5 000 公吨，于是要求卖方退还短量部分的货款。我方的要求是否合理？为什么？

六、技能操作题

1. 根据项目三表 1-3-5 所示的信用证以及下述补充资料缮制装箱单（见表 1-6-1）。

补充资料如下。

合同号：2500020184　　日期：2018-01-10

商业发票号：HMC18-107　　日期：2018-04-11

货物描述：

货名	件数	包装	毛重	净重	体积
SLOW COOKER ZIP123	3,226PCS	@2PCS/CTN	@4KGS/PCS	@3.5KGS/PCS	67.75M3
SLOW COOKER ZIP456	3,226PCS	@2PCS/CTN	@4.8KGS/PCS	@4.15KGS/PCS	83.88M3
GIFT BOX	24PCS	4CTNS	@0.42KGS/PCS	@0.33KGS/PCS	0.62M3
SPARE PARTS	48PCS	30CTNS	@1.5KGS/PCS	@1.2KGS/PCS	1.06M3

B/L DATE：2018-4-25

唛头：SPIL
2500020184
AUCKLAND
3,260CTNS

表 1-6-1 装箱单

<table>
<tr><td colspan="6">苏州艾可电器有限公司
SUZHOU AIKE ELECTRICS CO. ,LTD.</td></tr>
<tr><td colspan="3">SOLD TO:</td><td colspan="3">INVOICE NO. :
INVOICE DATE:
ORDER NO. :</td></tr>
<tr><td colspan="6">PACKING LIST</td></tr>
<tr><td colspan="3">FROM:</td><td colspan="2">TO:</td><td>VESSEL:</td></tr>
<tr><td colspan="6">ON BOARD DATE:</td></tr>
<tr><td>SHIPPING MARKS</td><td>DESCRIPTION OF GOODS</td><td>PACKING & QUANTITY</td><td>GROSS WEIGHT</td><td>NET WEIGHT</td><td>MEASUREMENT</td></tr>
<tr><td></td><td></td><td></td><td></td><td></td><td></td></tr>
<tr><td></td><td></td><td></td><td></td><td></td><td></td></tr>
<tr><td></td><td></td><td></td><td></td><td></td><td></td></tr>
<tr><td></td><td></td><td></td><td></td><td></td><td></td></tr>
<tr><td></td><td></td><td></td><td></td><td></td><td></td></tr>
<tr><td colspan="6"></td></tr>
<tr><td colspan="6">苏州艾可电器有限公司(章)
SUZHOU AIKE ELECTRICS CO. ,LTD.
张大虞(章)</td></tr>
</table>

2. 根据相关资料缮制装箱单(见表 1-6-2)。

相关资料如下。

合同号:TY20180610　　日期:2018-06-10

商业发票号:IY20180710　　日期:2018-07-10

客户名称及地址:TS MAPLE COMPANY 19 VTRA ORCHARD ROAD,SINGAPORE

价格条款:CIF SINGAPORE　　付款方式:D/P AT SIGHT

装运港:TIANJIN

货物描述:

SILK BLOUSES SIZE 7(160cm)　5,000SETS　@USD35.00/SET　USD175,000.00

SILK BLOUSES SIZE 9(170cm)　6,000SETS　@USD38.00/SET　USD228,000.00

装箱情况:PACKED IN 1 CARTON OF 20PCS EACH

项目	CTNS	G. W. (KGS)	N. W. (KGS)	MEAS(CBM)
SILK BLOUSES SIZE 7(160cm)	250	1.0KG/250	0.8KG/200	0.02M^3/5
SILK BLOUSES SIZE 9(170cm)	300	1.5KG/450	1.3KG/390	0.03M^3/9

唛头:N/M

表 1-6-2 装箱单

BEIJING TIANYE CLOTHING MANUFACTURE CO. ,LTD.
HAIDIAN DISTRICT,BEIJING,CHINA

TEL:0086-010-6238 7997
FAX:0086-010-6238 7996

INV. NO. : ________
DATE: ________
S/C NO. : ________

PACKING LIST

TO:

TRANSPORT AETAILS:

SHIPPING MARKS	DESCRIPTION OF GOODS	QTY(PCS)	CTNS	G. W. (KGS)	N. W. (KGS)	MEAS. (CBM)

TOTAL:

3. 根据项目五中的信用证(见表 1-5-3)及相关资料填制装箱单(见表 1-6-3)。

表 1-6-3 装箱单

<table>
<tr><td colspan="6">江 苏 好 跃 贸 易 公 司
JIANGSU HAO YUE TRADING CO.
12 HONGQI ROAD SUZHOU CHINA</td></tr>
<tr><td colspan="6">装 箱 单
PACKING LIST</td></tr>
<tr><td colspan="6">Messrs： (1)</td></tr>
<tr><td colspan="3">JANMES BROWN AND SONS
2116 N. W. 21 STREET MIAMI FL. 33142，U. S. A.</td><td colspan="3">Date：
Invoice No.：
Invoice Date：</td></tr>
<tr><td colspan="6">Exporter：</td></tr>
<tr><td colspan="3">JIANGSU HAO YUE TRADING CO.
12 HONGQI ROAD SUZHOU，CHINA</td><td colspan="3">Transport Details：
SEA FREIGHT
FROM SHANGHAI TO MIAMI U. S. A.</td></tr>
<tr><td>件号
Ctn. Nos.</td><td>件数
Quantity</td><td>货名
Description of goods</td><td>净重
Net weight</td><td>毛重
Gross weight</td><td>尺码
Measurement</td></tr>
<tr><td></td><td></td><td>(3)</td><td>(4)</td><td>(5)</td><td>(6)</td></tr>
<tr><td>(2)</td><td></td><td></td><td></td><td></td><td></td></tr>
<tr><td></td><td>220Ctns</td><td>2，640pairs，Art. No. JB702</td><td></td><td></td><td></td></tr>
<tr><td></td><td>300Ctns</td><td>3，600pairs，Art. No. JB703</td><td></td><td></td><td></td></tr>
<tr><td>(7)</td><td></td><td></td><td></td><td></td><td></td></tr>
<tr><td colspan="6">(8)</td></tr>
<tr><td colspan="6">(9)</td></tr>
<tr><td colspan="6">江苏好跃贸易公司(章)
JIANGSU HAO YUE TRADING CO.
(10)(章)</td></tr>
</table>

项目七　缮制报检单

一、常用术语中英文互译

1. 商品检验____________________________

2. 品质检验证书__________________________

3. 数量检验证书__________________________

4. 重量/体积检验证书______________________

5. 出入境检验检疫局_______________________

6. Inspection certificate of sanitary or health ____________________

7. Inspection certificate of disinfection __________________________

8. Inspection certificate of fumigation __________________________

9. Inspection certificate of hold ________________________________

10. China commodity inspection bureau __________________________

二、单项选择题

1. 以下不属于国家商检机构主要职能的是(　　)。

A. 法定商检　　B. 公正鉴定　　C. 通关检验　　D. 委托检验检疫

2. 在国际货物买卖合同中,对于货物检验时间和地点的规定方法中,使用较多的是(　　)。

A. 在出口国检验

B. 在进口国检验

C. 在出口国装运港检验,进口国目的港复验

D. 在第三国检验

3. 出境货物电子转单的程序是:由产地检验检疫机构将相关信息传送到________并出具________,出口商凭报检号、转单号及密码到出境地检验检疫机构申请________。(　　)

A. 电子转单中心　《出境货物通关单》《出境货物换证凭条》

B. 电子转单中心　《出境货物换证凭条》《出境货物通关单》

C. 出境地检验检疫办公场所　《出境货物换证凭条》《出境货物通关单》

D. 出境地检验检疫办公场所　《出境货物通关单》《出境货物换证凭条》

4. (　　)不是国家质量监督检验检疫总局的主要职责。

A. 主管全国质量、计量　　B. 出入境商品检疫

C. 出入境卫生检疫　　D. 流通领域商品质量监督管理

5. 对产地和报关地一致的出境货物,经检验检疫合格的,出具(　　)。

A.《出境货物通关单》　　B.《出境货物换证凭单》

C.《出境货物换证凭条》　　D.《出境货物不合格通知单》

6. 对于需要在产地实施检验检疫、口岸报关出境的货物，由产地检验检疫机构出具________，由口岸检验检疫机构经验证或者核查货证合格后，换发________。（　　）

A.《出境货物通关单》《出境货物换证凭条》

B.《出境货物换证凭条》《出境货物通关单》

C. 品质证书　《出境货物通关单》

D. 品质证书　《出境货物换证凭条》

7. 一般出口商品应在出口报关或装运前（　　）天报检。

A. 3　　B. 5　　C. 7　　D. 9

8.（　　）不是在所有出口报检时都要提供的单证。

A. 信用证　　B. 商业发票

C. 合同　　D. 出境货物报检单

9. 出境货物报检单上的重量一般填写报检货物的（　　）。

A. 法定重量　　B. 净重　　C. 毛重　　D. 公量

10. 入境货物报检单所列各栏必须填写完整、准确、清晰，没有内容填写的栏目应以（　　）表示，不得留空。

A. /　　B. ***　　C. NULL　　D. Blank

三、多项选择题

1. 检验检疫证书是检验检疫机构签发的用以证明出口货物品质、数量、卫生等的书面文件，它是（　　）。

A. 履行合同的法律依据　　B. 议付的有效单据

C. 出入境货物通关的重要凭证　　D. 索赔、仲裁等重要法律文件

2. 出入境检验检疫卫生证书是证明可供食用的出口动物产品、食品等经卫生检验、检疫合格的证书，适用的商品有（　　）等。

A. 肠衣　　B. 罐头　　C. 蛋品　　D. 乳制品

3. 为方便出口、提高工作效率，检验检疫机构对某些常年出口且信誉良好的出口企业，对非易腐烂变质、非易燃易爆的货物，接受（　　）报检。

A. 电话预约　　B. 传真报检　　C. 书面　　D. 邮寄

4. 入境货物报检单上的货物总值应与（　　）上所列一致。

A. 报关单　　B. 合同　　C. 发票　　D. 装箱单

E. 海运提单

5. 出入境检验检疫报检单位有（　　）。

A. 出入境检验检疫局　　B. 自理报检

C. 代理报检　　D. 第三方报检机构

6. 以下说法正确的是（　　）。

A. 品质检验的，还应提供国外品质证书或质量保证书、产品使用说明书及有关标准和技术资料

B. 凭样成交的，须加附成交样品

C. 以品级或公量计价结算的，应同时申请重量鉴定

D. 报检入境运输工具、集装箱时，只需提供检疫证明

E. 报检入境废物时，提供国家环保部门签发的“进口废物批准证书”即可

7. 在我国的出口业务中，实施法定检验的有(　　)。

A. 列入《商检机构实施检验的进出口商品种类表》的进口商品

B. 有关国际条约规定须商检机构检验的进口商品

C. 进口商品的残损鉴定和海损鉴定

D. 其他法律、行政法规规定须经商检机构检验的进口商品

8. 对检验时间、地点的规定方法，符合惯例的有(　　)。

A. 出口国检验　　B. 进口国检验

C. 出口国检验，进口国复验　　D. 离岸重量，到岸品质

9. 进口报检应随附的单据或证件有(　　)。

A. 核销单　　B. 国外商业发票和装箱清单

C. 运输单据　　D. 进口货物通知书

10. 一般情况下，出境货物报检需提交的单证有(　　)。

A. 汇票　　B. 发票　　C. 合同　　D. 包装性能结果单

四、判断题

1. 只有列入《商检机构实施检验的进出口商品种类表》的进出口商品，才属于法定检验的商品。(　　)

2. 出境货物的报检程序是先检验检疫，后放行通关。而入境货物的报检程序是先放行通关，后检验检疫。因为只有先放行提取货物，才能将提到的货物做法定检验检疫。(　　)

3. 商检证书是买卖合同的一个组成部分。(　　)

4. 经商检机构检验合格发给检验证单的出口商品，应当在商检机构规定的期限内报关出口，超过期限的，可向商检机构申请延长检验证单的期限。(　　)

5. 从欧盟进口的货物，如果未使用木质包装材料，进口时需提交输出国民间机构出具的《非木质包装声明书》。(　　)

6. 重量检验证书中的数量和重量的填报应以装箱单和提单为依据。(　　)

7. 检验检疫证书“收货人”栏一般不必填写，若出口商为中间商，收货人栏可填为“To Whom It May Concern”或“To Order”。(　　)

8. 若出口商品的木质包装已按要求实施熏蒸，商检机构对熏蒸后的木包装加盖了进口国认可的标识，在这种情况下，出口商同样需要商检机构出具“熏蒸/消毒证书”，以交进口商。(　　)

9. 对列入《法检目录》的出口商品，由检验检疫机构实施强制性检验，对合格商品检验检疫机构签发《出境货物通关单》。此《出境货物通关单》必须在向海关申报时交给海关审核，若没有提交纸制通关单，即使检验检疫机构的信息系统有合格记录，海关也不予放行。(　　)

10. 所有出口货物都需要经过法定检验后，才能报关出运。(　　)

五、简答题

1. 简述我国进出口商品检验的工作环节。

2. 检验检疫证书的含义及作用有哪些？

3. 简述我国检验检疫机构的基本任务。

六、技能操作题

1. 业务员张琪 2018 年 4 月 20 日申请报检，4 月 25 日领取报检单。请根据项目三表 1-3-5 中的信用证以及下述相关资料填写一份出境货物报检单（见表 1-7-1）。

报检单位编号：3202001516　　联系人：张琪

电话：6645320　　H. S. 编码：8516609000

货物存放地点：公司仓库　　许可证编号：QR201832020888

合同号：2500020184　　日期：2018-01-10

商业发票号：HMC18-107　　日期：2018-04-11

发货日期：2018 年 4 月 27 日

货物描述：

货名	件数	包装	毛重	净重	体积
SLOW COOKER ZIP123	3,226PCS	@2PCS/CTN	@4KGS/PCS	@3.5KGS/PCS	67.75M3
SLOW COOKER ZIP456	3,226PCS	@2PCS/CTN	@4.8KGS/PCS	@4.15KGS/PCS	83.88M3
GIFT BOX	24PCS	4CTNS	@0.42KGS/PCS	@0.33KGS/PCS	0.62M3
SPARE PARTS	48PCS	30CTNS	@1.5KGS/PCS	@1.2KGS/PCS	1.06M3

B/L DATE：2018-4-25

唛头：SPIL
2500020184
AUCKLAND
3,260CTNS

表 1-7-1　出境货物报检单

中华人民共和国出入境检验检疫

出境货物报检单

报检单位（加盖公章）：　　*编　号

报检单位登记号：　　联系人：　　电话：　　报检日期：　　年　月　日

<table>
<tr><td rowspan="2">发货人</td><td>（中文）</td><td colspan="5"></td></tr>
<tr><td>（外文）</td><td colspan="5"></td></tr>
<tr><td rowspan="2">收货人</td><td>（中文）</td><td colspan="5"></td></tr>
<tr><td>（外文）</td><td colspan="5"></td></tr>
<tr><td colspan="2">货物名称（中/外文）</td><td>H. S. 编码</td><td>产地</td><td>数/重量</td><td>货物总值</td><td>包装种类及数量</td></tr>
<tr><td colspan="2"></td><td></td><td></td><td></td><td></td><td></td></tr>
<tr><td colspan="2">运输工具名称号码</td><td colspan="2"></td><td>贸易方式</td><td></td><td>货物存放地点</td></tr>
<tr><td>合同号</td><td colspan="3"></td><td>信用证号</td><td></td><td>用途</td></tr>
<tr><td>发货日期</td><td></td><td colspan="2">输往国家（地区）</td><td></td><td>许可证/审批号</td><td></td></tr>
</table>

续表

<table>
<tr><td>启运地</td><td></td><td>到达口岸</td><td></td><td>生产单位注册号</td><td></td></tr>
<tr><td colspan="2">集装箱规格、数量及号码</td><td colspan="4"></td></tr>
<tr><td colspan="2">合同、信用证订立的检验检疫条款或特殊要求</td><td>标记及号码</td><td colspan="3">随附单据(划"√"或补填)</td></tr>
<tr><td colspan="2"></td><td></td><td colspan="2">□合同
□信用证
□发票
□换证凭单
□装箱单
□厂检单</td><td>□包装性能结果单
□许可/审批文件
□报检委托书
□型式试验报告书
□
□</td></tr>
<tr><td colspan="4">需要证单名称(划"√"或补填)</td><td colspan="2">* 检验检疫费</td></tr>
<tr><td colspan="2" rowspan="3">□品质证书 __正__副
□重量证书 __正__副
□数量证书 __正__副
□兽医卫生证书 __正__副
□健康证书 __正__副
□卫生证书 __正__副
□动物卫生证书 __正__副</td><td colspan="2" rowspan="3">□植物检疫证书 __正__副
□熏蒸/消毒证书 __正__副
□出境货物换证凭单 __正__副
□
□
□
□</td><td>总金额
(人民币元)</td><td></td></tr>
<tr><td>计费人</td><td></td></tr>
<tr><td>收费人</td><td></td></tr>
<tr><td colspan="4" rowspan="3">报检人郑重声明:
1. 本人被授权报检。
2. 上列填写内容正确属实,货物无伪造或冒用他人的厂名、标志、认证标志,并承担货物质量责任。

签名:____________</td><td colspan="2">领取证单</td></tr>
<tr><td>日期</td><td></td></tr>
<tr><td>签名</td><td></td></tr>
</table>

注:有"*"号栏由出入境检验检疫机关填写。 ◆国家出入境检验检疫局制

[1-2(2000.1.1)]

2. 请根据以下材料(见表 1-7-2)和相关资料填制出境货物报检单(见表 1-7-3)。

表 1-7-2 商业发票

<table>
<tr><td colspan="2">杭州立新电器股份有限公司
HANGZHOU LIXIN ELECTRIC CO. ,LTD.
842 MOGANSHAN ROAD HANGZHOU,CHINA</td></tr>
<tr><td colspan="2">商业发票
COMMERCIAL INVOICE</td></tr>
<tr><td colspan="2">To:</td></tr>
<tr><td>THOMAS IMP. AND EXP. COMPANY
31 BLUEBIRD STREET SINGAPORE</td><td>Invoice No. :TB-M85062
Invoice Date:JULY 25. ,2018
S/C No. :SM9806263
L/C No. :HU65926</td></tr>
</table>

续表

Marks & Nos.	Description of goods	Quantity	Unit Price	Amount
Transport details: FROM SHENZHEN TO SINGAPORE BY VESSEL PER S. S. :TAO LA V. 441		Terms of payment: BY L/C		
Marks & Nos.	Description of goods	Quantity	Unit Price	Amount
THOMAS SINGAPORE NOS. 1-500	COLOUR TELEVISION		CIF SINGAPORE	
	SET MODEL RT560	500SETS	USD160. 00	
	WITH REMOTE		PER SET	USD80,000. 00
	CONTROL,PACKED IN			
	EXPORT CARTONS OF			
	ONE SET EACH			
TOTAL		500SETS		USD80,000. 00
杭州立新电器股份有限公司(章) HANGZHOU LIXIN ELECTRIC CO. ,LTD.				

相关资料如下。

商品编码：8528. 1291　　CONTAINER NO. :1×40′COSU829234-2

发货日期：AUG. 10,2018　　货物存放地点：中山南头

用途：其他　　产地：浙江杭州

报检人：李月　　报检日期：2018 年 7 月 27 日

报验时提交的随附单据：合同、信用证、发票、装箱单。

需要的证单：品质证书(1 正 2 副),出境货物换证凭单(1 正 1 副)。

表 1-7-3　出境货物报检单

中华人民共和国出入境检验检疫

出境货物报检单

报检单位(加盖公章)：　　　　*编　　号

报检单位登记号：　　联系人：　　电话：　　报检日期：　　年　月　日

发货人	(中文)				
	(外文)				
收货人	(中文)				
	(外文)				

货物名称(中/外文)	H. S. 编码	产地	数/重量	货物总值	包装种类及数量

续表

<table>
<tr><td>运输工具名称号码</td><td colspan="2"></td><td>贸易方式</td><td></td><td>货物存放地点</td><td></td></tr>
<tr><td>合同号</td><td colspan="2"></td><td>信用证号</td><td></td><td>用途</td><td></td></tr>
<tr><td>发货日期</td><td></td><td>输往国家(地区)</td><td colspan="2"></td><td>许可证/审批号</td><td></td></tr>
<tr><td>启运地</td><td></td><td>到达口岸</td><td colspan="2"></td><td>生产单位注册号</td><td></td></tr>
<tr><td colspan="2">集装箱规格、数量及号码</td><td colspan="5"></td></tr>
<tr><td colspan="3">合同、信用证订立的检验检疫条款或特殊要求</td><td>标记及号码</td><td colspan="3">随附单据(划"√"或补填)</td></tr>
<tr><td colspan="3"></td><td></td><td colspan="2">□合同
□信用证
□发票
□换证凭单
□装箱单
□厂检单</td><td>□包装性能结果单
□许可/审批文件
□
□
□
□</td></tr>
</table>

<table>
<tr><td colspan="2">需要证单名称(划"√"或补填)</td><td colspan="2">*检验检疫费</td></tr>
<tr><td rowspan="3">□品质证书 __正__副
□重量证书 __正__副
□数量证书 __正__副
□兽医卫生证书 __正__副
□健康证书 __正__副
□卫生证书 __正__副
□动物卫生证书 __正__副</td><td rowspan="3">□植物检疫证书 __正__副
□熏蒸/消毒证书 __正__副
□出境货物换证凭单 __正__副
□
□
□
□</td><td>总金额
(人民币元)</td><td></td></tr>
<tr><td>计费人</td><td></td></tr>
<tr><td>收费人</td><td></td></tr>
<tr><td colspan="2" rowspan="3">报检人郑重声明:
1. 本人被授权报检。
2. 上列填写内容正确属实,货物无伪造或冒用他人的厂名、标志、认证标志,并承担货物质量责任。

签名:______________</td><td colspan="2">领取证单</td></tr>
<tr><td>日期</td><td></td></tr>
<tr><td>签名</td><td></td></tr>
</table>

注:有"*"号栏由出入境检验检疫机关填写。

◆国家出入境检验检疫局制

[1-2(2000.1.1)]

3. 请根据商业发票(见表 1-7-4)和相关资料填制出境货物报检单(见表 1-7-5)。

表 1-7-4 商业发票

<table>
<tr><td colspan="2">广东省轻工家电有限公司
GUANGDONG LIGHT ELECTRICAL APPLIANCES CO.,LTD.
52 DEZHENG ROAD SOUTH,GUANGZHOU,CHINA</td></tr>
<tr><td colspan="2">商业发票
COMMERCIAL INVOICE</td></tr>
<tr><td>Messrs:
BRUSSELSLACES AND GIFTS SERV. SA
RUE DE LUSAMBO. 21/23
1190 BRUXELLES,BE</td><td>INVOICE NO.:GD05753
INVOICE DATE:FEB. 28,2018
L/C NO.:21036414276424
S/C NO.:D/269/97</td></tr>
</table>

续表

<table>
<tr><td colspan="5">Exporter:
GUANGDONG LIGHT ELECTRICAL
APPLIANCES COMPANY LIMTIED</td></tr>
<tr><td colspan="3">Transport details:
FROM GUANGZHOU TO ANTWERP BELGIUM
W/T HONGKONG BY VESSEL
PER S. S. :DAQI V. 117</td><td colspan="2">Terms of Payment:
BY L/C</td></tr>
<tr><td>MARKS AND NUMBERS</td><td>DESCRIP. OF GOODS</td><td>QUANTYTY</td><td>UNIT PRICE</td><td>AMOUNT</td></tr>
<tr><td>AL SHAMALI
ANTWERP</td><td>H. S. CODE.: 6303.5900
COTTON PRINTED VELVET TOWELS</td><td>3,936PCS</td><td>@USD3.64/PC</td><td>USD14,327.04</td></tr>
<tr><td colspan="5">CIF ANTWERP USD14,327.04
TOTAL QUANTITY: 3,936PCS PACKING:160CATRONS
TOTAL: U. S. DOLLARS FOURTEEN THOUSAND AND THREE HUNDRED TWENTY-SEVEN POINT FOUR ONLY.

GUANGDONG LIGHT ELECTRICAL
APPLIANCES COMPANY LIMITED
(签章)</td></tr>
</table>

相关资料如下。

集装箱号：1×20′COSU82901-2　　发货日期：MAR. 15,2018

货物存放地点：大朗仓库　　用途：其他

产地：广州　　报检人：杨怡

报检日期：2018 年 3 月 1 日

报检时提交的随附单据：合同、信用证、发票、装箱单。

需要证单：品质证书(1 正 2 副)，卫生检验证书 1 正 1 副，出境货物换证凭单(1 正 1 副)。

表 1-7-5　出境货物报检单

中华人民共和国出入境检验检疫

出境货物报检单

报检单位(加盖公章)：　　*编　号________

报检单位登记号：　联系人：　电话：　报检日期：　年　月　日

<table>
<tr><td rowspan="2">发货人</td><td>(中文)</td><td colspan="5"></td></tr>
<tr><td>(外文)</td><td colspan="5"></td></tr>
<tr><td rowspan="2">收货人</td><td>(中文)</td><td colspan="5"></td></tr>
<tr><td>(外文)</td><td colspan="5"></td></tr>
<tr><td colspan="2">货物名称(中/外文)</td><td>H. S. 编码</td><td>产地</td><td>数/重量</td><td>货物总值</td><td>包装种类及数量</td></tr>
<tr><td colspan="2"></td><td></td><td></td><td></td><td></td><td></td></tr>
</table>

续表

<table>
<tr><td>运输工具名称号码</td><td colspan="2"></td><td>贸易方式</td><td></td><td>货物存放地点</td><td></td></tr>
<tr><td>合同号</td><td colspan="2"></td><td>信用证号</td><td></td><td>用途</td><td></td></tr>
<tr><td>发货日期</td><td></td><td>输往国家（地区）</td><td colspan="2"></td><td>许可证/审批号</td><td></td></tr>
<tr><td>启运地</td><td></td><td>到达口岸</td><td colspan="2"></td><td>生产单位注册号</td><td></td></tr>
<tr><td>集装箱规格、数量及号码</td><td colspan="6"></td></tr>
<tr><td colspan="2">合同、信用证订立的检验检疫条款或特殊要求</td><td>标记及号码</td><td colspan="4">随附单据（划“√”或补填）</td></tr>
<tr><td colspan="2"></td><td></td><td colspan="2">□合同
□信用证
□发票
□换证凭单
□装箱单
□厂检单</td><td colspan="2">□包装性能结果单
□许可/审批文件
□
□
□
□</td></tr>
<tr><td colspan="4">需要证单名称（划“√”或补填）</td><td colspan="3">＊检验检疫费</td></tr>
<tr><td colspan="2" rowspan="3">□品质证书 __正__副
□重量证书 __正__副
□数量证书 __正__副
□兽医卫生证书 __正__副
□健康证书 __正__副
□卫生证书 __正__副
□动物卫生证书 __正__副</td><td colspan="2" rowspan="3">□植物检疫证书 __正__副
□熏蒸/消毒证书 __正__副
□出境货物换证凭单 __正__副
□
□
□
□</td><td>总金额（人民币元）</td><td colspan="2"></td></tr>
<tr><td>计费人</td><td colspan="2"></td></tr>
<tr><td>收费人</td><td colspan="2"></td></tr>
<tr><td colspan="4" rowspan="3">报检人郑重声明：
1. 本人被授权报检。
2. 上列填写内容正确属实，货物无伪造或冒用他人的厂名、标志、认证标志，并承担货物质量责任。
签名：__________</td><td colspan="3">领取证单</td></tr>
<tr><td>日期</td><td colspan="2"></td></tr>
<tr><td>签名</td><td colspan="2"></td></tr>
</table>

注：有“＊”号栏由出入境检验检疫机关填写。

◆国家出入境检验检疫局制

[1-2(2000.1.1)]

项目八　缮制原产地证书

一、常用术语中英文互译

1. 目的地国家________　　2. 签证机构________
3. 收货方________　　4. 发票号码和日期________
5. 运输方式和路线 ________　　6. Certificate of origin ________
7. GSP ________　　8. Origin criterion ________
9. Chamber of commerce ________　　10. Competent authorities ________

二、单项选择题

1. 在我国,签发普惠制原产地证书 FORM A 的机构是(　　)。

A. 海关总署及各省市海关　　B. 各省市出入境检验检疫局
C. 商务部及各省市经贸厅　　D. 出口商

2. 根据我国有关规定,出口企业最迟于货物出运前 3 天,持签证机构规定的正本文件向签证机构申请办理一般原产地证书。申请一般原产地证书时不需要的文件是(　　)。

A.《一般原产地证书申请单》　　B.《中华人民共和国原产地证书》
C. 正本商业发票　　D. 商检证书

3. 信用证规定“Certificate of origin G. S. P. Form A in duplicate”,根据要求,该产地证的签发机构是(　　)。

A. 贸促会(商会)　　B. 出境地海关
C. 生产地公证处　　D. 出入境检验检疫局

4. 以下有关一般原产地证书“商品名称、包装种类及件数”一栏填报的陈述,不正确的是(　　)。

A. 商品名称必须与 H. S. 编码准确对应,可以使用商品总称
B. 包装件数必须用阿拉伯数字和文字同时表示
C. 商品名称填完后要在下一行加上“*********”表示结束,以防伪造或添加
D. 若信用证中要求产地证中显示信用证号,可加注在此栏结束符号下方

5. 某批出口到俄罗斯的货物,货物原料有进口成分,但进口成分价值为产品离岸价的28%,则原产地证中“原产地标准”栏应填报(　　)。

A. P　　B. Y28%　　C. W HS28%　　D. F 28%

6. 信用证条款有 Certificate of Origin in two fold indicating that goods are of Chinese origin issued by Chamber of Commerce,根据该条款,原产地证的签发机构为(　　)。

A. 贸促会(商会)　　B. 出境地海关
C. 生产地公证处　　D. 出入境检验检疫局

7. 普惠制是(　　)对发展中国家出口产品给予的一种关税优惠制度。

A. 发达国家　　B. 发展中国家　　C. 美国　　D. 欧盟

8. 不属于普惠制原则的是(　　)。

A. 普遍原则　　B. 非互惠原则

C. 严格符合原则　　D. 非歧视原则

9. 普惠制原产地证书 FORM A 原产地标准栏目中,如果出口商品完全是出口国自产的且不含有进口成分的商品,出口到所有给惠国应填写(　　)。

A. P　　B. Y　　C. W　　D. F

10. 在一般原产地证书中,商品名称栏目填完后,在下面一行加上(　　)表示填写结束。

A. *********　　B. 。。。。。。。。

C. +++++++++　　D. ---------

三、多项选择题

1. 出口企业申请签发普惠制原产地证书应提供的单证和资料有(　　)。

A. 普惠制原产地证书申请书一份

B. 普惠制原产地证书(FORM A)一套

C. 正式的出口商业发票正本一份,装箱单一份

D. 含有进口成分的产品,应提交《含进口成分商品成本明细单》

2. 产地证书是由出口国政府有关机构签发的一种证明货物原产地或制造地的证明文件,通常用于不需要提供(　　)的国家和地区。

A. 海关发票　　B. 领事发票　　C. 形式发票　　D. 厂商发票

E. 商业发票

3. 如果信用证中没有特别规定,原产地证可以由(　　)出具。

A. 商检局　　B. 贸促会　　C. 生产企业　　D. 出口企业

4. 普惠制产地证书第 12 栏"出口商声明"(Declaration by the exporter)应填写的内容有(　　)。

A. 出口国国名　　B. 进口国国名

C. 出口商申请日期　　D. 签证当局盖章

5. 特殊原产地证书主要有(　　)。

A. 普惠制产地证书　　B. 厂商产地证书

C. 区域性优惠原产地证书　　D. 专用原产地证书

6. 出口企业在办理原产地证时,必须提交的单证有(　　)。

A. 中华人民共和国出口货物原产地证书/加工装配证明申请书》

B. 中华人民共和国出口货物原产地证书

C. 出口货物商业发票

D. 签证机构认为必要的其他证明文件

7. 给予我国普惠制待遇的有(　　)。

A. 保加利亚　　B. 美国　　C. 新西兰　　D. 加拿大

8. 普惠制原产地证书 FORM A 的申报日期可以(　　)。

A. 早于发票日期　　B. 不得早于发票日期

C. 与发票日期同日　　D. 与提单日期同日

9. 下列属于区域性优惠原产地证书的有(　　)。

A. FORM A　　B. FORM E　　C. FORM F　　D. FORM B

10. 专用原产地证书包括(　　)。

A. 纺织品证书　　B. 化工产品安全证书

C. 手工制品证书　　D. 烟草真实性证书

四、判断题

1. 我国某贸易商把进口布料剪裁缝制为服装再出口至印度,因为布料是进口的,不能申请办理普惠制产地证书 FORM A。(　　)

2. 原产地证书应由检验检疫局、贸促会或商务部出具,不能由出口商或生产厂家出具。(　　)

3. 在我国,国家质量监督检验检疫总局及所属机构是签发普惠制产地证书的唯一机构。(　　)

4. 我国出口企业对美国出口纺织品时,除了提交原产地声明书以外,还需提交普惠制产地证书。(　　)

5. 一般原产地证书的"签证机构证明"一栏(Certification)应由签证机构签字、盖章,并填写日期、地点,签发日期可以早于发票日期。(　　)

6. 普惠制原产地证书 FORM A 一般用英文填制,应进口商的要求,也可使用法文,除此之外,证书填制不得使用其他文种。(　　)

7. 普惠制原产地证书 FORM A 的"收货人"一栏应填写最终收货人的名称。如果信用证未明确最终收货人,可以填写商业发票的抬头人名称,或者填写中间商的名称。(　　)

8. 如果普惠制产地证书已签发,因遗失或损毁等原因向出入境检验检疫局申请补发证书时,经出入境检验检疫局审批后可以补发,并在证书上盖"DUPLICATE"红色印章。(　　)

9. 普惠制的原则有非普遍原则、非互惠原则和非歧视原则。(　　)

10. 含有进口成分的产品,出口到欧盟,普惠制原产地证书 FORM A 的原产地标准栏目填"W"。(　　)

五、简答题

1. 简述原产地证书的含义及作用。

2. 我国原产地证书的种类有哪些?

3. 简述原产地证书的申请与签发程序。

六、技能操作题

1. 广东省纺织品进出口针织品有限公司向希腊某商出口一批塑胶玩具，该出口公司产地证申报员李月拟于2018年10月7日向广州检验检疫局申报，公司电话：020-7878 7878。请根据商业发票（见表1-8-1）帮李月填制一般原产地证书（见表1-8-2）。

表1-8-1 商业发票

广东省纺织品进出口针织品有限公司
GUANGDONG TEXTILES IMP. & EXP. KNITWEARS COMPANY LIMITED
15/F.,GUANGDONG TEXTILES MANSION 168 XIAOBEI ROAD,GUANGZHOU,CHINA

商业发票
COMMERCIAL INVOICE

Messrs:
JOHNSON
KREONTOS 30 STR. GREECE

INVOICE NO.: YSM1999B
INVOICE DATE: OCT. 05,2018
L/C NO.: KDTT524250
L/C DATE: AUG. 20,2018
S/C NO.: GD-98TX2509

Exporter:
GUANGDONG TEXTILES IMP. & EXP. KNITWEARS COMPANY LIMTIED
15/F.,GUANGDONG TEXTILES MANSION 168 XIAOBEI ROAD,GUANGZHOU,CHINA

Transport details:
FROM GUANGZHOU TO PIRAEUS GREECE
BY VESSEL SAILING DATE: OCT. 15,2018

Terms of payment:
BY L/C

MARKS AND NUMBERS	DESCRIP. OF GOODS	QUANTYTY	UNIT PRICE	AMOUNT
JOHNSON	H. S. NO.: 9509900000		FOB GUANGZHOU	
97KCS05111	PLASTIC TOYS	10,000PCS	USD1.20/PC	USD12,000.00
NO. 1-500				
MADE IN CHINA				

USD12,000.00

TOTAL QUANTITY: 10,000PCS PACKING:500CATRONS
TOTAL: U.S. DOLLARS TWELVE THOUSAND ONLY.

广东省纺织品进出口针织品有限公司
GUANGDONG TEXTILES IMP. & EXP. KNITWEARS COMPANY LIMITED
（签章）

表 1-8-2 一般原产地证书

<table>
<tr><td colspan="2">1. Exporter</td><td colspan="3" rowspan="2">Certificate No.

**CERTIFICATE OF ORIGIN
OF
THE PEOPLE'S REPUBLIC OF CHINA**</td></tr>
<tr><td colspan="2">2. Consignee</td></tr>
<tr><td colspan="2">3. Means of transport and route</td><td colspan="3" rowspan="2">5. For certifying authority use only</td></tr>
<tr><td colspan="2">4. Country/region of destination</td></tr>
<tr><td>6. Marks and numbers</td><td>7. Number and kind of packages; description of goods</td><td>8. H. S. code</td><td>9. Quantity</td><td>10. Number and date of invoices</td></tr>
<tr><td colspan="2">11. Declaration by the exporter
The undersigned hereby declares that the above details and statements are correct; that all the goods were produced in China and that they comply with the Rules of Origin of the People's Republic of China.

Place and date, signature and stamp of authorized signatory</td><td colspan="3">12. Certification
It is hereby certified that the declaration by the exporter is correct.

Place and date, signature and stamp of certifying authority</td></tr>
</table>

2. 广东省轻工家电有限公司出口一批到比利时的产品，该产品完全为我国江西浪花毛织厂自产，不含任何进口成分，请你根据商业发票(见表1-8-3)帮助该公司产地证申报员李月(2018年3月18日申报，预定出口装运日期为3月22日)填制"普惠制产地证书FORM A"(见表1-8-4)。

表1-8-3 商业发票

广东省轻工家电有限公司

GUANGDONG LIGHT ELECTRICAL APPLIANCES COMPANY LIMITED

52 DEZHENG ROAD SOUTH, GUANGZHOU, CHINA

商业发票

COMMERCIAL INVOICE

Messrs:
BRUSSELSLACES AND GIFTS SERV. SA
RUE DE LUSAMBO. 21/23
1190 BRUXELLES, BE

INVOICE NO.: GD05753
INVOICE DATE: FEB. 28, 2018
L/C NO.: 21036414276424
S/C NO.: D/269/97

Exporter:
GUANGDONG LIGHT ELECTRICAL APPLIANCES COMPANY LIMTIED

Transport details:
FROM GUANGZHOU TO ANTWERP BELGIUM
W/T HONGKONG BY VESSEL
PER S. S.: DAQI V. 117

Terms of payment:
BY L/C

MARKS AND NUMBERS	DESCRIP. OF GOODS	QUANTYTY	UNIT PRICE	AMOUNT
AL SHAMALI ANTWERP	H. S. CODE.: 6303.5900 COTTON PRINTED VELVET TOWELS	3,936PCS	CIF ANTWERP @USD5.64/PC	USD22,199.04
				USD22,199.04

TOTAL QUANTITY: 3,936PCS PACKING: 160CATRONS

TOTAL: U. S. DOLLARS TWENTY-TWO THOUSAND AND ONE HUNDRED NINETY-NINE POINT FOUR ONLY.

广东省轻工家电有限公司
GUANGDONG LIGHT ELECTRICAL APPLIANCES COMPANY LIMITED
(签章)

表 1-8-4 普惠制产地证书 FORM A

<table>
<tr>
<td colspan="3">1. Goods consigned from (Exporter's business name, address, country)</td>
<td colspan="3" rowspan="2">Reference No.

GENERALIZED SYSTEM OF PREFERENCES
CERTIFICATE OF ORIGIN
(Combined declaration and certificate)
FORM A
Issued in THE PEOPLE'S REPUBLIC OF CHINA
(country)
See Notes Overleaf</td>
</tr>
<tr>
<td colspan="3">2. Goods consigned to (Consignee's name, address, country)</td>
</tr>
<tr>
<td colspan="3">3. Means of transport and route(as far as known)</td>
<td colspan="3">4. For official use</td>
</tr>
<tr>
<td>5. Item number</td>
<td>6. Marks and numbers of packages</td>
<td>7. Number and kind of packages; description of goods</td>
<td>8. Origin criterion (see notes overleaf)</td>
<td>9. Gross weight or other quantity</td>
<td>10. Number and date of invoices</td>
</tr>
<tr>
<td colspan="3">11. Certification
It is hereby certified, on the basis of control carried out, that the declaration by the exporter is correct.

....
Place and date, signature and stamp of certifying authority</td>
<td colspan="3">12. Declaration by the exporter
The undersigned hereby declares that the above details and statements are correct; that all the goods were produced in
CHINA
(country)
and that they comply with the origin requirements specified for those goods in the Generalized System of Preferences for goods exported to
....
(importing country)

....
Place and date, signature of authorized signatory</td>
</tr>
</table>

项目九　缮制报关单

一、常用术语英译中

1. Brussels tariff nomenclature ________________

2. Customs co-operative council ________________

3. Combined certificate of value and origin ________________

4. Custom house ________________　　5. Clearance of goods ________________

6. Customs broker ________________　　7. Customs invoice ________________

8. Customs duty ________________　　9. Import licence ________________

10. Import quota ________________

二、单项选择题

1. 关于报关单份数的说法正确的是(　　)。

A. 一份电子出口报关单最多填报 20 项商品

B. 一份纸质出口报关单最多填报 5 项商品

C. 一份纸质出口报关单可允许附带最多 1 张纸质报关单

D. 一份纸质出口报关单可允许附带最多 2 张纸质报关单

2. 若某货物由上海吴淞港(关区代码：2202)出运，在出口报关单“出口口岸”栏应填报(　　)。

A. 上海口岸　　B. 吴淞海关 2202　　C. 吴淞口岸　　D. 上海口岸 2202

3. 进口商在货物到达目的港后，应在运输工具进境之日起(　　)日内向海关申报。

A. 3　　B. 7　　C. 14　　D. 15

4. 根据《中华人民共和国海关法》规定，进口货物的收货人向海关申报的时限是(　　)。

A. 自运输工具申报进境之日起 7 日内

B. 自运输工具申报进境之日起 10 日内

C. 自运输工具申报进境之日起 14 日内

D. 自运输工具申报进境之日起 15 日内

5. 按照《中华人民共和国海关法》规定，不需要办理报关手续的是(　　)。

A. 进出境的运输工具　　B. 进出境的货物

C. 进出境的行李物品　　D. 进出境的人员

6. 北京 ABC 外商投资公司委托大连化工进出口公司与日本一家供货商签订了一份进口某型电动车的合同，在进口货物报关单“经营单位”和“备注栏”内按规定应分别填报(　　)。

A. 北京 ABC 外商投资公司　大连化工进出口公司

B. 北京 ABC 外商投资公司　北京 ABC 外商投资公司

C. 大连化工进出口公司　大连化工进出口公司

D. 大连化工进出口公司　北京ABC外商投资公司

7. 出口货物报关单上的征免性质一栏，应按海关核发的《征免税证明》中批注的征免性质或海关规定的《征免性质代码表》填报相应征免性质的简称或其代码。一份报关单允许填报(　　)种征免性质。

A. 1　B. 2　C. 3　D. 4

8. 贸易方式若是一般贸易，出口报关单的"征免性质"栏和"征免"栏应分别填报(　　)。

A. 一般征税　照章征税　B. 照章征免　一般纳税

C. 一般纳税　照章征免　D. 照章征税　一般征免

9. 我国某进口商从菲律宾购进澳大利亚生产的羊毛，用船运至香港地区再转车进入深圳。进口报关单上起运国(地区)和运抵国(地区)两栏应填报(　　)。

A. 澳大利亚　中国　B. 菲律宾　中国

C. 香港　中国　D. 菲律宾　香港

10. 我国某进出口公司从中国香港购进一批SONY牌电视机，该电视机为日本品牌，其中显像管由韩国生产，集成电路板由新加坡生产，其他零件均由马来西亚生产，最后由韩国组装成整机。该公司向海关申报进口该电视机时，原产地应填报(　　)。

A. 日本　B. 韩国　C. 新加坡　D. 马来西亚

三、多项选择题

1. 按照海关规定的《结汇方式代码表》，出口货物报关单"结汇方式"栏可以填写(　　)。

A. 信汇　B. 信用证　C. 汇票　D. 电汇

2. 某合资企业从韩国进口一批机器设备，该企业委托A进出口公司代办进口手续。A进出口公司与外商订货后，随即委托B公司具体办理货物运输事宜，同时委托上海C报关公司负责办理进口报关手续。下列出现在报关单有关栏目内的单位，填写错误的有(　　)。

A. 经营单位：A进出口公司　B. 收货单位：某合资企业

C. 申报单位：B公司　D. 收货单位：A进出口公司

3. 我国由海关代征的进口环节税包括(　　)。

A. 增值税　B. 消费税　C. 营业税　D. 所得税

4. 报关程序按时间先后分为三个阶段：前期阶段、进出境阶段、后续阶段。对于进出口货物的收、发货人，进出境阶段包括(　　)等环节。

A. 进出口申报　B. 缴纳税费　C. 备案、销案　D. 配合查验

5. 进出口报关时不必在报关单随附单据栏目中填写的必备的随附单证有(　　)。

A. 商业发票　B. 通关单　C. 装箱单　D. 许可证

6. 进口企业向海关提交(　　)等单据进行报关，海关审核无误后，在报关单上盖放行章，进口企业凭该报关单和提单等有关证件在船公司提货。

A. 进口货物报关单　B. 发票

C. 提单　D. 商品检验证

7. 出口货物报关单是由海关总署统一格式印制的，由出口企业或其代理人在装运前填制并凭以向海关申报通关，经海关审核并签发的法律文件。出口货物报关单是(　　)。

A. 海关依法监管货物出口的法律证书

B. 海关征收关税、税费的重要凭证

C. 出口货物核销、退税的重要依据

D. 海关编制海关统计的原始凭证

8. 按海关规定，在报关单的“备案号”栏内应填报(　　)的编号。

A.《加工贸易登记手册》　　B.《征免税证明》

C.《出口货物通关单》　　D.《电子账册》

9. 根据海关对报关单上“运输方式”项目的分类规定，“其他运输”包括(　　)。

A. 管道运输　　B. 驼畜运输　　C. 自行车装运　　D. 人力扛运

10. 某进出口公司报关员制作了一份进口报关单，在“标记唛码及备注”栏应填写的内容是(　　)。

A. NO MARK　　B. 付汇核销单编号

C. 商检证1份及其编号　　D. 进料加工合同共2本手册及全部编号

四、判断题

1. 报关单上“商品名称、规格型号”栏目，正确地填写内容应有中文商品名称、规格型号以及商品的英文名称和品牌。(　　)

2. 某外贸公司与境外贸易商以FOB价、D/P at sight方式结算订立出口棉麻衬衣的一般贸易出口合同，按规定申报时应填写一式四联报关单，分别是海关留存联、海关统计联、企业留存联、出口退税专用联。(　　)

3. 进口报关单上的进口日期应填报实际货物进境的日期。(　　)

4. 进出口货物收发货人、报关行、国际货运代理都可作为报关单位。(　　)

5. 报关企业是经海关批准、在海关办理了注册登记的境内法人，因此可以从事进出口业务。(　　)

6. 在我国，有进出口经营权的企业就享有海关报关权。(　　)

7. 加工贸易报关单上的收、发货单位可以与《加工贸易登记手册》中的“货主单位”不一致。(　　)

8. 报关单上的“杂费”指成交价格以外的、应计入完税价格或从完税价格中扣除的费用，如手续费、佣金、回扣等。(　　)

9. 报关单上的“收货单位”应为进口货物在境内的最终消费、使用的单位名称，“发货单位”应为出口货物在境内的生产或销售的单位名称。(　　)

10. 一批精密仪表在大连机场海关申报出口并转关运输至北京出境，其出口报关单“出口口岸”栏应按实际申请海关所在地填为“大连机场”。(　　)

五、简答题

1. 简述出口货物通关的程序。

2. 简述进口货物通关时集中审单的审核结果情况。

3. 出口货物报关时应提交的单据有哪些?

4. 进口货物报关时应提交的单据有哪些?

六、技能操作题

1. 请根据商业发票(见表1-9-1)和相关资料填制出口货物报关单(见表1-9-2)。

表 1-9-1 商业发票

JIAXING RICH TRAVEL PRODUCTS CO. ,LTD.
Xiucai Road,XiuZhou Industrial Park,Jiaxing,Zhejiang,China
Tel:86-573-8269 6629　　Fax:86-573-8279 1833
Commercial Invoice

Ship to: ELSA AB　　No. BG1601033
VIKENS INDUSTRIOMRODE 123,65　　OCT. 22,2018
SANDARED SWEDEN
Shipment: Per sailing from SHANGHAI,CHINA to GOTHENBURG SWEDEN on,OCT. 28,2018
Payment: BY T/T
Terms: FOB SHANGHAI

	Description	Quantity	Price	Amount
	40CM ALUMINUMPLATE PLASTIC	2,000PCS	USD4.1	USD8,200.00
	55CM ALUMINUMPLATE PLASTIC	1,000PCS	USD5.14	USD5,140.00
Total:		3,000PCS		USD13,340.00

Total Amount: U. S. DOLLARS THIRTEEN THOUSAND THREE HUNDRED AND FORTY ONLY.
Remarks: COUNTRY OF ORIGIN:CHINA
WE HEREBY CERTIFY THAT THIS SHIPMENT CONTAINS NO SOLID WOOD PACKING MATERIALSSHIPPING MARK:
ITEM DESCRIPTION
QTY:

JIAXING RICH TRAVEL PRODUCTS CO. ,LTD.
嘉兴瑞奇旅游制品有限公司
General Manager 周慧

相关资料如下。

经营单位海关注册号：913304007338001234

运输工具名称：EVELYN MAERSK V. 615W　B/L NO. :957003535W

毛重：837KGS　净重：909.5KGS　共装：75CTNS

出口口岸：上海海关　预录入编号：223120160888000789

许可证号：BG1606123

发货单位：鑫苑贸易有限公司　H. S. NO. :76152.000.00

有无特殊关系：否；价格影响确认：否；支付特许权使用费确认：否

用途：打扫卫生用；成分：铝；品牌：无；型号：无

表 1-9-2 出口货物报关单

中华人民共和国海关出口货物报关单

预录入编号：　海关编号：　（××海关）　页码/页数：

境内发货人	出境关别	出口日期	申报日期	备案号
境外收货人	运输方式	运输工具名称及航次号	提运单号	
生产销售单位	监管方式	征免性质	许可证号	

续表

合同协议号	贸易国(地区)		运抵国(地区)		指运港		离境口岸	
包装种类	件数	毛重(千克)	净重(千克)	成交方式	运费	保费	杂费	
随附单证及编号								
标记唛码及备注								
项号	商品编号	商品名称及规格型号	数量及单位	单价/总价/币制	原产国(地区)	最终目的国(地区)	境内货源地	征免
报关人员　　报关人员证号　　电话 兹申明对以上内容承担如实申报、依法纳税之责任 申报单位　　　　申报单位(签章)							海关批注及签章	

2. 请根据项目五中表 1-5-5 所示的商业发票及相关资料填制出口货物报关单(表 1-9-3)。相关资料如下。

经营单位海关注册号：3215587629

运输工具名称：COSCO HONG KONG 456W　　B/L NO.：EGLV152600784920

毛重：19,335KGS　　净重：17,765KGS　　出口口岸：上海海关

预录入编号：222920160791000789　　总运费：USD1,550

有无特殊关系：否；价格影响确认：否；支付特许权使用费确认：否

H. S. NO.：8477.3010.00　　申报日期：2018-9-8

用途：制造中空制品；品牌：阳光；型号：ABLB75-1，ABLB75-2

表 1-9-3　出口货物报关单

中华人民共和国海关出口货物报关单

预录入编号：　　　　海关编号：　　　（××海关）　　　　　　　　　页码/页数：

<table>
<tr><td>境内发货人</td><td colspan="2">出境关别</td><td colspan="2">出口日期</td><td>申报日期</td><td colspan="2">备案号</td></tr>
<tr><td>境外收货人</td><td colspan="2">运输方式</td><td colspan="2">运输工具名称及航次号</td><td colspan="3">提运单号</td></tr>
<tr><td>生产销售单位</td><td colspan="2">监管方式</td><td colspan="2">征免性质</td><td colspan="3">许可证号</td></tr>
<tr><td>合同协议号</td><td colspan="2">贸易国（地区）</td><td colspan="2">运抵国（地区）</td><td>指运港</td><td colspan="2">离境口岸</td></tr>
<tr><td>包装种类</td><td>件数</td><td>毛重（千克）</td><td>净重（千克）</td><td>成交方式</td><td>运费</td><td>保费</td><td>杂费</td></tr>
<tr><td colspan="8">随附单证及编号</td></tr>
<tr><td colspan="8">标记唛码及备注</td></tr>
</table>

项号	商品编号	商品名称及规格型号	数量及单位	单价/总价/币制	原产国（地区）	最终目的国（地区）	境内货源地	征免

<table>
<tr><td>报关人员　　报关人员证号　　电话
兹申明对以上内容承担如实申报、依法纳税之责任
申报单位　　　　　　　　　　　　申报单位（签章）</td><td>海关批注及签章</td></tr>
</table>

项目十　缮制保险单据

一、常用术语中英文互译

1. 保险单________________

2. 仓至仓条款__________

3. 预约保险单__________

4. 中国人民保险公司海洋运输货物保险条款________________

5. 保费________________

6. Insurance certificate ________________

7. Covering all risks and war risks ________________

8. Amount insured ________________

9. Institute cargo clauses ________________

10. Insured ________________

二、单项选择题

1. 以CIF术语达成的交易，如信用证没有特别规定，保险单的被保险人一栏应填写(　　)。

A. 开证申请人的名称　　　　B. 受益人的名称

C. TO ORDER　　　　D. TO WHOM IT MAY CONCERN

2. 我方按CIF条件出口一批陶瓷制品，由于信用证中没有规定具体投保险别，我方在办理投保手续时，一般可按(　　)投保。

A. 一切险＋碰损破碎险　　　　B. 平安险＋水渍险

C. 平安险＋碰损破碎险　　　　D. 一切险＋水渍险

3. 进口商往往要求出口商出具(　　)年以下船龄的证明，因为该年限以上的船为超龄船，保险公司不愿承保。

A. 15　　B. 20　　C. 30　　D. 25

4. CIC"特殊附加险"是指在特殊情况下要求保险公司承保的险别，该险别(　　)。

A. 一般可以单独投保

B. 不能单独投保

C. 可单独投保两项以上

D. 在被保险人同意的情况下可以单独投保

5. 根据中国保险条款规定，不能单独投保的险别是(　　)。

A. 平安险　　B. 水渍险　　C. 战争险　　D. 一切险

6. 预约保险单(Open Policy)又称开口保险单，是(　　)。

A. 保险人签发正式保单前出立的临时证明

B. 保险单出立后，根据投保人的需求，对保险内容补充或变更而出具的一种凭证

C. 经常有相同类型货物需要陆续装运的保险

D. 投保人与保险人订立保险合同时，在还有一些条件尚未确定而投保人又急需保险凭证的情况下，由保险人先行开立的

7. 保险单中，保险赔偿赔付地点一般填写(　　)。

A. 起运港(地)　　B. 目的港(地)

C. 投保人所在地　　D. 保险公司所在地

8. 转让保险单时，如信用证未明确规定背书方式，应采用(　　)。

A. 空白背书　　B. 记名背书　　C. 记名指示背书　　D. 不必背书

9. 仓至仓条款是(　　)。

A. 承运人负责运输责任起讫的条款　　B. 出口商负责运输责任起讫的条款

C. 保险人负责保险责任起讫的条款　　D. 进口商负责运输责任起讫的条款

10. 如信用证没有特别规定，按国际保险市场惯例，保险金额一般在发票金额的基础上(　　)填写。

A. 加一成　　B. 加两成　　C. 加三成　　D. 加四成

三、多项选择题

1. 以下关于保险凭证的表述，正确的有(　　)。

A. 保险凭证俗称小保单，是一种简化的保险单

B. 保险凭证既有正面内容，又有背面条款

C. 保险凭证与保险单具有同等效力

D. 在实务中，保险凭证可以代替保险单

2. 出口的茶叶为防止运输途中串味，办理保险时应投保(　　)。

A. 串味险　　B. 平安险加串味险

C. 水渍险加串味险　　D. 一切险加串味险

3. 根据伦敦保险协会制定的《协会货物条款》，以下险别能单独投保的有(　　)。

A. ICC(A)　　B. ICC(B)　　C. 战争险　　D. 恶意损害险

4. 按照我国《海洋货物运输保险条款》的规定，以下险别，属于我国海洋运输货物保险中的基本险的是(　　)。

A. FPA　　B. ICC(A)　　C. WPA　　D. WAR RISKS

5. 我国保险条款中属于一般附加险别的有(　　)。

A. 淡水、雨淋险　　B. 短量险　　C. 钩损险　　D. 黄曲霉素险

E. 拒收险

6. 我国《海运货物运输保险条款》中，适用“仓至仓条款”的险别是(　　)。

A. WAR RISKS　　B. STRIKE RISK　　C. FPA　　D. WPA

E. ALL RISKS

7. 在有具体唛头的情况下，保险单唛头一栏可填写(　　)。

A. 发票上的唛头　　B. As per Invoice No. ...(发票号码)

C. N/M　　D. N/N

8. 一切险所承保的责任范围包括(　　)。

A. 淡水雨淋险　　B. 拒收险　　C. 钩损险　　D. 渗漏险

9. 保险单是(　　)。

A. 物权凭证　　B. 索赔证明　　C. 保险合同　　D. 货物收据

E. 运输契约的证明

10. 我国海洋运输货物保险条款中的基本险别包括(　　)。

A. 平安险　　B. 战争险　　C. 水渍险　　D. 一切险

E. 罢工险

四、判断题

1. 某出口合同按CIF伦敦条件成交,载货船舶经台湾海峡时曾一度搁浅,后经施救浮起继续航行,至马六甲海峡又遇暴风巨浪,致使茶叶公司交运的1000箱茶叶中,有200箱遭到不同程度的损坏,幸亏事先投保了水渍险,否则买方将不能从保险公司获得赔偿。(　　)

2. 按CIF术语出口时,我出口商在国内投保一切险,出口商承担的风险起讫应为"仓至仓"。(　　)

3. 保险单和海运单都是一种权利凭证,都可以背书转让。(　　)

4. 按国际保险市场惯例,大保单与小保单具有同等法律效力。(　　)

5. 保险单可以做成空白背书,方便卖方在交单时把保险单的求偿权转让给买方。(　　)

6. 在出口业务中,保险单日期不能迟于海运提单日期。(　　)

7. 当信用证要求提交的保险单份数为"IN TWO COPIES"时,我方应提交两份副本。(　　)

8. L/C在保险条款中规定I. O. P.,则出口商交单的保险单上必须显示免赔率。(　　)

9. 保险单俗称"大保单",保险凭证俗称"小保单",由于保险凭证背面没有列入保险条款,因而它们不具有同等的法律效力。(　　)

10. 如信用证规定按ICC条款投保,根据中国人民保险公司的现行规定是不能接受的,应要求对方修改信用证。(　　)

五、简答题

1. 简述我国进出口业务中的保险条款与基本险别。

2. 简述保险单的含义及主要形式。

3. 我国某公司以CIF条件出口一批羊肉到非洲某国,信用证规定投保平安险加战争险、罢工险。货到目的港后由于码头工人罢工而致无人卸货,一个星期后由于无法补充燃料,货轮上的冷冻设备停止运转。罢工结束,该批羊肉已变质无法食用。保险公司对于该损失是否赔偿?为什么?

六、技能操作题

1. 请根据以下资料填制保险单(见表1-10-1)。

(1) 信用证条款。

APPLICANT: *50: ZELLERS ING. ,ATIN. IMPORT DEPT.
401 BAY STREET,10/FL.
TORONTO ON MJH. 2Y4,CANADA

BENEFICIARY：＊59：G. M. G. HARDWEAR & TOOLS IMP. & EXP. COMPANY LTD.
726 DONGFENG ROAD EAST，GUANGZHOU，CHINA
LOADING IN CHARGE：44A：GUANGZHOU，CHINA
FOR TRANSPORT TO …：44B：VANCOUVER，CANADA
DESCRIPT. OF GOODS：45 A：HANDLE TOOLS

ITEM NO.	QUANTITY	UNTI PRICE
A0214	2，000DOZ	USD10.50
A0012	1，000DOZ	USD11.50
M0120	500DOZ	USD28.00

AS PER SALES CONFIRMATION NO. 02GP520471
DD 18 JAN. 12
CIF VANCOUVER CANADA

DOCUMENTS REQUIRED：46A：

＋MARINE INSURANCE POLICY OR CERTIFICATE IN DUPLICATE，ENDORSED IN BLANK，FOR FULL INVOICE VALUE PLUS 10 PERCENT，STATING CLAIM PAYABLE IN CANADA COVERING INSTITUTE CARGO CLAUSES(A) AND WAR RISKS.

（2）其他资料。

发票号码：KW-180419　　发票日期：2018 年 4 月 10 日
发票金额：USD46 500.00　　提单日期：2018 年 4 月 19 日
船名：CHAOHE/ZIM CANADA V.44E(在中国香港地区转运)
唛头：ZELLERS CANADA/VANCOUVER　　保险单号码：KC18-85362
货物装箱情况：10DOZ/PACKAGE　　350PACKAGES

表 1-10-1　保险单

中保财产保险有限公司
The People's Insurance (Property) Company of China，Ltd.

发票号码 Invoice No.	保险单号次 Policy No.

海洋货物运输保险单
MARINE CARGO TRANSPORTATION INSURANCE POLICY

被保险人：
Insured：

中保财产保险有限公司(以下简称本公司)根据被保险人的要求，及其所缴付约定的保险费，按照本保险单承担险别和背面所载条款与下列特别条款承保下列货物运输保险，特签发本保险单。

This policy of Insurance witnesses that the People's Insurance (Property) Company of China，Ltd. (hereinafter called "The Company")，at the request of the Insured and in consideration of the agreed premium paid by the Insured，undertakes to insure the undermentioned goods in transportation subject to conditions of the Policy as per the Clauses printed overleaf and other special clauses attached hereon.

续表

<table>
<tr><td colspan="2">保险货物项目
Descriptions of Goods</td><td>包装
Packing</td><td>单位
Unit</td><td>数量
Quantity</td><td>保险金额
Amount Insured</td></tr>
<tr><td colspan="2">承保险别
Conditions</td><td colspan="4">货物标记
Marks of Goods</td></tr>
<tr><td colspan="6">总保险金额：
Total Amount Insured：</td></tr>
<tr><td>保费
Premium</td><td colspan="2">载运输工具
Per conveyance S. S.</td><td colspan="3">开航日期
Slg. on or abt</td></tr>
<tr><td colspan="2">起运港
Form</td><td colspan="4">目的港
To</td></tr>
<tr><td colspan="6">所保货物，如发生本保险单项下可能引起索赔的损失或损坏，应立即通知本公司下述代理人查勘。如有索赔，应向本公司提交保险单正本（本保险单共有____份正本）及有关文件。如一份正本已用于索赔，其余正本则自动失效。
In the event of loss or damage which may result in acclaim under this Policy, immediate notice must be given to the Company's Agent as mentioned hereunder. Claims, if any, one of the Original Policy which has been issued in original (s) together with the relevant documents shall be surrendered to the Company. If one of the Original Policy has been accomplished, the others to be void.</td></tr>
<tr><td colspan="6">赔款偿付地点
Claim payable at</td></tr>
<tr><td colspan="2">日期
Date</td><td colspan="4">在
at</td></tr>
<tr><td colspan="6">地址：
Address：</td></tr>
</table>

2. 请根据以下资料，以保险公司业务员身份填制保险单（见表 1-10-2）。

（1）信用证条款。

APPLICANT： ＊50：INTERCONTOR，ZENTRALEINKAUF UND HANDELS
SIGMUND STR. 220 90431 NUERNBERG

BENEFICIARY： ＊59：GUANGDONG TEXTILES IMP. & EXP. COTTON
MANUFACTURED GOODS COMPANY LTD.
14/F.，GUANGDONG TEXTILES MANSION
NO. 168 XIAOBEI ROAD，GUANGZHOU，CHINA

LOADING IN CHARGE： 44A：GUANGZHOU，CHINA

FOR TRANSPORT TO …： 44B：HAMBURG

DESCRIPT. OF GOODS： 45A：GUITAR

ITEM NO. QUANTITY UNTI PRICE

948　　1,700PCS　　USD7.42

AS PER SALES CONFIRMATION NO. 2002MCGS02007 DD 8.3.2018

CIF HAMBURG

DOCUMENTS REQUIRED：46A：

+MARINE INSURANCE POLICY OR CERTIFICATE IN DUPLICATE, ENDORSED IN BLANK, FOR FULL INVOICE VALUE PLUS 10 PERCENT, STATING CLAIM PAYABLE IN HAMBURG COVERING INSTITUTE CARGO CLAUSES (A) AND WAR RISKS, MARKED PREMIUM PAID.

（2）其他资料。

发票号码：180603GTB	发票日期：2018年6月20日
发票金额：USD46,500.00	提单日期：2018年6月25日
船名：NANTU V.832	货物装箱情况：10PCS/CTN
唛头：KCHCSB/HAMBURG	保险单号码：KC536487

表1-10-2　保险单

中保财产保险有限公司
The People's Insurance (Property) Company of China, Ltd.

发票号码 Invoice No.	保险单号次 Policy No.

海洋货物运输保险单
MARINE CARGO TRANSPORTATION INSURANCE POLICY

被保险人：
Insured：

中保财产保险有限公司（以下简称本公司）根据被保险人的要求，及其所缴付约定的保险费，按照本保险单承担险别和背面所载条款与下列特别条款承保下列货物运输保险，特签发本保险单。

This policy of Insurance witnesses that the People's Insurance (Property) Company of China, Ltd. (hereinafter called "The Company"), at the request of the Insured and in consideration of the agreed premium paid by the Insured, undertakes to insure the undermentioned goods in transportation subject to conditions of the Policy as per the Clauses printed overleaf and other special clauses attached hereon.

保险货物项目 Descriptions of Goods	包装 Packing	单位 Unit	数量 Quantity	保险金额 Amount Insured

续表

承保险别 Conditions	货物标记 Marks of Goods	
总保险金额： Total Amount Insured：		
保费 Premium	载运输工具 Per conveyance S. S.	开航日期 Slg. on or abt
起运港 Form	目的港 To	
所保货物，如发生本保险单项下可能引起索赔的损失或损坏，应立即通知本公司下述代理人查勘。如有索赔，应向本公司提交保险单正本(本保险单共有____份正本)及有关文件。如一份正本已用于索赔，其余正本则自动失效。 In the event of loss or damage which may result in acclaim under this Policy, immediate notice must be given to the Company's Agent as mentioned hereunder. Claims, if any, one of the Original Policy which has been issued in original (s) together with the relevant documents shall be surrendered to the Company. If one of the Original Policy has been accomplished, the others to be void.		
赔款偿付地点 Claim payable at		
日期 Date	在 at	
地址： Address：		

3. 根据信用证(见表 1-10-3)和相关资料审核保险单据(见表 1-10-4)，并回答问题。

表 1-10-3　信用证

Form of Doc. Credit	* 40A：IRREVOCABLE
Doc. Credit Number	* 20：BL-181805
Date of Issue	31C：180325
Expiry	* 31D：Date 180531 Place CHINA
Applicant	* 50：THOMASIMP. AND EXP. COMPANY 32 BLUEBIRD STREET BANGKOK THAILAND
Applicant bank	51：KRUNG THAI BANK PUBLIC CO.,LTD. BANGKOK
Beneficiary	* 59：HANGZHOU HOPESHOW GARMENTS CO.,LTD. 842 MOGANSHAN ROAD HANGZHOU, CHINA
Amount	* 32B：Currency USD Amount 36,300,00
Available with/by	* 41D：ANY BANK BY NEGOTIATION
Draft at ...	42C：AT SIGHT FOR FULL INVOICE VALUE
Drawee	42D：KRUNG THAI BANK PCL SUANMALI IBC BANGKOK

续表

Partial Shipments	43P：PROHIBITED
Transshipment	43T：PERMIT
Port of loading	44E：SHANGHAI
Port of discharge	44F：BANGKOK
Descript. of Goods	45 A： 65 PCT COTTON 35 PCTRAYON LADIES' COATS CIF BANGKOK ITEM NO. 3501T,1,000PCS,USD9.00/PC ITEM NO. 3501B,1,000PCS,USD9.50/PC ITEM NO. 3502T,1,000PCS,USD8.80/PC ITEM NO. 3502B,1,000PCS,USD9.00/PC
Documents required	46 A： +MANUALLY SIGNED COMMERCIAL INVOICE IN QUADRUPLICATE CERTIFYING THAT ALL DETAILS ARE AS PER PROFORMA INVOICE NO. TH120316 DATED Mar. 16, 2018 AND ALSO SHOW THE FREIGHT CHARGE, PREMIUM, FOB VALUE AND COUNTRY OF ORIGIN SEPARATELY +FULL SET CLEAN ON BOARD OCEAN BILLS OF LADING MADE OUT TO OUR ORDER MARKED FREIGHT PREPAID NOTIFY APPLICANT AND SHOWING THE NAME AND ADDRESS OF THE SHIPPING AGENT AT DESTINATION +SIGNED PACKING ASSORTED LIST IN QUADRUPLICATE STATING THAT ONE PC IN ONE PP BAG AND 48PCS IN AN EXPORT CARTON. +SIGNED CERTIFICATE OF ORIGIN IN DUPLICATE SHOWING THE NAME OF THE MANUFACTURER +INSURANCE POLICY IN DUPLICATE FOR 110 PCT OF THE INVOICE VALUE COVERING ALL RISKS AS PER CIC OF PICC DATE Jan. 1, 1981 WAREHOUSE TO WAREHOUSE CLAUSE INCLUDE IN THE SAME CURRENCY OF THE DRAFTS CLAIM PAYABLE IN THAILAND +BENEFICIARY'S CERTIFICATE STATING THAT ONE SET OF N/N SHIPPING DOCUMENTS HAS BEEN SENT TO THE APPLICANT DIRECTLY IMMEDIATELY AFTER SHIPMENT EFF-ECTED
Additional Cond.	47 A： +ALL DOCUMENTS MUST SHOW THE CREDIT NUMBER AND DATE AND NAME OF THE ISSUING BANK +A DISCREPANCY HANDLING FEE OF USD100.00 SHOULD BE DEDUCTED AND INDICATED ON THE BILL SCHEDULE FOR EACH PRESENTATION OF DISCREPANT DOCUMENTS UNDER THIS CREDIT +THIS DOCUMENTARY CREDIT IS SUBJECT TO UNIFORM CUSTOMS AND PRACTICE FOR DOCUMENTARY CREDIT ICC PUBLICATION NO. 600

续表

Presentation Period	48：WITHIN 15 DAYS AFTER THE DATE OF B/L BUT WITHIN THE VALIDITY OF THIS CREDIT
Confirmation	*49：WITHOUT
Advising through	57：THIS CREDIT IS ADVISED THROUGH BANK OF CHINA HANGZHOU BRANCH
Details of Charges	71 B：ALL BANKING CHARGES OUTSID ETHAILAND ARE FOR THE ACCOUNT OF BENEFICIARY
Instruction	78：ON RECEIPT OF DOCUMENTS CONFIRMING TO THE TERMS OF THIS DOCUMENTARY CREDIT，WE UNDERTAKE TO REIMBURSE YOU IN THE CURRENCY OF THE CREDIT IN ACCORDANCE WITH YOUR INSTRUCTIONS，WHICH SHOULD INCLUDE YOUR UID NUMBER AND THE ABA CODE OF THE RECEIVING BANK
Send. to rec. info.	72：DOCUMENTS TO BE DISPATCHED BY COURIER SERVICE IN ONE LOT TO BANK OF CHINA BANGKOK BRANCH TRADE SERVICES，26 BOLIDEN ROAD，BANGKOK，THAILAND

相关资料如下。

发票号码：HS18E0428	发票日期：2018年4月28日
提单号码：COS1205851	提单日期：2018年5月10日
船名：ZHEN HUA V.007S	原产地证号：6838002
商品编号：6209.9000	货物装箱情况：20尺拼箱，CFS/CFS
集装箱号：COSU561753	封号：18153
毛重：16千克	净重：14.5千克
外箱尺码：60×40×40CMS	保单号码：201831001789626
合同号码：HS180316	合同日期：2018年3月16日
海运费：864美元	保险费：80美元

议付银行：中国银行杭州分行

船公司在目的港的代理的名称与地址：

COSCO BANGKOK BRANCH

36 JERVA ROAD，BANGKOK，THAILAND

生产厂家名称：

HANGZHOU LINGLONG GARMENTS FACTORY

唛头：

THOMAS

HS180316

BANGKOK

NOS.1-80

（1）请用中文回答该信用证要求受益人提交的单证名称。

（2）改正保险单上的错误。

表 1-10-4 保险单

PICC

中国人民财产保险股份有限公司
PICC Property and Casualty Company Limited
总公司设于北京　　一九四九年创立
Head Office Beijing　　Established in 1949

货 物 运 输 保 险 单
CARGO TRANSPORTATION INSURANCE POLICY

发票号码 Invoice No. HS18E0428
合同号码 Contract No. HS180316　　　　保单号次 Policy No. 201831001789626
信用证号 Credit No. BL-181805
被保险人 Insured：HANGZHOU HOPESHOW GARMENTS CO.，LTD.

中保财产保险有限公司（以下简称本公司）根据被保险人的要求，及其所缴付约定的保险费，按照本保险单承担险别和背面所载条款与下列特别条款承保下列货物运输保险，特签发本保险单。
This policy of Insurance witnesses that The People Insurance (Property) Company of China, Ltd. (hereinafter called the Company) at the request of the Insured and in consideration of the agreed premium paid by the Insured, undertakes to insure the under mentioned goods in transportation subject to the conditions of this Policy as per the Clauses printed overleaf and other special clauses attached hereon.

标记 Marks & No.	包装及数量 Quantity	保险货物项目 Description of goods	保险金额 Amount Insured
AS PER INV. NO. HSE180428	60CTNS	35 PCT COTTON 65 PCT RAYON LADIES' COATS	USD36,300.00

总保险金额
Total Amount Insured：SAY U.S. DOLLARS THIRTY SIX THOUSAND THREE HUNDRED ONLY.

保险费 Premium　As arranged　启运日期 Date of commencement　AS PER B/L　装载运输工具 Per conveyance　S.S.：ZHEN HUA V.007S

自 From　SHANGHAI　　经 Via　　至 To　BANGKOK

承保险别 Conditions：
COVERING ALL RISKS AS PER CIC OF PICC DATED 01/01/1981 WAREHOUSE TO WAREHOUSE CLAUSE INCLUDED CREDIT NO. BL-081805 DATED 25 MAR.，2018 ISSUED BY KRUNG THAI BANK PUBLIC CO.，LTD.，BANGKOK

所保货物，如发生本保险单项下可能引起索赔的损失或损坏，应立即通知本公司下述代理人查勘。如有索赔，应向本公司提交保险单正本（本保险单共有 2 份正本）及有关文件。如一份正本已用于索赔，其余正本则自动失效。
In the event of damage which may result in a claim under this Policy, immediate notice be given to the Company Agent as mentioned here under. Claims, if any, one of the Original Policy which has been issued in **TWO** Original(s) together with the relevant documents shall be surrendered to be Company, if one of the Original Policy has been accomplished, the others to be void.

续表

Insurance agent at destination: THAILAND INSURANCE CO. ,LTD. 29 DADA ROAD,BANGKOK,THAILAND 赔款偿付地点 Claim payable at BANGKOK 出单日期 Issuing date APR. 30,2018 地址：中国浙江省杭州市中山北路 321 号 邮编(Post Code)：310000 电话(Tel)：0571-2880 2220 传真(Fax)：0571-2880 2226	中国人民财产保险股份有限公司浙江省分公司 PICC Property and Casualty Company Limited,Zhejiang Branch 姜小葵 Authorized Signature

项目十一　缮制运输单据

一、常用术语中英文互译

1. 全套清洁已装船提单__________　　2. 指示提单__________

3. 托运人__________　　4. 装运港__________

5. 卸货港__________　　6. Freight prepaid __________

7. Freight collect __________　　8. S. T. C. __________

9. Blank endorsed __________　　10. Made out to order __________

二、单项选择题

1. 纸质托运单一式十联单，其中的(　　)是托运单的核心。此联在海关放行后被海关盖上“放行章”，船公司据此联才可以将货物装船。

A. 第二联船代留底　　B. 第五联装货单

C. 第七联场站收据　　D. 第九联配舱回单

2. 若货物从广州运往荷兰的鹿特丹港口，再运至德国的一个内陆城市SCHORNDORF，贸易术语为CIF ROTTERDAM，则托运单的目的港应填(　　)。

A. ROTTERDAM　　B. NETHERLAND

C. SCHORNDORF　　D. GERMANY

3. 按照海运运输的业务要求，进口商办理租船订舱手续，必须由委托人填写(　　)。

A. 海运提单　　B. 海运货运委托书

C. 海运单　　D. 配舱单

4. 对于海运卸货港的选择，一般行使选择权的是(　　)。

A. 船公司　　B. 货运代理人　　C. 买方　　D. 卖方

5. 我国集装箱运输中的三大单证不包括(　　)。

A. 装箱单　　B. 场站收据

C. “交货记录”联单　　D. 设备交接单

6. 按照有关规定，不同包装种类的货物混装在一个集装箱内，这时货物的总件数显示数字之和，包装种类用(　　)表示。

A. Cartons　　B. Pieces　　C. Packages　　D. Pallets

7. 在集装箱运输中，能够实现“门到门”运输的集装箱货物交接方式的是(　　)。

A. LCL/LCL　　B. FCL/FCL　　C. LCL/FCL　　D. FCL/LCL

8. 若信用证同时列明3个装运港XINGANG/QINHUANGDAO/TANGSHANG，在填制托运单时应填写(　　)。

A. XINGANG/QINHUANGDAO/TANGSHANG

B. XINGANG

C. 根据 L/C 提供的港口,只填写实际装运港的名称

D. GUANGZHOU

9. 我国出口业务中,出口商委托货代代为办理出口货物托运手续,首先应由外贸企业填制(　　)。

A. 托运单　　B. 订舱委托书　　C. 装货单　　D. 配舱回单

10. 开证行 HANGSENG BANK 开来的信用证中,要求 FULL SET OF B/L MADE OUT TO OUR ORDER,则填托运单时在 CONSIGNEE 一栏应填(　　)。

A. TO ORDER

B. TO OUR ORDER

C. TO ORDER OF HANGSENG BANK

D. HANGSENG BANK

11. 经过背书才能转让的提单是(　　)。

A. 转船提单　　B. 指示提单　　C. 记名提单　　D. 不记名提单

12. 对于成交量小、批次多、交货港口分散的货物运输,比较适宜的运输方式是(　　)。

A. 班轮运输　　B. 租船运输　　C. 不定期船运输　　D. 定程租船

13. 海运提单的抬头是指提单的(　　)。

A. Shipper　　B. Consignee　　C. Notify Party　　D. Carrier

14. 信用证条款如下。

APPLICANT:ABC CO.

BENEFICIARY:GD TRADING CO.,LTD.

DOCUMENTS REQUIRED:FULL SET OF CLEAN ON BOARD BILL OF LADING CONSIGNED TO THE ORDER OF APPLICANT, MARKED FREIGHT PREPAID, NOTIFY APPLICANT.

信用证未对提单做任何其他规定,则提单的收货人应为(　　)。

A. TO THE ORDER OF APPLICANT

B. TO ORDER

C. TO THE ORDER OF ABC CO.

D. CONSIGNED TO THE ORDER OF APPUCANT

15. 海运提单日期应理解为(　　)。

A. 签订运输合同的日期　　B. 货物开始装船的日期

C. 货物装船过程中的任何一天　　D. 货物装船完毕的日期

16. 假定货物由承运人 COSCO 承运,船长为张三。提单由其代理 ABC SHIPPING CO. 签署,签发人为李四。如果提单表面已经表明了承运人的身份,则提单的签发应该是(　　)。

A. ABC SHIPPING CO. 李四 AS CARRIER

B. COSCO 张三 AS CARRIER

C. ABC SHIPPING CO. 李四 AS AGENT FOR THE CARRIER NAMED ABOVE

D. ABC SHIPPING CO. 张三 AS AGENT FOR THE CARRIER NAMED ABOVE

17. 在海上货物运输实践中,被称为"下货纸"的单证是(　　)。

A. 提单　　B. 装货单　　C. 收货单　　D. 提货单

18. 航空货运单中的运费，应采用的货币币种为（　　），并用IATA货币代码表示。

A. 美元　　B. 人民币

C. 目的港所在国家的货币　　D. 始发站所在国家的货币

19. 一票货物于2018年4月10日开始装船，并于同月12日全部装上船，同日船舶开航。如果在同月11日，应托运人要求，承运人签发已装船提单，则此提单被称为（　　）。

A. 倒签提单　　B. 顺签提单　　C. 预借提单　　D. 待运提单

20. 提单收货人栏记载“TO THE HOLDER”表明（　　）。

A. 该提单是记名提单

B. 该提单是不记名提单

C. 收货人是“TO THE HOLDER”公司

D. 该提单是指示提单

三、多项选择题

1. 对托运人而言，选择海上货物承运人时，主要考虑的因素包括（　　）。

A. 运输服务的定期性　　B. 运输时间

C. 运输费用　　D. 运输的可靠性

E. 承运人的经营状况和责任

2. 出口货物托运人缮制《国际货物托运委托书》所依据的文件有（　　）。

A. 外销出仓单　　B. 销售合同　　C. 信用证　　D. 配舱回单

3. （　　）是结汇单据，如果缮制错漏、延误等，就会影响安全结汇。

A. 汇票　　B. 发票　　C. 托运单　　D. 受益人证明书

4. 租船订舱所需要的单据有（　　）。

A. 托运单　　B. 装货单　　C. 装箱单　　D. 海运提单

5. 根据集装箱货物装箱数量和方式，集装箱的装箱方式分为（　　）。

A. 混装　　B. 整箱　　C. 分装　　D. 拼箱

6. 托运单收货人栏目填写为（　　），则其对应的提单可通过背书转让。

A. ABC CO.　　B. TO ORDER

C. TO ORDER OF SHIPPER　　D. TO ORDER OF XXXBANK

7. 海运托运单（　　）。

A. 是收货人凭以提货的物权凭证

B. 是承运人收到托运人货物的收据

C. 是承运人与托运人之间运输合同契约的证明

D. 经过背书，可以转让

8. 托运单栏目中，须由船公司填写的是（　　）。

A. 提单编号　　B. 船名　　C. 船期　　D. 托运单编号

9. 托运单的运费缴付方式，根据实际情况可填写（　　）。

A. FREIGHT PREPAID

B. FREIGHT PAID

C. FREIGHT COLLECT

D. FREIGHT PAYABLE AT DESTINATION

10. 承运人从起运地到目的地都采用整箱交接货物方式的有(　　)。

A. CY TO CY　　B. CY TO CFS　　C. DOOR TO CY　　D. CFS TO CY

11. 在海运实践中,有权签发提单的当事人是(　　)。

A. 承运人本人　　B. 货代公司

C. 载货船长　　D. 经承运人授权的代理人

12. 海运提单做成指示性抬头时,提单收货人一栏可以填写(　　)。

A. to order of shipper　　B. to order of issuing bank

C. to issuing bank　　D. to order

13. 在出口业务中,卖方可凭以结汇的运输单据有(　　)。

A. 海运提单　　B. 铁路提单正本　　C. 承运货物收据　　D. 大副收据

14. 班轮提单是(　　)。

A. 物权凭证

B. 承运人签发给托运人的货物收据

C. 承运人与托运人之间运输契约的证明

D. 出口人纳税的依据

15. 提单或航空货运单中的"SHIPPER"是(　　)。

A. 销售合同中的供货商　　B. 买卖合同中的购货商

C. 将货物交给承运人的人　　D. 与承运人签订代理合同的人

16. 根据 UCP 600 的规定,即使信用证禁止转运,运输单据也可以被银行接受的条件有(　　)。

A. 空运单据注明货物将发生转运或可能发生转运,只要同一空运运单包括运输全程

B. 空运单注明货物已发生转运,只要同一空运运单包括运输全程

C. 海运提单注明货物将发生转运,同时提单注明货物已由集装箱、拖车及/或子母船运输,并且同一提单包括海运全程运输

D. 海运提单含有承运人声明保留转运权利的条款

17. 关于已装船提单,下面叙述中正确的有(　　)。

A. 提单上印就"已装船"字样或加盖"已装船"戳记

B. 注明船名和装船日期

C. 属于可转让的清洁提单

D. 由船公司收到货物时签发

18. 按不同的运输方法,提单可以分为(　　)。

A. 直达提单　　B. 无船承运人提单

C. 转船提单　　D. 多式联运提单

19. 根据 UCP 600 的规定,海运提单中货物的描述(　　)。

A. 只要不与信用证的描述相抵触,可使用货物的统称

B. 必须使用货物的全称

C. 必须与商业发票的货物描述完全一致

D. 符合信用证或合同的,与实际货物的名称、规格、型号、成分、品牌等一致

20. 下列关于提单份数的表述,正确的有(　　)。

A. 发货人按信用证规定的提单份数提交正本提单给银行

B. 每份提单具有同等效力

C. 收货人持凭其中的任意一份提单提取货物后,其他提单即刻自动失效

D. 发货人持凭其中的任意一份提单作电放,其他正本提单给银行

四、判断题

1. 装运期就是交货期。 ( )

2. 若合同或信用证没有特别说明,通常情况下,托运单中的货物说明也必须详细列出货物的型号、规格,不能只写大类名称或统称。 ( )

3. 承运人接受的托运人保函具有对抗收货人的效力。 ( )

4. 如来证中要求两个或两个以上的公司为收货人,托运单栏内写不下,可只填写一个收货人。 ( )

5. 若信用证中规定装运港为 Chinese main port,则在托运单中的装运港应填 Chinese main port,以保持单证一致。 ( )

6. 如在托运单收货人一栏留空,这种表示方法称为空白指示。 ( )

7. 被通知人的职责是及时接受船方发出的到货通知并及时提货。 ( )

8. 如出口 10 万码花布,分别用粗胚布捆成 100 捆,则填写数目这一栏时应填写 100 捆。 ( )

9. 货物装船后,大副在收货单上签收。托运人凭已签名的收货单向船公司或船代理换取全套正本提单。 ( )

10. 托运单号码一般就是提单号码。 ( )

11. 正本提单如出具一式三份,每份的效力都不同。 ( )

12. 信用证规定装运港为 Chinese Port,缮制提单时,装运港一栏应照样填写 Chinese Port,以免单证不符。 ( )

13. 提单正面通常印有“不知条款”,表示承运人不知道集装箱内实际装入的货物品质和件数,与之有关的货损、货差、货物短缺、货物不实等责任均由托运人承担。 ( )

14. 海运提单、铁路运单和航空运单都属于物权凭证,均可通过背书转让。 ( )

15. 各种单证的签发日期应当符合逻辑性和国际惯例,通常提单日期是确定各种单证日期的关键。( )

16. 空白抬头提单是指提单的“Consignee”栏内不填写任何内容,谁持有该提单谁就有权提货。( )

17. 承运人签发提单时,将提单上原先印就的 Clean on board 中的 Clean 字样划去,没做另外批注,使该套提单变成了不清洁提单。 ( )

18. 银行一般不受理过期提单,提单持有人也不能凭单向承运人提货。 ( )

19. 承运人或船长的任何签字或证实,不必表明“承运人”或“船长”的身份。 ( )

20. 航空货运单收货人一栏,若显示“TO ORDER”或“TO ORDER OF SHIPPER”等字样,则表示受托运人指示。 ( )

五、简答题

1. 货主托运货物时,选择承运人应考虑哪些因素?

2. 简述海运出口货物托运的程序。

3. 简述集装箱的装箱方式。

4. 简述集装箱运输的优越性。

5. 简述海运提单的定义和作用。

6. 某提单显示：Shipper： ABC IMP. &EXP. CO. ,LTD.

Consignee： TO ORDER

Notify Party： SHANGHAI INTERNATIONAL CO. ,LTD.

请问：

(1) 该提单属于哪种类型的提单？

(2) 该提单是否可以转让？如果可以转让提单，它通过什么方式转让？

(3) 该提单由谁首先背书？

(4) 该提单是否一定要经过 SHANGHAI INTERNATIONAL CO. ,LTD. 背书？

7. 船公司 2018 年 4 月 16 日签发了一张“备运提单”，但在该提单上又加注“2018 年 5 月 8 日装××船”。假设信用证规定该批货物应于 2018 年 5 月 12 日前装船，并应提交“已装船提单”，上述提单是否符合信用证规定？

8. 什么是航空总运单和航空分运单？

9. 甲出口公司收到国外开来的不可撤销自由议付信用证，证中规定最迟装船日期为 2018 年 5 月 9 日，有效期为 2018 年 6 月 1 日，到期地点为中国，要求提交的单据为海运提单，信用证对交单的期限没有任何规定。甲公司于 2018 年 4 月 28 日将货物装船并取得已经装船提单，于 2018 年 5 月 25 日将全套单据向议付行交单。议付行以单据不符合为由不付款(迟交)，议付行的做法是否正确？

六、技能操作题

1. 请根据以下材料，以广东纺织品进出口广通贸易有限公司制单员李宁的名义，于 2019 年 2 月 26 日填制出口货物委托运输合同(见表 1-11-1)，委托广东远航通国际货运代理公司代为办理货物运输手续。

(1) 信用证条款。

ISSUING BANK：HABIB BANK AG ZURICH DUBAI. U. A. E.

CREDIT NUMBER：SK/25067/2018

DATE OF ISSUE：DEC. 27,2018

EXPIRY：DATE 190327 PLACE CHINA

APPLICANT：MAHARAJA DEIRA L. L. C,DUBAI(UAE) P. O. BOX NO. 6093, DUBAI(UAE),FAX NO. 263745

BENEFICIARY：GUANGDONG TEXTILES IMP. AND EXP. GRANDTON TRADING CO. ,LTD. 7/F.,GUANGDONG TEXTILES MANSION, NO. 168 XIAOBEI ROAD,GUANGZHOU,CHINA

AMOUNT：USD99,960.00

AVAILABLE WITH/BY：AVAILABLE WITH ANY BANK IN CHINA NEGOTIATION

DRAFTS AT：AT SIGHT

PATRIAL SHIPMENTS：ALLOWED

TRANSSHIPMENT：ALLOWED(AT HONGKONG PORT ONLY)

SHIPMENT PERIOD: AT THE LATEST MARCH 12,2019

(SHIPMENT FROM CHINA PORTS TO DUBAI BY STEAMER)

COVERING: 4,000 DOZEN LADIES LYCRA LONG PANT
CIFC2 DUBAI USD25.5 PER DOZEN
ALL OTHER DETAILS ARE AS PER S/C NO. 2018/2495
PACKING 10DOZ/CTN

SHIPPING MARKS: MAHARAJA/264553/DUBAI/NO. 1-400

DOCUMENTS REQUIRED: * FULL SET OF CLEAN "SHIPPED ON BOARD" OCEAN BILLS OF LADING MADE OUT TO THE ORDER OF HABIB BANK AG ZURICH DUBAI. U. A. E. AND NOTIFY APPLICANT, SHOWING "FREIGHT PREPAID" MENTIONING L/C NO.

ADDITIONAL CONDITION: SHIPMENT TO BE EFFECTED BY 1×20′CONTAINER (FCL).

PRESENTATION PERIOD: NOT LATER THAN 15 DAYS AFTER THE DATE OF THE SHIPPING DOCUMENTS BUT WITHIN THE VALIDITY OF THE CREDIT.

(2) 其他资料。

发票号码：GD-TX-9057	托运日期：JAN. 2,2019
单位毛重：15KGS/CTN	单位净重：12KGS/CTN
单位尺码：60CM×20CM×50CM/CTN	货物堆存地点：大松岗

表 1-11-1 出口货物委托运输合同

<table>
<tr><td rowspan="8">**出口货物委托运输合同**
(货物明细单)
受托人(承运人或货运代理人)：
广东远航通国际货运代理有限公司
委托人(即托运人)：

(Shipper)：

日期：　年　月　日
根据《中华人民共和国合同法》与《中华人民共和国海商法》的规定，就出口货物委托运输事宜订立合同。</td><td>银行编号</td><td colspan="2"></td><td>运输编号</td><td>2018-GD-00010000121</td></tr>
<tr><td>信用证号</td><td colspan="2"></td><td>开证日期</td><td></td></tr>
<tr><td>合同号</td><td colspan="4"></td></tr>
<tr><td>海关编号</td><td colspan="4">6204620029</td></tr>
<tr><td>贸易国别</td><td colspan="2"></td><td>消费国别</td><td></td></tr>
<tr><td>贸易性质</td><td></td><td>佣金%</td><td></td><td>扣除方式　</td></tr>
<tr><td>汇票期限</td><td></td><td>折扣%</td><td></td><td>其他费用　</td></tr>
<tr><td>选择增减</td><td colspan="4"></td></tr>
</table>

续表

<table>
<tr><td colspan="3" rowspan="7">标志唛头：</td><td>出口口岸</td><td colspan="7"></td></tr>
<tr><td>目的港</td><td colspan="7"></td></tr>
<tr><td>装期</td><td colspan="2"></td><td>可否转船</td><td colspan="2"></td><td>可否分批</td><td></td></tr>
<tr><td>效期</td><td colspan="2"></td><td>交单期</td><td colspan="4"></td></tr>
<tr><td>运费预付</td><td></td><td>运费到付</td><td></td><td>正本提单</td><td></td><td>副本提单</td><td></td></tr>
<tr><td>毛重（千克）</td><td colspan="2"></td><td>净重（千克）</td><td colspan="4"></td></tr>
<tr><td>体积（M^3）</td><td colspan="2"></td><td>总数量</td><td colspan="4"></td></tr>
<tr><td colspan="2">制定货代信息</td><td colspan="2"></td><td>总件数</td><td colspan="2"></td><td colspan="2">包装</td><td colspan="2"></td></tr>
<tr><td colspan="2">货代电话邮政编码</td><td></td><td>运费</td><td></td><td>确认</td><td></td><td>总货名</td><td colspan="3"></td></tr>
<tr><td rowspan="2">提单或承运收据</td><td>抬头人</td><td colspan="3"></td><td>开证行</td><td colspan="5"></td></tr>
<tr><td>通知人</td><td colspan="9"></td></tr>
<tr><td colspan="2">托运人本公司注意事项</td><td colspan="7">货物描述</td><td colspan="2">总值（价格条件）</td></tr>
<tr><td colspan="2">请另打印一份，报关用。</td><td colspan="7" rowspan="3"></td><td colspan="2" rowspan="3"></td></tr>
<tr><td colspan="2">许可证号码：</td></tr>
<tr><td colspan="2">法定商检：</td></tr>
<tr><td>有进料不超过</td><td></td><td>来料加工</td><td></td><td>来料费</td><td></td><td>加工费</td><td></td><td>FOB 价</td><td colspan="2"></td></tr>
<tr><td rowspan="2">受托人注意事项</td><td colspan="7"></td><td>发运信息</td><td colspan="2" rowspan="2">红印</td></tr>
<tr><td colspan="7">附件单据：1 票 2 份　装箱单 1 份　报关单　份
核销单 1 份　许可证 2 份</td><td>制单员</td></tr>
</table>

2. 根据第1题的资料填制一份托运单(见表 1-11-2)。

表 1-11-2 托运单

SHIPPER(发货人)		B/L No.
CONSIGNEE(收货人)		中远集装箱运输有限公司 COSCO CONTAINER LINES 集装箱货物托运单
NOTIFY PARTY(通知人)		
Pre-carriage by(前程承运人)	Place of Receipt(收货地点)	装货单 SHIPPING ORDER

Ocean Vessel(船名)	Voy. No.(航次)	Port of Loading(装货港)	Date(日期)
Port of Discharge(卸货港)	Place of Delivery(交货地点)	Final Destination for the Merchant's Reference(目的地)	

Container No.(集装箱号)	Seal No.(铅封号) Marks & Nos.(标记与号码)	No. of container or packages(箱数或件数)	Kind of Packages; Description of Goods(包装种类与货名)	Gross Weight 毛重(千克)	Measurement 尺码(立方米)

TOTAL NUMBER OF CONTINERS OR PACKAGES(JIN WORDS) 集装箱数或件数合计(大写)	

FREIGHT & CHARGES(运费与附加费)	Revenue Tons(运费吨)	Rate(运费率)	Per(每)	Prepaid(运费预付)	Collect(运费到付)

Service Type on Receiving □—CY □—CFS □—DOOR	Service Type on Delivery □—CY □—CFS □—DOOR	Reefer Temperature Required(冷藏温度)	℉	℃

TYPE OF GOODS(货类)	□Ordinary(普通) □Reefer(冷藏) □Dangerous(危险品) □Auto(裸装车辆)	危险品	IMCO Class: UN No.:
	□Liquid(液体) □Live Animal(活动物) □Bulk(散货)		IMDG Code Page: Property:

可否转船:	可否分批:	装期:	Received by the Carrier the total number of containers or other packages or units stated above to be transported subject to the terms and conditions of the Carrier's regular form of Bill of Lading(for combined Transport to Port shipment) which shall be deemed to be incorporated herein Date: as Agent only
货价:	信用证号码:	No. of original B(S)/L:	
特约事项:	合同号码:	托运人盖章:	

3. 请根据信用证资料及其他资料，以货运代理人身份填制海运提单(见表 1-11-3)。

(1) 信用证条款。

Issuing Bank: METITA BANK LTD. FIN-00020 METITA, FINLAND
Term of Doc. Credit: IRREVOCABLE
Credit Number: KHL18-22457
Date of Issue: 180505
Expiry: Date 180716 Place CHINA
Applicant: FFK CORP. AKEKSANTERINK AUTO
P. O. BOX 9, FINLAND
Beneficiary: GUANGDONG RONGHUA TRADE CO., LTD.
168 DEZHENG ROAD SOUTH, GUANGZHOU, CHINA
Amount: Currency USD Amount 38,400.00
Pos. /Neg. Tol. (%): 5/5
Available with/by: ANY BANK IN ADVISING COUNTRY BY NEGOTIATION
Partial Shipments: Not Allowed
Transshipment: Allowed
Loading in Charge: GUANGZHOU
For Transport to: HELSINKI
Shipment Period: AT THE LATEST JULY 16, 2018
Description of Goods: 9,600PCS OF WOMEN'S SWEATERS
Unit Price: USD4.00/PC
OTHER DETAILS AS PER S/C NO. 98GQ468001
Packing: 12PCS/CTN CFR HELSINKI(INCOTERMS 2010)
Documents Required: FULL SET OF CLEAN ON BOARD MARINE BILLS OF LADING, MADE OUT TO ORDER OF ISSUING BANK, MARKED "FREIGHT PREPAID" AND DDC COLLECT, SHOWING INSURANCE PREMIUM, SURCHARGE AND TRADE TERMS NOTIFY APPLICANT
Additional Cond.: 1. T. T. REIMBURSEMENT IS PROHIBITED
2. ALL DOCUMENTS MUST BE MARKED THE S/C NO. AND L/C NO.

(2) 其他资料。

提单号码：KTT1245678　　货物总毛重：6 500KGS
货物总尺码：25CBMS　　唛头：ABC/HELSINKI/NO. 1-800
船名：第一程 DONGFANG，第二程 MAKIS V. 002　　转运港：中国香港
集装箱号码：SIHU365487-2(20') SEAL NO. 123456 CY/CY
保险费：USD100.00　　附加费：USD300.00
提单签发日期：2018 年 7 月 10 日　　提单签发地点：广州
承运人：ABC SHIPPING CO.　　承运人代理人：XYZ SHIPPING CO.
提单签发人：李四　　提单装船批注日期：2018 年 7 月 11 日

货物由托运人负责装箱、计数及封箱；整箱装；由集装箱堆场至集装箱堆场。

表 1-11-3　海运提单

<table>
<tr><td colspan="2">Shipper Insert Name, Address and Phone</td><td rowspan="4">B/L No.
中远集装箱运输有限公司
COSCO CONTAINER LINES
TLX：33057 COSCO CN
FAX：+86(021) 6545 8984
ORIGINAL</td></tr>
<tr><td colspan="2"></td></tr>
<tr><td colspan="2">Consignee Insert Name, Address and Phone</td></tr>
<tr><td colspan="2"></td></tr>
<tr><td colspan="2">Notify Party Insert Name, Address and Phone
(It is agreed that no responsibility shall attach to the Carrier or his agents for failure to notify)</td><td rowspan="8">Port-to-Port or Combined Transport
BILL OF LADING
RECEIVED in external apparent good order and condition except as other-Wise noted. The total number of packages or unites stuffed in the container, the description of the goods and the weights shown in this Bill of Lading are furnished by the Merchants, and which the carrier has no reasonable means of checking and is not a part of this Bill of Lading contract. The carrier has Issued the number of Bills of Lading stated below, all of this tenor and date, One of the original Bills of Lading must be surrendered and endorsed or signed against the delivery of the shipment and whereupon any other original Bills of Lading shall be void. The Merchants agree to be bound by the terms and conditions of this Bill of Lading as if each had personally signed this Bill of Lading.
SEE clause 4 on the back of this Bill of Lading (Terms continued on the back hereof, please read carefully).
* Applicable Only When Document Used as a Combined Transport Bill of Lading.</td></tr>
<tr><td colspan="2"></td></tr>
<tr><td>Combined Transport *
Pre-carriage by</td><td>Combined Transport *
Place of Receipt</td></tr>
<tr><td></td><td></td></tr>
<tr><td>Ocean Vessel Voy. No.</td><td>Port of Loading</td></tr>
<tr><td></td><td></td></tr>
<tr><td>Port of Discharge</td><td>Combined Transport *
Place of Delivery</td></tr>
<tr><td></td><td></td></tr>
</table>

<table>
<tr><td>Marks & Nos.
Container/Seal No.</td><td>No. of Packages & Description of Goods</td><td>Gross Weight Kgs</td><td>Measurement</td></tr>
<tr><td></td><td></td><td></td><td></td></tr>
<tr><td></td><td colspan="3">Description of Contents for Shipper's Use Only (Not part of This B/L Contract)</td></tr>
<tr><td colspan="4">Total Number of containers and/or packages (in words)</td></tr>
<tr><td colspan="4">Subject to Clause 7 Limitation</td></tr>
</table>

续表

<table>
<tr><td>Freight & Charges</td><td>Revenue Tons</td><td>Rate</td><td>Per</td><td>Prepaid</td><td>Collect</td></tr>
<tr><td></td><td rowspan="3"></td><td rowspan="3"></td><td rowspan="3"></td><td rowspan="3"></td><td rowspan="3"></td></tr>
<tr><td>Declared Value Charge</td></tr>
<tr><td></td></tr>
</table>

<table>
<tr><td>Ex. Rate:</td><td>Prepaid at</td><td>Payable at</td><td>Place and date of issue</td></tr>
<tr><td rowspan="3"></td><td></td><td></td><td></td></tr>
<tr><td>Total Prepaid</td><td>No. of Original B(s)/L</td><td>Signed for the Carrier,
COSCO CONTAINER LINES</td></tr>
<tr><td></td><td></td><td></td></tr>
<tr><td colspan="4">LADEN ON BOARD THE VESSEL</td></tr>
</table>

DATE		BY	

4. 以下是相关资料及所填制好的海运提单，请指出其中的错误并加以修改。

(1) 相关资料一。

广东省荣华贸易有限公司与芬兰 ABC 公司成交一笔出口交易。芬兰 ABC 公司按期开来信用证，广东荣华公司按期出运，并填制好海运提单。

Issuing Bank: METITA BANK LTD. FIN-00020 METITA, FINLAND

Term of Doc. Credit: IRREVOCABLE

Credit Number: LRT9802457

Date of Issue: 180505

Expiry: Date 180716 Place CHINA

Applicant: ABC CORP. AKEKSANTERINK AUTO
P. O. BOX 9, FINLAND

Beneficiary: GUANGDONG RONGHUA TRADE CO., LTD.
168 DEZHENG ROAD SOUTH, GUANGZHOU, CHINA

Amount: Currency USD Amount 36,840.00 (SAY U.S. DOLLARS THIRTY SIX THOUSAND FOUR HUNDRED AND EIGHTY ONLY.)

Pos./Neg. Tol. (%): 5/5

Available with/by: ANY BANK IN ADVISING COUNTRY BY NEGOTIATION

Partial Shipments: Not Allowed

Transshipment: Allowed

Loading in Charge: GUANGZHOU

For Transport to: HELSINKI

Shipment Period: AT THE LATEST JULY 16, 2018

Description of Goods: 9,600PCS OF WOMEN'S SWEATERS
Unit Price: USD3.80/PC
OTHER DETAILS AS PER S/C NO. 98GQ468001
Packing: 12PCS/CTN TOTAL 800CTNS
CFR HELSINKI (INCOTERMS 2010)

Documents Required: FULL SET OF CLEAN ON BOARD MARINE BILLS OF LADING, MADE OUT TO ORDER OF METITA BANK LTD., FINLAND, MARKED "FREIGHT PREPAID" AND NOTIFY APPLICANT(AS INDICATE ABOVE)

Additional Cond.: 1. T. T. REIMBURSEMENT IS PROHIBITED

2. ALL DOCUMENTS MUST BE MARKED THE S/C NO. AND L/C NO.

3. SHIPPING MARKS: ABC/HELSINKI/NO. 1-800

(2) 相关资料二。

填制完成的海运提单见表 1-11-4。

表 1-11-4 海运提单

<table>
<tr><td colspan="2">1. Shipper Insert Name, Address and Phone</td><td colspan="2" rowspan="12">B/L No.

Port-to-Port or Combined Transport
BILL OF LADING
RECEIVED in external apparent good order and condition except as other—Wise noted. The total number of packages or unites stuffed in the container, the description of the goods and the weights shown in this Bill of Lading are furnished by the Merchants, and which the carrier has no reasonable means of checking and is not a part of this Bill of Lading contract. The carrier has Issued the number of Bills of Lading stated below, all of this tenor and date, One of the original Bills of Lading must be surrendered and endorsed or signed against the delivery of the shipment and whereupon any other original Bills of Lading shall be void. The Merchants agree to be bound by the terms and conditions of this Bill of Lading as if each had personally signed this Bill of Lading.
SEE clause 4 on the back of this Bill of Lading (Terms continued on the back hereof, please read carcfully).
* Applicable Only When Document Used as a Combined Transport Bill of Lading.</td></tr>
<tr><td colspan="2">GUANGDONG RONGHUA TRADE CO., LTD.
168 DEZHENG ROAD SOUTH, GUANGZHOU, CHINA
①</td></tr>
<tr><td colspan="2">2. Consignee Insert Name, Address and Phone</td></tr>
<tr><td colspan="2">ABC CORP. AKEKSANTERINK AUTO
P. O. BOX 9, FINLAND
②</td></tr>
<tr><td colspan="2">3. Notify Party Insert Name, Address and Phone</td></tr>
<tr><td colspan="2">METITA BANK LTD.
FIN-00020 METITA, FINLAND
③</td></tr>
<tr><td>4. Combined Transport * Pre-carriage by</td><td>5. Combined Transport * Place of Receipt</td></tr>
<tr><td></td><td></td></tr>
<tr><td>6. Ocean Vessel Voy. No.</td><td>7. Port of Loading</td></tr>
<tr><td>SUISUN 103</td><td>GUANGZHOU</td></tr>
<tr><td>8. Port of Discharge</td><td>9. Combined Transport * Place of Delivery</td></tr>
<tr><td>HELSINKI VIA HONGKONG</td><td></td></tr>
<tr><td>Marks & Nos. Container/Seal No.</td><td>No. of Containers or Packages Description of Goods(If Dangerous Goods, See Clause 20)</td><td>Gross Weight Kgs</td><td>Measurement</td></tr>
<tr><td>N/M
④</td><td>9,600PCS WOMEN'S SWEATERS
⑤
TOTAL: EIGHT HUNDRED CARTONS ONLY.
⑥
S/C NO. LRT9802457
⑦</td><td>13,600.00KGS

FREIGHT COLLECT
⑧</td><td>25CBM</td></tr>
</table>

续表

<table>
<tr><td></td><td colspan="5">Description of Contents for Shipper's Use Only (Not part of This B/L Contract)</td></tr>
<tr><td colspan="6">10. Total Number of containers and/or packages (in words)</td></tr>
<tr><td>Subject to Clause 7 Limitation</td><td colspan="5"></td></tr>
<tr><td>11. Freight & Charges</td><td>Revenue Tons</td><td>Rate</td><td>Per</td><td>Prepaid</td><td>Collect</td></tr>
<tr><td></td><td rowspan="3"></td><td rowspan="3"></td><td rowspan="3"></td><td rowspan="3"></td><td rowspan="3"></td></tr>
<tr><td>Declared Value Charge</td></tr>
<tr><td></td></tr>
</table>

<table>
<tr><td>Ex. Rate:</td><td>Prepaid at</td><td>Payable at</td><td>Place and date of issue</td></tr>
<tr><td rowspan="3"></td><td></td><td></td><td>GUANGZHOU,MAY 20,2018</td></tr>
<tr><td>Total Prepaid</td><td>No. of Original B(s)/L</td><td>Signed for the Carrier,
COSCO CONTAINER LINES</td></tr>
<tr><td></td><td>THREE(3)</td><td>ABC SHIPPING CO.
刘五 AS MASTER</td></tr>
<tr><td colspan="4">LADEN ON BOARD THE VESSEL</td></tr>
</table>

DATE		BY	

请指出错误并修改：

5. 根据给出的资料填制航空运单(见表 1-11-5)。

(1) 信用证条款。

Applicant: YYY TRADING CO. ,LTD.
220 SIGMUND STR.
80035 NOLA(ITALY)

Beneficiary: GUANGDONG ABC IMPORT & EXPORT COMPANY LTD.
NO. 188 XIAOGANG ROAD,GUANGZHOU

Loading in Charge: GUANGZHOU

For Transport to: MILAN,ITALY

Description of Goods: 1,700PCS OF LADIES' 55% RAMIE 36% WOOL 9% NYLON KNITTED SWEATER CFR MILAN AIRPORT AS PER SALES CONFIRMATION NO. 2018MCGS02007 DD8. 3. 2018 TOTAL AMOUNT USD12,614. 00

Documents Required: CLEAN AIRWAYBILL FOR GOODS AIRFREIGHTED TO

YYY TRADING CO. , LTD. 220 SIGMUND STR. 80035 NOLA (ITALY) MARKED FREIGHT PREPAID AND EVIDENCING THAT ORIGINAL INVOICE AND PACKING LIST ACCOMPANY THE GOODS, NOTIFY APPLICANT

(2) 其他资料。

航空运单填开日期：2018 年 5 月 25 日

航空运单填开地点：广州

始发站：广州

货物装箱情况：1 700PCS/40CTNS

航班号及日期：CA1234/26, MAY 2018

总毛重：400KGS

唛头：YYY/MILAN/NOS1-40

计费重量：420KGS

计费货币：美元

航空运单号码：03030030509

填开货运单的代理人名称：XYZ CARGO.

空运单注明没有声明价值和没有商业价值

尺码：30CM×40CM×20CM

表 1-11-5 航空运单

<table>
<tr><td colspan="6">Shipper's name and address</td><td colspan="5">NOT NEGOTIABLE
Air Waybill 中国国际航空公司
Issued by
AIR CHINA</td></tr>
<tr><td colspan="6">Consignee's name and address</td><td colspan="5">It is agreed that the goods described herein are accepted in apparent good order and condition (except as noted) for carriage SUBJECT TO THE CONDITIONS OF CONTRACT ON THE REVERSE HEREOF, ALL GOODS MAY BE CARRIDE BY ANY OTHER MEANS. INCLUDING ROAD OR ANY OTHER CARRIER UNLESS SPECIFIC CONTRARY INSTRUCTIONS ARE GIVEN HEREON BY THE SHIPPER. THE SHIPPER'S ATTENTION IS DRAWN TO THE NOTICE CONCERNING CARRIER'S LIMITATION OF LIABILITY. Shipper may increase such limitation of liability by declaring a higher value of carriage and paying a supplemental charge if required.</td></tr>
<tr><td colspan="6">Issuing Carrier's Agent Name and City</td><td colspan="5" rowspan="3">Accounting Information</td></tr>
<tr><td colspan="2">Agents IATA Code</td><td colspan="4">Account NO.</td></tr>
<tr><td colspan="6">Airport of Departure (Add. of First Carrier) and Requested Routing</td></tr>
<tr><td rowspan="2">To</td><td rowspan="2">By first carrier</td><td rowspan="2">To</td><td rowspan="2">By</td><td rowspan="2">To</td><td rowspan="2">By</td><td rowspan="2">Currency</td><td colspan="2">WT/VAL</td><td rowspan="2">Declared Value for Carriage</td><td rowspan="2">Declared Value for Customs</td></tr>
<tr><td>PP</td><td>CC</td></tr>
</table>

续表

<table>
<tr><td rowspan="2">Airport of Destination</td><td colspan="2">Flight/Date</td><td rowspan="2">Amount of Insurance</td><td colspan="5" rowspan="2">INSURANCE— if carrier offers insurance and such insurance is requested in accordance with the conditions thereof indicate amount to be insured in figures in box marked "Amount of Insurance".</td></tr>
<tr><td></td><td></td></tr>
<tr><td colspan="9">Handling Information

(for USA only) Those commodities licensed by US for ultimate destination ... Diversion contrary to US law is prohibited.</td></tr>
<tr><td>No. of Pieces</td><td>Gross Weight</td><td>Kg lb</td><td>Rate Class</td><td>Chargeable Weight</td><td>Rate/Charge</td><td>Total</td><td colspan="2">Nature and Quantity of Goods</td></tr>
<tr><td></td><td></td><td></td><td></td><td></td><td></td><td></td><td colspan="2"></td></tr>
<tr><td>Prepaid</td><td>Weight charge</td><td>Collect</td><td colspan="6">Other Charges</td></tr>
<tr><td colspan="3">Valuation Charge</td><td colspan="6" rowspan="4"></td></tr>
<tr><td colspan="3"></td></tr>
<tr><td colspan="3">Tax</td></tr>
<tr><td colspan="3"></td></tr>
<tr><td colspan="3">Total Other Charges Due Agent</td><td colspan="6" rowspan="4">Shipper certifies that the particulars on the face hereof are correct and that insofar as any part of the consignment contains dangerous goods, such part is properly described by name and is in proper condition for carriage by air according to the applicable Dangerous Goods Regulations.
....
Signature of Shipper or his agent</td></tr>
<tr><td colspan="3"></td></tr>
<tr><td colspan="3">Total Other Charges Due Carrier</td></tr>
<tr><td colspan="3"></td></tr>
<tr><td>Total Prepaid</td><td colspan="2">Total Collect</td><td colspan="6" rowspan="4">Executed on ____ at ____ Signature of issuing Carrier or as Agent</td></tr>
<tr><td></td><td colspan="2"></td></tr>
<tr><td>Currency Conversion Rates</td><td colspan="2">CC Charges in des. Currency</td></tr>
<tr><td></td><td colspan="2"></td></tr>
<tr><td>For Carrier's Use Only at Destination</td><td colspan="2">Charges at Destination</td><td colspan="3">Total Collect Charges</td><td colspan="3">AIR WAYBILL NUMBER
999-80693231</td></tr>
</table>

项目十二　缮制商业汇票

一、常用术语中英文互译

1. 商业汇票____________________　　2. 即期汇票____________________
3. 远期汇票____________________　　4. 提示____________________
5. 承兑____________________　　6. Drawer ____________________
7. Drawee ____________________　　8. Payee ____________________
9. Drawn on ____________________　　10. Draw under ____________________

二、单项选择题

1. 关于汇票的出票人，下列表述正确的是(　　)。
   A. 出票人一般都位于汇票的左下角
   B. 出票人通常为信用证申请人
   C. 出票人通常为信用证议付行
   D. 出票人一般位于汇票右下角，通常为出口人或信用证的受益人，应有企业全称和负责人的签字盖章

2. 一张汇票规定见票后 60 天付款，而持票人于 2018 年 9 月 28 日提示承兑，则付款到期日为(　　)。
   A. 2018 年 11 月 26 日　　B. 2018 年 11 月 27 日
   C. 2018 年 11 月 28 日　　D. 2018 年 11 月 29 日

3. 汇票的抬头有三种填写方式，根据我国《票据法》规定，签发(　　)的汇票无效。
   A. 限制性抬头　　B. 指示性抬头
   C. 持票人或来人抬头　　D. 记名抬头

4. 如果信用证显示 Available with any bank，在缮制汇票时，受款人栏目(　　)。
   A. 只能填写 ANY BANK　　B. 可以由受益人指定
   C. 只能由开证行指定　　D. 可以由进口商指定

5. 汇票的号码一般填写(　　)。
   A. 汇票号码　　B. 商业发票号码
   C. 提单号码　　D. 银行指定号码

6. 若信用证上未注明汇票的付款人，则根据 UCP 600 的规定，汇票的付款人应该是(　　)。
   A. 开证申请人　　B. 开证行　　C. 议付行　　D. 出口人

7. 全套汇票的正本份数应该是(　　)。
   A. 视不同国家而定　　B. 两份
   C. 三份　　D. 一份

8. 若信用证上关于汇票的条款规定是 AVAILABLE BY YOUR DRAFT AT 30 DAYS SIGHT DRAWN ON APPLICANT,则此汇票应填写(　　)。

A. 付款期限为 AT 30 DAYS SIGHT,付款人为开证申请人的名称

B. 付款期限为 AT 30 DAYS SIGHT,付款人为开证行的名称

C. 付款期限为 AT XXXSIGHT,付款人为开证行的名称

D. 付款期限为 AT 30 DAYS SIGHT,付款人为"APPLICANT"

9. 在我国出口业务中,出口公司开出的汇票在信用证结算方式下的出票条款应填写(　　)。

A. 合同号码及签订日期　　B. 发票号码及签发日期

C. 提单号码及签发日期　　D. 信用证号、开证日期、开证行名称

10. 出票人是工商企业或个人,付款人可以是工商企业或个人,也可以是银行的汇票是(　　)。

A. 银行汇票　　B. 商业承兑汇票　　C. 商业汇票　　D. 银行承兑汇票

三、多项选择题

1. 根据 UCP 600 的规定,信用证项下汇票的付款人应规定为(　　)。

A. 开证行　　B. 开证行指定的银行

C. 开证申请人　　D. 开证申请人指定的银行

2. 如果信用证没有规定出票根据,汇票中一般要填写的内容有(　　)。

A. 开证行名称　　B. 开证申请人名称

C. 信用证号码　　D. 开证日期

3. 在信用证项下,对汇票的要求有(　　)。

A. 按照信用证的要求制作汇票

B. 按照买卖合同的要求制作汇票

C. 汇票的抬头应做成凭议付行指示

D. 汇票号就是商业发票的号码

E. 汇票的金额与货币应与商业发票的金额和货币一致

4. 按《中华人民共和国票据法》规定,汇票抬头的填写方法有(　　)。

A. 限制性抬头　　B. 指示性抬头

C. 持票人或来人抬头　　D. 记名抬头

5. 汇票的抬头限定"PAY TO ABC CO. ONLY",表明(　　)。

A. 限付给 ABC CO.　　B. 凭 ABC CO. 指示

C. 可以转让　　D. 不能转让

6. 当来证规定"INVOICE MUST SHOW CIF VALUE INCLUDING 5% COMMISSION AT THE TIME OF NEGOTIATION, 5% COMMISSION MUST BE DEDUCTED FROM DRAWINGS UNDER THIS CREDI",汇票金额应该(　　)。

A. 小于发票金额　　B. 大于发票金额

C. 是不含佣的 CIF 价　　D. 是含佣的 CIF 价

7. 以下情况,属于拒付的有(　　)。

A. 付款人破产

B. 付款人虽不拒绝付款,但承诺延缓 1 个月付款

C. 付款人拒绝付款

D. 付款人虽不拒绝付款,但承诺到期付款,并办理了承兑手续

8. 用于议付信用证项下结算的汇票可以是(　　)。

A. 即期汇票　　B. 远期汇票　　C. 商业汇票　　D. 银行汇票

E. 以上都对

9. 根据我国《票据法》的规定,汇票上必须记载的事项包括(　　)。

A. 确定的金额　　B. 出票日期　　C. 付款人姓名　　D. 汇票编号

E. 付款项目

10. 汇票小写金额为58,673.56港币,汇票大写正确的是(　　)。

A. HONGKONG DOLLARS FIFTY EIGHT THOUSAND SIX HUNDRED AND SEVENTY THREE CENTS FIFTY SIX ONLY.

B. HONGKONG DOLLARS FIFTY EIGHT THOUSAND SIX HUNDRED AND SEVENTY THREE 56/100 ONLY.

C. HONGKONG DOLLARS FIFTY EIGHT THOUSAND SIX HUNDRED AND SEVENTY THREE POINT FIFTY SIX ONLY.

D. HONGKONG DOLLARS FIFTY EIGHT THOUSAND SIX HUNDRED AND SEVENTY THREE 56% ONLY.

四、判断题

1. 作为可以支取信用证金额的凭证,汇票在本质上是一种单据,而不是票据。(　　)

2. 通常情况下,汇票、提单和保险单的抬头人分别是付款人、收货人、被保险人。(　　)

3. 根据UCP 600的规定,汇票的受票人可做成开证申请人。(　　)

4. 汇票是出票人承诺在见票时或在未来某一规定的或可以确定的时间,对持票人或其指定人支付一定金额的书面文件。(　　)

5. 如果汇票上加注"按某号信用证开立""按某合同装运某货物",则构成支付的附加条件,该汇票无效。(　　)

6. 根据我国《票据法》规定,票据金额以中文大写和数码同时记载的,两者必须一致。若两者不一致,则以中文大写为准。(　　)

7. 出票人签字是承认自己的债务,收款人因此有了债权,若汇票上没有出票人的签字,则票据也能成立。(　　)

8. 商业汇票和银行汇票的主要区别在于前者的付款人是商业企业,后者的付款人是银行。(　　)

9. 汇票出票人应该是信用证指定的受益人。(　　)

10. 远期汇票只有经过承兑才能转让。(　　)

五、简答题

1. 简述汇票记载出票日期的作用。

2. 汇票的抬头有哪几种?在实务中是如何应用的?

3. 请根据下面已填写好的汇票回答相关问题。

BILL OF EXCHANGE

NO. HLK356 EXCHANGE FOR USD14,200.00 DATE JAN. 10,2018

AT ××× DAYS AFTER SIGHT OF THIS FIRST OF EXCHANGE (SECOND OF EXCHANGE BEING UNPAID)

PAY TO THE ORDER OF BANK OF CHINA,GUANGZHOU BRANCH

THE SUM OF U. S. DOLLARS FOURTEEN THOUSAND TWO HUNDRED ONLY.

DRAWN UNDER THIS CREDIT NO. 002-10358

TO HONGKONG ABC CO.

3/F GUANGTEX BUILDING TAIKOKTSUI

KOWLOON,HONGKONG

GUANGZHOU HUADA FOOD CO. ,LTD.

(1) 汇票出票人、付款人分别是谁?

(2) 汇票是即期还是远期?

(3) 有几张汇票?

(4) 该笔业务的受款人是谁?

六、技能操作题

1. 请根据相关资料填制商业汇票(见表 1-12-1)。

相关资料如下。

INVOICE NO.: TU231

ISSUING BANK: KUWAIT REAL ESTATE BANK

L/C NO.: SP00256 DATED MAR. 21,2018

INVOICE AMOUNT: USD9,785.00

BENEFICIARY: BEIJING NATIONAL NATIVE PRODUCE IMP. & EXP. CORPORATION

APPLICANT: HAMEED ALI AL TUHOO CO. ,KUWAIT

NEGOTIATING BANK: THE INDUSTRIAL & COMMERCIAL BANK OF CHINA

DATE OF NEGOTIATION: APR. 18,2018

... AVAILABLE WITH YOUR DRAFT AT SIGHT DRAWN ON US FOR THE FULL INVOICE VALUE. ALL DRAFTS MUST BE MARKED"DRAWN UNDER KUWAIT REAL ESTATE BANK".

表 1-12-1 商业汇票

BILL OF EXCHANGE

NO. Date:

EXCHANGE FOR

At DAYS AFTER Sight of THIS SECOND BILL of EXCHANGE

(First of the tenor and date being unpaid)

Pay to the order of or order the sum of

Drawn under

L/C NO. Dated

TO.

2. 请根据相关资料填制商业汇票(见表 1-12-2)。

相关资料如下。

COVERING 3,000 DOZ OF GARMENTS AT JPY20.2 PER DOZ. UNDER CONTRACT NO.:02PI744. THE BUYERS SHALL DULY ACCEPT THE DOCUMENTARY DRAFT DRAWN BY THE SELLERS AT 90 DAYS UPON FIRST PRESENTATION AND MAKE PAYMENT ON ITS MATURITY. THE SHIPPING DOCUMENTS ARE TO BE DELIVERED AGAINST PAYMENT ONLY.

COLLECTING BANK: THE BANK OF TOKYO,LTD.
P. O. BOX 240,NAGOYA-NAKA,NAGOYA,460-91 JAPAN

PRINCIPAL: SHANHAI FENGHUA TEXTILES I/E CO.
25 GUANGDONG ROAD,SHANGHAI,CHINA

PAYER: TOYOHANM AND CO.,LTD.
58 NISHIKI 6-CHOME,NAKAKU

INVOICE NO.: YU25868

DATE OF NEGOTIATION: APR. 14,2018

表 1-12-2 商业汇票

BILL OF EXCHANGE	
NO.	Date:
EXCHANGE FOR	
At	Sight of THIS SECOND BILL of EXCHANGE
(First of the tenor and date being unpaid)	
Pay to	or order the sum of
Drawn under	
L/C NO.	Dated
TO.	

项目十三　缮制其他常用结汇单据

一、常用术语中英文互译

1. 商品检验________________　　2. 品质检验证书________________

3. 受益人证明书________________　　4. 装船通知________________

5. 预定到达时间________________

6. China commodity inspection bureau ________________

7. estimated time of departure(ETD)________________

8. I. O. P. (irrespective of percentage)________________

9. P. T. O. (please turn over)________________

10. Shipping company's certificate ________________

二、单项选择题

1. 下列各项中,不属于收汇单证的附属单据是(　　)。

A. 装船通知　　B. 船公司证明

C. 出口商或受益人证明　　D. 提单

2. 按照国际贸易惯例,采用(　　)贸易术语时,合同的卖方尤其需要及时向买方发出装船通知。

A. FOB　　B. CFR　　C. CIF　　D. CIP

3. 受益人声明可以是一份单独的文件,也可以与(　　)合并,在上面加注声明即可。

A. 装船通知　　B. 船公司证明　　C. 商业发票　　D. 提单

4. 按惯例,装运通知应以快捷方式及时发送。"及时"一般应是货物装船以后的(　　)个工作日之内。

A. 1　　B. 2　　C. 3　　D. 4

5. 制作装船通知的日期,应在提单日期后的(　　)天之内,信用证项下应符合信用证的规定。

A. 1　　B. 2　　C. 3　　D. 4

6. 装船通知中"预计开船日期"一般表示为(　　)。

A. MESSERS　　B. STD　　C. ETA　　D. ETD

7. 装船通知中商品描述部分应与(　　)的内容一致。

A. 商业发票　　B. 船公司证明　　C. 托运单　　D. 提单

8. 受益人证明是指在(　　)支付方式下,出口商出具自己履行了某些规定义务的证明。

A. 汇付　　B. 电汇　　C. 托收　　D. 信用证

9. 出口许可证所填制的内容必须与(　　)一致,不能有相互矛盾的地方。
A. 原产地证书　B. 报关单　C. 合同　D. 报检单

10. 装船通知的主要作用是为了方便进口商做好(　　)准备。
A. 投保　B. 订舱　C. 报关报检　D. 接货

三、多项选择题

1. 出口商证明等附属单据上可显示(　　),表示与同批货物其他单据关联。
A. 提单号　B. 发票号
C. 合同号　D. 出口收汇核销单号

2. 装运通知是指出口商在出口货物装运后,向收货人或其通知人发出货物装运情况的书面文件,其主要作用有(　　)。
A. CIF 条件下告知进口商做好接货准备
B. FOB、CFR 条件下提请进口商办理保险
C. 该副本是议付货款的单证之一
D. FOB、CFR 条件下自动承保的证明

3. 制作受益人证明等附属单据时,必须注意(　　)。
A. 单据名称和出具人签署应符合信用证要求
B. 单据内容应符合信用证要求,并与其他单据相关内容不矛盾
C. 应该至少提供一份正本
D. 应注明出单日

4. 按惯例,装运通知应以快捷方式及时发送,这里的“快捷方式”主要包括(　　)。
A. 电传(TELEX)　B. 电子邮件(E-Mail)
C. 传真(FAX)　D. 简电通知

5. 阿拉伯国家的来证中要求不得使用以色列籍的船舶且航程不得经过以色列转运,此证明一般由(　　)出具。
A. 船代理　B. 船公司　C. 出口商　D. 进口商

6. 下列说法正确的有(　　)。
A. 出口许可证所填制的内容必须与报关单一致,不能有相互矛盾的地方
B. 出口许可证所允许出口的数量,在实际出运时可以视情况超出
C. 出口许可证的任何更改都要经过原发证机关办理,任何涂改和伪报都要追究责任
D. 出口许可证是国家批准某些商品出口的证明文件

7. 实务中,需要卖方在货物装船后及时发送装运通知的术语有(　　)。
A. FOB　B. CFR　C. CIF　D. CIP

8. 因信用证的规定由出口商出具的说明其已履行某种义务或办理某项工作的声明文件有(　　)。
A. 关于商品品质的声明
B. 关于商品包装的声明
C. 关于商品原产地的声明
D. 关于已发装船通知、已寄样品或已寄副本单据的声明

9. 属于“非单据条件”的信用证规定有(　　)。

A. 载货船舶的船龄不超过 15 年　　B. 载货船舶挂巴拿马国旗

C. 装船后立即通知申请人装货细节　　D. 货物原产于中国并提供原产地证书

E. CIF 条件下的保险单

10. 装运通知的抬头可以是(　　)。

A. 买方　　B. 开证申请人

C. 买方指定的保险公司　　D. 卖方

四、判断题

1. 进出口许可证制是我国乃至世界上大多数国家采用的管理进出口秩序的重要手段。(　　)

2. 对外已签合同的进口货物,在进口许可证有效期限内尚未进口的,可到原发证机构申请进口许可证的展延。(　　)

3. 对欧盟纺织品出口专用产地证(EEC 产地证)是由商务部签发的,而不是由贸促会签发的。(　　)

4. 附属单据不属于结汇单据。(　　)

5. 装运通知的签发人应为卖方。(　　)

6. 按照我国习惯做法,如以 CFR 和 FOB 成交,进口商在接到国外进口商发来的装船通知后,即应填制投保单或预约保险起运通知书,向保险公司投保。(　　)

7. 在 CFR 条件下,如合同未规定卖方在货物装船后发装船通知,卖方就没有该义务。(　　)

8. 对外已签合同的进口货物,在进口许可证有效期限内尚未进口的,可到原发证机构申请进口许可证的展期。(　　)

9. 附属单据大致可分为除商业发票外的其他发票、包装单据、商检单据、原产地证明书、进出口许可证和其他附属单据等。(　　)

10. 根据信用证的要求,出口商有时还要提供一些有关运输方面的证明,例如装船通知、船籍及航程证明、船龄证明、船级证明以及班轮公会船只证明等。(　　)

五、简答题

1. 装船通知的作用及主要内容是什么?

2. 什么是受益人声明? 实务中有哪些常见的受益人声明?

3. 有关运输方面的证明单据有哪些?

六、技能操作题

1. 受益人证明书填制练习。

(1) 信用证条款。

BENEFICIARY: SHANGHAI MACHINERY IMP. & EXP. CORPORATION

L/C NO.: HU65926

DOCUMENTS REQUIRED: * BENEFICIARY'S CERTIFICATE CERTIFYING THAT COMMERCIAL INVOICE, PACKING LIST AND ORIGINAL EXPORT LICENCE HAVE

BEEN DESPATCHED BY COURIER DIRECTLY
TO YOUTA TRADING COMPANY.

(2) 其他资料。

INVOICE NO.：TB-M85062

DATE OF ISSUING THE BENEFICIARY'S CERTIFICATE：AUG. 3,2018

(3) 填制要求。

请根据上述信用证资料及其他资料填制受益人证明书(见表 1-13-1)。

表 1-13-1 受益人证明书

BENEFICIARY'S CERTIFICATE DATE：

2. 装船通知书填制练习。

(1) 信用证资料。

Date of Issue：181020

Form of Doc. Credit：IRREVOCABLE

Doc. Credit Number：M20K2710NS00032

Expiry：DATE 181115 PLACE IN BENEFICIARY'S COUNTRY

Applicant：SE BANG TRADING CO. ,LTD.
148 NAMCHEON-2 DONG,SUYOUNG-KU
PUSAN,KOREA

Beneficiary：GUANGZHOU ARTS & CRAFTS IMP. & EXP. CO.
628 GUANGZHOU DADAO ZHONG ROAD
GUANGZHOU,CHINA

Partial Shipments：ALLOWED

Transshipment：ALLOWED

Loading of Charge：GUANGZHOU,CHINA

For Transport to...：PUSAN,KOREA

Latest Date of Ship.：181105

Descript. of Goods：CHINA ORIGIN

ARTIFICIAL FLOWERS
AB-06001 5,184DOZ @USD2.50/DOZ
AB-07049 2,880DOZ @USD2.80/DOZ
AS PER S/C NO. 97A/KF002A DATE OCT. 15,2018
CIF PUSAN

Documents Required: SHIPMENT ADVICE IN FULL DETAILS INCLUDING SHIPPING MARKS, CONTAINER NUMBERS, VESSEL NAME, B/L NUMBER, VALUE AND QUANTITY OF GOODS MUST BE SENT ON THE DATE OF SHIPMENT TO APPLICANT.

(2) 其他资料。

INV. NO.: 97KF335　　B/L DATE: OCT. 28,2018
B/L NO.: DSA97-1102　　SHIPPING MARKS: SE BANG/PUSAN
PACKING: AB-06001 36DOZ/CTN　G. W.: 23KGS/CTN　N. W.: 18KGS/CTN
AB-07049 36DOZ/CTN　G. W.: 19KGS/CTN　N. W.: 13KGS/CTN
MEASUREMENT: 40CM×50CM×80CM/CTN　DATE OF ADVICE: OCT. 29,2018
CONTAINER NO. MSCU4097561(20′)　MSCU4097615(40′)
NAME OF STEAMER: SUI 301/NORASIA V. 49-3 W/T HONGKONG

(3) 填制要求。

请根据上述信用证资料及其他资料填制装船通知书(表 1-13-2)。

表 1-13-2　装船通知书

广州工艺进出口公司
GUANGZHOU ARTS & CRAFTS IMP. & EXP. CO.
628 GUANGZHOU DADAO ZHONG ROAD,GUANGZHOU,CHINA
SHIPPING ADVICE

DATE:

To Messrs.:

Name of Commodity:
Quantity:
Invoice Value:
Name of Carrying Steamer:
Date of Shipment:
Shipping Marks:
Credit No.:
Port of Loading:
Port of Discharge:
B/L No.:
Container No.:

项目十四　填写开证申请书

一、常用术语中英文互译

1. 议付________________　　2. 延期付款________________

3. 空运单________________　　4. 账号________________

5. 到期日________________　　6. Airmail________________

7. Acceptance________________　　8. Sight payment________________

9. Price term________________　　10. Express delivery________________

二、单项选择题

1. 在信用证支付方式下,只要单据表面与信用证条款符合,开证行就必须按规定付款,进口商(　　)。

A. 应在申请开证时,按合同有关规定转化成有关单据,具体规定在信用证内

B. 只要在信用证申请书中详细阐明即可,不用列明应提交与之相应的单据

C. 应与出口人建立深厚的友谊

D. 应委托一个机构全权监督出口方的行为

2. 在以信用证为支付方式的进口贸易中,依据合同规定,进口商的首要义务是(　　)。

A. 开立信用证　　B. 申请进口货物许可证

C. 办理租船订舱手续　　D. 办理保险手续

3. 进口商在申请开证前,要落实的事情是办理(　　)。

A. 进口批准手续及外汇来源　　B. 货物入境通关手续

C. 货物检验手续　　D. 货物的保险手续

4. 在信用证申请书中,汇票的付款人应填写(　　)。

A. 开证人　　B. 开证行或指定付款行

C. 通知行　　D. 受益人

5. 下列各单据中,不能归入进口到货单证类别的是(　　)。

A. 保险单据　　B. 运输单据

C. 入境货物通关单　　D. 进口货物报关单

6. 进口商填写开证申请书的主要依据是(　　)。

A. 发票　　B. 贸易合同　　C. 订单　　D. 进口许可证

7. 根据 UCP 600 的规定,开证行开立的信用证不会是(　　)。

A. 可撤销信用证　　B. 议付信用证

C. 跟单信用证　　D. 转让信用证

8. 我国出口到英国一批货物共计 10 万美元,分批交货,信用证支付。与我国供货商签订合同的是新加坡的一家公司,信用证由英国进口商开立,然后新加坡的有关银行按照信用

证的要求将该证转给我国供货商,这张信用证是(　　)。

A. 可转让信用证　　B. 不可转让信用证

C. 可循环信用证　　D. 可撤销信用证

9. 进口商申请开证时,银行通常进行"三查一保",其中"三查"不包括(　　)。

A. 审查开证申请书和开证申请人的声明

B. 审查开证申请人的资信情况

C. 审查信用证受益人的资信情况

D. 审查开证时应提供的有效文件

10. 信用证开立后,应由一家通知行进行通知,一般情况下确定通知行的做法是(　　)。

A. 由进口商和出口商商定　　B. 由受益人选择

C. 由开证行指定　　D. 由开证申请人指定

三、多项选择题

1. 申请开立信用证的具体程序是(　　)。

A. 递交有关合同的副本及附件　　B. 填写开证申请书

C. 缴付保证金　　D. 递交发票

2. 买方应按合同规定的开证时间填写开证申请书并办理开证手续,开证行对开证申请书审核无误后,收取(　　),按开证申请书的要求开出信用证。

A. 订单　　B. 保证金　　C. 开证手续费　　D. 合同书

3. 信用证申请书中常见的付款方式有(　　)。

A. 即期支付　　B. 承兑支付　　C. 议付　　D. 延期支付

4. 关于信用证中的"Date and place of expiry",表述正确的有(　　)。

A. 表明该证的到期日期和到期地点

B. 信用证的到期地点可以是开证行所在地也可以是受益人的所在地

C. 可以推算信用证的开证日期

D. 如果是开证行所在地,出口审单员一定要把握好交单日期和邮程,防止信用证失效

5. 关于 SWIFT,下列表述正确的有(　　)。

A. 使用 SWIFT 系统的银行必须加入该协会,方可使用 SWIFT 系统

B. 使用 SWIFT 信用证,必须遵守 SWIFT 使用手册的规定,使用 SWIFT 手册规定的代号

C. SWIFT 信用证必须按国际商会制定的 UCP 600 的规定处理

D. SWIFT 系统具有自动收发储存信息、自动收押和核押等功能

E. SWIFT 系统可每周 24 小时连续运转

6. 信用证中,表示开证人的常见词或词组有(　　)。

A. Principal　　B. Opener　　C. Applicant　　D. account of...

E. Accountee

7. 信用证的开证方式主要有(　　)。

A. 邮寄　　B. 传真　　C. 电开本　　D. 信开本

8. 下列信用证条款中，属于佣金条款的有（ ）。

A. Port congestion surcharges, if any, at the time of shipment is for opener's account

B. Signed invoices must show 5% commission

C. 5% commission to be deducted from the invoice value

D. Beneficiary's drafts are to be made out for 95% of invoice value, being 5% commission payable to credit opener

9. 信用证中，表示受益人的常见词或词组有（ ）。

A. Beneficiary B. in favour of... C. Opener D. in your favour

10. 使用（ ）术语时，应在信用证申请书中的保单条款前的括号内打"×"。

A. CIF B. FOB C. CFR D. CIP

四、判断题

1. 进口人对卖方的要求，在申请开证时，应按合同有关规定转化成有关单据，具体规定在信用证中。（ ）

2. 如在信用证申请书中采用延期付款方式，卖方一般会将货价定得比采用承兑支付方式时高。（ ）

3. 开证行开立信用证后，一般把信用证副本寄交出口商，把正本交给开证申请人，以作为审核备查。（ ）

4. 我国银行一般不开可转让信用证，因为对第二受益人资信难于了解，特别是对于跨地区和国家的转让更难掌握。（ ）

5. 在信用证业务中，信用证的开立以买卖合同为基础，因此，信用证条款与买卖合同条款严格相符是开证行向受益人承担付款责任的前提条件。（ ）

6. 申请人资信好，或办理了抵押、质押手续的，或有其他金融机构、有实力的公司为其出面担保的，开证银行可免收申请人的保证金。（ ）

7. 在 FOB 术语、信用证支付方式的进口业务中，开证申请工作一般是在租船订舱工作之后。（ ）

8. 在我国出口业务中，我出口公司收到进口商寄来的开证申请书后即可据此备货，委托出运。（ ）

9. 开证申请书的开证人声明，是开证申请人申请开立信用证应承担的义务和责任的书面承诺。（ ）

10. 2018 年 6 月 21 日在 SWIFT 电文中表示为 210618。（ ）

五、简答题

1. 申请开立信用证的程序是什么？

2. 银行开立信用证时的"三查一保"是什么意思？

3. 简述信用证与买卖合同的关系。

4. 我国某公司与非洲某商按 CIF 条件签订一笔大宗商品出口合同，合同规定装运期为 7 月，但未规定具体开证日期。外商拖延开证，我国公司见装运期快到，从 6 月底就开始连续多次电催外商开证。7 月 5 日，收到开证的简电通知，我国公司因怕耽误装运期，即按简电通知内容办理装运。7 月 28 日，外商开来信用证正本，正本上对有关单据做了与合同不符的规定。我国公司审证时未予以注意，交银行议付时，银行发现单证不符，无法付款，建议改成 D/P 托收。外商提出按 D/P after 30 days T/R 办理，我国公司只好答应。最后外商以 T/R 将单据借走，借走后不见踪影，最后我国公司钱货两空。请问我国公司应通过此事件吸取哪些教训?

六、技能操作题

1. 请根据销售合同(见表 1-14-1)和相关合同资料，用英文缮制开证申请书(见表 1-14-2)。

(1) 销售合同见表 1-14-1。

表 1-14-1 销售合同

明基贸易有限公司

MJ TRADE CO. ,LTD.

12F 7 BLDG SHATOUJIAO FREE TRADE ZONE,YANTIAN,SHENZHEN,CHINA 416061

销售合同

SALE CONTRACT

To:

COMPANHIA BRASILEIRA DE　　　　Contract No.: TR100566

DISTRIBUICAO ROD. ANHANGUERA,KM 17,8　　　　Date: JULY 16,2018

OSASCO-SP-BRASIL

This sales contract is made between the sellers and buyers whereby the seller agree to sell and the buyers agree to buy the undermentioned goods according to the terms and conditions stipulated below:

Description of Goods	Quantity	Unit Price	Amount CIF SANTOS
PENGUIM HUMIDIFIER (BLACK BODY -WHITE DETAIL)-127V	1,280PCS	@USD13.70/PC	USD17,536.00
PENGUIM HUMIDIFIER (BLACK BODY -WHITE DETAIL)-220V	600PCS	@USD13.70/PC	USD8,220.00
TOTAL:	1,880PCS		USD25,756.00

5% MORE OR LESS AMOUNT AND QUANTITY ARE ALLOWED.

Total amount in words　SAY U.S. DOLLARS Twenty Five Thousand Seven Hundred And Fifty Six ONLY.

Packing　4Pc in one Ctn,total packed in 470Ctns.

Delivery　Sea freight from Shanghai to SanTos allowing partial shipments and transshipment

Shipping Mark　MJ HONGKONG/100566/SANTOS. 1-470

Time of Shipment　On or before SEP. 12,2018

Terms of Payment　By 100pct irrevocable letter of credit in favour of the Seller to be available By darfts at sight to open and to reach the seller before July 25,2018 and to remain valid for negotiation in China until the 15th days after the foresaid time of the shipment. The L/C must mention this contract number. All banking charges outside BRAZIL are for of the beneficiary.

Insurance　To be effected by the sellers for 110 pct of the invoice value covering all risks and war risk of Institute Cargo Clause (A)

Documents required

1. Signed invoice in 3 originals plus 1 copy.
2. Full set clean on board Bill of Lading made out to order blank endorsed notify the buyer.

续表

3. Insurance policy in duplicate. 4. Packing list in 3 originals plus 1 copy. 5. Certificate of Origin in duplicate.
The Seller MJ Trade Co. ,Ltd. 张三 签署   The Buyer COMPANHIA BRASILEIRA HARK Signature

（2）相关合同资料。

最迟开证日期：2018 年 7 月 21 日

开户行及账号：BANK OF BRAZIL RIO DE JANEIRO,2357924680

法人代表：HARK

开证方式：电开

表 1-14-2 开证申请书

IRREVOCABLE DOCUMENTARY CREDIT APPLICATION

To: Date:

<table>
<tr><td colspan="2" rowspan="2">Beneficiary(full name and address)</td><td>L/C No.
Ex-Card No.
Contract No.</td></tr>
<tr><td>Date and place of expiry of the credit</td></tr>
<tr><td>Partial shipment
□allowed □not allowed</td><td>Transshipment
□allowed □not allowed</td><td rowspan="2">□Issued by airmail
□With brief advice by teletransmission
□Issued by express delivery
□Issued by teletransmission (which shall be the operative instrument)</td></tr>
<tr><td colspan="2" rowspan="2">Loading on board/dispatch/taking in charge at/from
Not late than
For transportation to</td></tr>
<tr><td>Amount (both in figures and words)</td></tr>
<tr><td colspan="2" rowspan="2">Description of goods:

Packing:</td><td>Credit available with
□by sight payment □by acceptance
□by negotiation □by deferred payment
at against the documents detailed herein
□and beneficiary's drafts for ____% of the invoice value
at
on</td></tr>
<tr><td>□FOB □CFR □CIF
□or other terms</td></tr>
</table>

续表

Documents required: (marked with ×)
1. ( ) Signed Commercial invoice in ________ copies indication
2. ( ) Full set of clean on board ocean Bill of Lading made out ________ and ( ) blank endorsed, marked "freight" ( ) collect/( ) prepaid Notify.
3. ( ) Air Waybill showing "freight ( ) to collect/( ) prepaid ( ) indicating freight amount" and consigned to ________.
4. ( ) Memovandum issued by ________ consigned to ________.
5. ( ) Insurance Policy/Certificate in ________ copies for 110% of the invoice value showing claims payable in China in currency of the draft, blank endorsed, covering ( ) Ocean Marine Transportation/( ) Air Transportation/( ) Over Land transportation ( ) All risks, war risk.
6. ( ) Packing List in ________ copies indication gross and net weights for each package and packing conditions as called for by the L/C.
7. ( ) Certificate of Quantity/Weight in ________ copies issued by an independent surveyor at the loading port, indicating the actual surveyed quantity/weight of shipped goods as well as the packing condition.
8. ( ) Certificate of Quality in ________ copies issued by ( ) manufacturer/( ) public recognized surveyor/( ).
9. ( ) Beneficiary's Certified copy of cable/telex dispatched to the accountees within ________ hours after shipment advising ( ) name of vessel/( ) flight No./( ) wagon No., date, quantity, weight and value of shipment.
10. ( ) Beneficiary's Certificate certifying that extra copies of the documents have been dispatched according to the contract terms.
11. ( ) Shipping Co's certificate attesting that the carrying vessel is chartered or booked by accountee or their shipping agents.
12. ( ) Other documents, if any:

Additional Instructions:
1. ( ) All banking charges outside opening bank are for beneficiary's account.
2. ( ) Documents must be presented within ________ days after the date of issuance of the transport documents but within the validity of this credit.
3. ( ) Third party as shipper is not acceptable. Short form/Blank back B/L is not acceptable.
4. ( ) Both quantity and amount ________% more or less are allowed.
5. ( ) Prepaid freight drawn in excess of L/C amount is acceptable against presentation of original charges voucher issued by( ) Shipping Co./Air Line/or it's agent.
6. ( ) All documents to be forwarded in one cover, unless otherwise stated above.
7. ( ) Other terms, if any:

Account No.: with ________________ (name of bank)
Transacted by: (Applicant: name signature of authorized person)
Telephone No.: (with seal)

2. 根据合同资料，用英文缮制进口开证申请书(见表 1-14-3)。

合同资料如下。

买方：DAFA TRADING CO.
NO. 200 NANFANG ROAD HANGHZOU CHINA
大发贸易公司
中国杭州南方路 200 号

电话：0571-8765 4329

卖方：ABC IMP. AND EXP. INC.
　　　NO. 396 GIANT STREET SAN FRANCISCO U. S. A.

品名：ENERGY SAVING ELECTRONIC LAMP
　　　ART NO. FCL-22，22W，1，040PCS，UNIT PRICE USD3.50
　　　ART NO. FCL-32，32W，1，040PCS，UNIT PRICE USD5.50

总金额：9 360.00 美元

包装：40 个 1 纸箱，牢固出口纸箱

装运：2018 年 9 月 30 日前，不允许分批装运和转运

装运港：旧金山

目的港：上海

贸易术语：CIF 上海

支付：不可撤销即期跟单信用证

最迟开证日期：2018 年 8 月 10 日

允许金额与数量各有 5%的增减幅度

保险：按发票金额加一成投保一切险和战争险

单据条款：商业发票一式五份，注明信用证号码和合同号
　　　　　装箱单一式四份
　　　　　全套清洁以装船正本提单，做成"凭指示"抬头，空白背书，注明运费预付，通知开证申请人
　　　　　检验检疫机构出具的品质检验证书两份
　　　　　保险单正本一式两份，做空白背书

合同号：DTE084956

开户行及账号：中国银行杭州分行，1357924680

法人代表：卢华

开证方式：电开

表 1-14-3　开证申请书

IRREVOCABLE DOCUMENTARY CREDIT APPLICATION

To：　　　　　　　　　　　　　　　　　　　　　　　　Date：

<table>
<tr><td colspan="2" rowspan="2">Beneficiary(full name and address)</td><td>L/C No.
Ex-Card No.
Contract No.</td></tr>
<tr><td>Date and place of expiry of the credit</td></tr>
<tr><td>Partial shipment
□allowed □not allowed</td><td>Transshipment
□allowed □not allowed</td><td rowspan="2">□Issued by airmail
□With brief advice by teletransmission
□Issued by express delivery
□Issued by teletransmission (which shall be the operative instrument)</td></tr>
<tr><td colspan="2" rowspan="2">Loading on board/dispatch/taking in charge at/from

Not late than
For transportation to</td></tr>
<tr><td>Amount (both in figures and words)</td></tr>
</table>

续表

Description of goods: Packing:	Credit available with □by sight payment □by acceptance □by negotiation □by deferred payment at against the documents detailed herein □and beneficiary's drafts for ____% of the invoice value at on □FOB □CFR □CIF □or other terms

Documents required: (marked with ×)

1. ( ) Signed Commercial invoice in ________ copies indication.
2. ( ) Full set of clean on board ocean Bill of Lading made out ________ and ( ) blank endorsed, marked"freight" ( ) collect/( ) prepaid Notify.
3. ( ) Air Waybill showing"freight( ) to collect/( ) prepaid ( ) indicating freight amount" and consigned to ________.
4. ( ) Memovandum normal issued by ________ consigned to ________.
5. ( ) Insurance Policy/Certificate in ________ copies for 110% of the invoice value showing claims payable in China in currency of the draft, blank endorsed, covering ( ) Ocean Marine Transportation/( ) Air Transportation/( ) Over Land transportation ( ) All risks, war risk.
6. ( ) Packing List in ________ copies indication gross and net weights for each package and packing conditions as called for by the L/C.
7. ( ) Certificate of Quantity/Weight in ________ copies issued by an independent surveyor at the loading port, indicating the actual surveyed quantity/weight of shipped goods as well as the packing condition.
8. ( ) Certificate of Quality in ________ copies issued by ( ) manufacturer/( ) public recognized surveyor/( ).
9. ( ) Beneficiary's Certified copy of cable/telex dispatched to the accountees within ________ hours after shipment advising ( ) name of vessel/( ) flight No. /( ) wagon No. , date, quantity, weight and value of shipment.
10. ( ) Beneficiary's Certificate certifying that extra copies of the documents have been dispatched according to the contract terms.
11. ( ) Shipping Co's certificate attesting that the carrying vessel is chartered or booked by accountee or their shipping agents.
12. ( ) Other documents, if any:

Additional Instructions:

1. ( ) All banking charges outside opening bank are for beneficiary's account.
2. ( ) Documents must be presented within ________ days after the date of issuance of the transport documents but within the validity of this credit.
3. ( ) Third party as shipper is not acceptable. Short form/Blank back B/L is not acceptable.
4. ( ) Both quantity and amount ________% more or less are allowed.
5. ( ) Prepaid freight drawn in excess of L/C amount is acceptable against presentation of original charges voucher issued by( ) Shipping Co. /Air Line/or it's agent.
6. ( ) All documents to be forwarded in one cover, unless otherwise stated above.
7. ( ) Other terms, if any:

Account No. : with ________________ (name of bank)

Transacted by: (Applicant: name signature of authorized person)

Telephone No. : (with seal)

第二部分

独立完成综合制单实训

实训一　电汇方式下出口单据缮制

一、实训资料

1. 销售合同(见表 2-1-1)。

表 2-1-1　销售合同

JIANGSU HENGTANG FURNITURE CO. ,LTD.

No. 1111 MINYING DEVELOPMENT DISTRICT,TAOYUAN OF WUJIANG,JIANGSU,CHINA

TEL:+86-512-8753 9660　FAX:+86-512-8753 9661

SALES CONFIRMATION

MESSORS:　　DATE:JUNE 04,2018

RUBY HOME FURNISHINGS

ADDRESS:1205 PIONEER WAY EAST TACOMA WA 98443

SHIPMENT:From Shanghai China TO TACOMA WA,U. S. A. By Sea.

CONTRACT NO. :28317　　PAYMENT:T/T(Total payment against the copy of B/L)

DELIVERY TIME:JUNE 14,2018　　PRICE TERM:FOB SHANGHAI

INVOICE NO. :EM16015

2×40′HQ

MARKS	DESCRIPTION	QUANTITY(PCS)	UNIT PRICE	AMOUNT
N/M	FABRIC SOFA	54	$ 286.90	$ 15,492.60
	FABRIC CHAIR	54	$ 142.20	$ 7,678.80
	OTTOMAN	82	$ 66.00	$ 5,412.00
TOTAL		190	FOB SHANGHAI	$ 28,583.40

SAY TOTAL U. S. DOLLARS TWENTY EIGHT THOUSTHAND FIVE HUNDRED AND EIGHTY THREE POINT FOUR ONLY.

ADVISING BANK:BANK OF COMMUNICATIONS SUZHOU BRANCH

ADD:28 SUHUI ROAD SUZHOU,JIANGSU CHINA

SWIFT CODE:COMMCNSHJXG

BENEFICIARY:JIANGSU HENGTANG FURNITURE CO. ,LTD.

ADD:No. 1111 MINYING DEVELOPMENT DISTRICT,TAOYUAN 215000,JIANGSU,CHINA

A/C NO. :29606801015633005639

江苏横塘家具有限公司

JIANGSU HENGTANG FURNITURE CO. ,LTD.

ELSA　　钟汉良

CONFIRMED BY　　SELLER'S SIGNATURE

2. 补充资料。

INVOICE NO.：HG6415-1

GOODS：

	G. W.	N. W.	MEAS	H. S. CODE
FABRIC SOFA	52KGS/CTN	48KGS/CTN	1.4CBM/CTN	9401619000
FABRIC CHAIR	23KGS/CTN	20KGS/CTN	0.6CBM/CTN	9403609990
OTTOMAN	17KGS/CTN	14KGS/CTN	0.3CBM/CTN	9403609990

PACKED IN 190 CARTONS,@1PCS/CTN

CERTIFICATE NO.：15B1245A4563

B/L NO.：SHCM54869500

B/L DATE.：JUNE 10,2018

VESSEL'S NAME：YM MOVEMENT V.0026E

报检单位登记号：323961234

报检单编号：007812345

海关编号：220128160×××××××××

预录入编号：222920160777000345

经营单位注册号：4205821264

境内货源地：桃源

商品用途：民用家具/民用餐厅家具

材质：桦木

品牌：无

报关员：张琪

电话：0512-88834567

随附单据：出口货物通关单

该货物是完全自产品。

发货单位与经营单位相同。

2018 年 6 月 8 日由上海天原报关有限公司向上海吴淞海关(2202)申报出口。

二、实训要求

请以“单证员”的工作角色，根据以上资料缮制商业发票(见表 2-1-2)、装箱单(见表 2-1-3)、原产地证书申请书(见表 2-1-4)、原产地证书(见表 2-1-5)、出境货物报检单(见表 2-1-6)、海运出口托运单(见表 2-1-7)、海运提单(见表 2-1-8)、出口货物报关单(见表 2-1-9)。

表 2-1-2 商业发票

<table>
<tr><td colspan="5">江苏横塘家具有限公司
No. 1111 MINYING DEVELOPMENT DISTRICT，TAOYUAN OF WUJIANG，JIANGSU，CHINA
TEL：+86-512-8753 9660 FAX：+86-512-8753 9661</td></tr>
<tr><td colspan="5">商业发票
COMMERCIAL INVOICE</td></tr>
<tr><td colspan="5">Messrs：</td></tr>
<tr><td colspan="2" rowspan="5"></td><td colspan="2">Invoice No.：</td><td>18HY34-95</td></tr>
<tr><td colspan="2">Invoice Date：</td><td>MAR. 31，2018</td></tr>
<tr><td colspan="2">Credit No.：</td><td>NBM-18007678</td></tr>
<tr><td colspan="2">Credit Date：</td><td>FEB. 08，2018</td></tr>
<tr><td colspan="2">Terms of Payment：</td><td></td></tr>
<tr><td colspan="5">Exporter：</td></tr>
<tr><td colspan="2" rowspan="2"></td><td colspan="3">Transport details：</td></tr>
<tr><td colspan="3"></td></tr>
<tr><td>Marks & Nos.</td><td>Description of Goods</td><td>Quantity</td><td>Unit Price</td><td>Amount</td></tr>
<tr><td></td><td></td><td></td><td colspan="2"></td></tr>
<tr><td></td><td></td><td></td><td></td><td></td></tr>
<tr><td></td><td></td><td></td><td></td><td></td></tr>
<tr><td></td><td></td><td></td><td></td><td></td></tr>
<tr><td></td><td></td><td></td><td></td><td></td></tr>
<tr><td colspan="5">江苏横塘家具有限公司
（章）
JIANGSU HENGTANG FURNITURE CO.，LTD.
钟汉良（章）</td></tr>
</table>

表 2-1-3 装箱单

<table>
<tr><td colspan="10">江苏横塘家具有限公司
JIANGSU HENGTANG FURNITURE CO. ,LTD.
No. 1111 MINYING DEVELOPMENT DISTRICT,TAOYUAN OF WUJIANG,JIANGSU,CHINA</td></tr>
<tr><td colspan="10">装箱单
PACKING LIST</td></tr>
<tr><td colspan="10">To:</td></tr>
<tr><td colspan="4" rowspan="3"></td><td colspan="2">Inv. No. :</td><td colspan="4"></td></tr>
<tr><td colspan="2">Inv. Date:</td><td colspan="4"></td></tr>
<tr><td colspan="6"></td></tr>
<tr><td>From:</td><td colspan="2"></td><td>To:</td><td colspan="2"></td><td colspan="2">By vessel</td><td colspan="2"></td></tr>
<tr><td>Marks & Nos.</td><td>Description of goods</td><td>Quantity (PCS)</td><td>CARTON (CTNS)</td><td colspan="2">G. Weight (KGS)</td><td colspan="2">N. Weight (KGS)</td><td colspan="2">Measurement (CBM)</td></tr>
<tr><td></td><td></td><td></td><td></td><td colspan="2"></td><td colspan="2"></td><td colspan="2"></td></tr>
<tr><td colspan="10"></td></tr>
<tr><td colspan="10">江苏横塘家具有限公司
（章）
JIANGSU HENGTANG FURNITURE CO. ,LTD.
钟汉良（章）</td></tr>
</table>

表 2-1-4　原产地证书申请书

<table>
<tr><td colspan="6">中华人民共和国出口货物
一般原产地证明书/加工装配证明书申请书
企业名称：____________________　　证书号：____________________</td></tr>
<tr><td colspan="6">申请人郑重声明：
本人被正式授权代表本企业办理和签署本申请书。
本申请书及中华人民共和国出口货物原产地证明书/加工装配证明书所列内容正确无误，如发现弄虚作假，冒充证书所列货物，擅改证书，本人愿按《中华人民共和国出口货物原产地条例》的有关规定接受处罚并承担法律责任，现将有关情况申报如下：</td></tr>
<tr><td colspan="2">商品名称(中英文)</td><td></td><td>H.S.编码
(八位数)</td><td colspan="2"></td></tr>
<tr><td colspan="2">商品 FOB 总值(以美元计)</td><td></td><td>最终目的
国/地区</td><td colspan="2"></td></tr>
<tr><td>转口国/地区</td><td></td><td>拟出运日期</td><td></td><td>发票号</td><td></td></tr>
<tr><td colspan="6">贸易方式和企业性质(请在适用处画“√”)</td></tr>
<tr><td colspan="2">一般贸易</td><td colspan="2">灵活贸易</td><td colspan="2">其他贸易</td></tr>
<tr><td>中资企业</td><td>外资企业</td><td>中资企业</td><td>外资企业</td><td>中资企业</td><td>外资企业</td></tr>
<tr><td></td><td></td><td></td><td></td><td></td><td></td></tr>
<tr><td colspan="2">数量或重量</td><td colspan="2"></td><td colspan="2">是否含有进口成分：是(　　)　否(　　)</td></tr>
<tr><td>证书种类(画“√”)</td><td>一般原产地</td><td colspan="2"></td><td>加工装配证</td><td></td></tr>
<tr><td colspan="2">该批货物实际生产企业</td><td colspan="4"></td></tr>
<tr><td colspan="6">现提交中国出口货物商业发票副本一本，中华人民共和国出口货物原产地证明书/加工装配证明书一正三副，以及其他附件________份，请予以审核签证。

申请单位盖章：　　　　　　　　申领人(签名)：
电话：
日期：　　年　　月　　日</td></tr>
<tr><td colspan="6">注：1. 灵活贸易：包括来料加工、补偿贸易、进料加工贸易。
2. 外资企业指所有含有外资的企业。
3. 其他贸易指一般贸易和灵活贸易以外的贸易，如展卖、易货、租赁等贸易方式。</td></tr>
</table>

表 2-1-5 原产地证书

<table>
<tr><td colspan="2">1. Exporter</td><td colspan="3" rowspan="2">Certificate No.

CERTIFICATE OF ORIGIN
OF
THE PEOPLE'S REPUBLIC OF CHINA</td></tr>
<tr><td colspan="2">2. Consignee</td></tr>
<tr><td colspan="2">3. Means of transport and route</td><td colspan="3" rowspan="2">5. For certifying authority use only</td></tr>
<tr><td colspan="2">4. Country/region of destination</td></tr>
<tr><td>6. Marks and numbers</td><td>7. Number and kind of packages; description of goods</td><td>8. H. S. code</td><td>9. Quantity</td><td>10. Number and date of invoices</td></tr>
<tr><td colspan="2">11. Declaration by the exporter
The undersigned hereby declares that the above details and statements are correct; that all the goods were produced in China and that they comply with the Rules of Origin of the People's Republic of China.

Place and date, signature and stamp of authorized signatory</td><td colspan="3">12. Certification
It is hereby certified that the declaration by the exporter is correct.

Place and date, signature and stamp of certifying authority</td></tr>
</table>

表 2-1-6　出境货物报检单

中华人民共和国出入境检验检疫
出境货物报检单

报检单位(加盖公章)：　　　　　　　　　　　　　　　　＊编　　号：________

报检单位登记号：　　　　联系人：　　　　电话：　　　　报检日期：　　年　月　日

发货人	(中文)	
	(外文)	
收货人	(中文)	
	(外文)	

货物名称(中/外文)	H. S. 编码	产地	数/重量	货物总值	包装种类及数量

运输工具名称号码		贸易方式		货物存放地点	
合同号		信用证号		用途	
发货日期		输往国家(地区)		许可证/审批号	
启运地		到达口岸		生产单位注册号	
集装箱规格、数量及号码					

合同、信用证订立的检验检疫条款或特殊要求	标记及号码	随附单据(划"√"或补填)	
		□合同 □信用证 □发票 □换证凭单 □装箱单 □厂检单	□包装性能结果单 □许可/审批文件 □ □ □ □

需要证单名称(划"√"或补填)		＊检验检疫费	
□品质证书　__正__副 □重量证书　__正__副 □数量证书　__正__副 □兽医卫生证书　__正__副 □健康证书　__正__副 □卫生证书　__正__副 □动物卫生证书　__正__副	□植物检疫证书　__正__副 □熏蒸/消毒证书　__正__副 □出境货物换证凭单　__正__副 □ □ □ □	总金额 (人民币元)	
		计费人	
		收费人	

报检人郑重声明：	领取证单	
1. 本人被授权报检。 2. 上列填写内容正确属实，货物无伪造或冒用他人的厂名、标志、认证标志，并承担货物质量责任。 签名：________	日期	
	签名	

注：有"＊"号栏由出入境检验检疫机关填写。　　　　◆国家出入境检验检疫局制

[1-2(2000.1.1)]

表 2-1-7 海运出口托运单

SHIPPER(发货人)	B/L No. 中远集装箱运输有限公司 COSCO CONTAINER LINES 集装箱货物托运单 装货单 SHIPPING ORDER
CONSIGNEE(收货人)	
NOTIFY PARTY(通知人)	
Pre-carriage by(前程承运人) Place of Receipt(收货地点)	

Ocean Vessel(船名)	Voy. No.(航次)	Port of Loading(装货港)	Date(日期)
Port of Discharge(卸货港)	Place of Delivery(交货地点)	Final Destination for the Merchant's Reference(目的地)	

Container No.(集装箱号)	Seal No.(铅封号) Marks & Nos.(标记与号码)	No. of container or packages(箱数或件数)	Kind of Packages; Description of Goods(包装种类与货名)	Gross Weight 毛重(千克)	Measurement 尺码(立方米)
TOTAL NUMBER OF CONTINERS OR PACKAGES(JIN WORDS) 集装箱数或件数合计(大写)					

FREIGHT & CHARGES(运费与附加费)	Revenue Tons(运费吨)	Rate(运费率)	Per(每)	Prepaid(运费预付)	Collect(运费到付)

Service Type on Receiving	Service Type on Delivery	Reefer Temperature Required(冷藏温度)	℉	℃
□—CY □—CFS □—DOOR	□—CY □—CFS □—DOOR			

TYPE OF GOODS(货类)	□Ordinary(普通) □Reefer(冷藏) □Dangerous(危险品) □Auto(裸装车辆)	危险品	IMCO Class: UN No.:
	□Liquid(液体) □Live Animal(活动物) □Bulk(散货)		IMDG Code Page: Property:

可否转船:	可否分批:	装期:	Received by the Carrier the total number of containers or other packages or units stated above to be transported subject to the terms and conditions of the Carrier's regular form of Bill of Lading(for combined Transport to Port shipment) which shall be deemed to be incorporated herein Date: as Agent only
货价:	信用证号码:	No. of original B(S)/L:	
特约事项:	合同号码:	托运人盖章:	

表 2-1-8　海运提单

<table>
<tr><td colspan="2">Shipper Insert Name, Address and Phone</td><td rowspan="4">B/L No.

中远集装箱运输有限公司
COSCO CONTAINER LINES
TLX：33057 COSCO CN
FAX：＋86(021) 6545 8984
ORIGINAL</td></tr>
<tr><td colspan="2"></td></tr>
<tr><td colspan="2">Consignee Insert Name, Address and Phone</td></tr>
<tr><td colspan="2"></td></tr>
<tr><td colspan="2">Notify Party Insert Name, Address and Phone
(It is agreed that no responsibility shall attach to the Carrier or his agents for failure to notify)</td><td rowspan="8">Port-to-Port or Combined Transport
BILL OF LADING
RECEIVED in external apparent good order and condition except as other-Wise noted. The total number of packages or unites stuffed in the container, the description of the goods and the weights shown in this Bill of Lading are furnished by the Merchants, and which the carrier has no reasonable means of checking and is not a part of this Bill of Lading contract. The carrier has Issued the number of Bills of Lading stated below, all of this tenor and date, One of the original Bills of Lading must be surrendered and endorsed or signed against the delivery of the shipment and whereupon any other original Bills of Lading shall be void. The Merchants agree to be bound by the terms and conditions of this Bill of Lading as if each had personally signed this Bill of Lading.
SEE clause 4 on the back of this Bill of Lading (Terms continued on the back hereof, please read carefully).
* Applicable Only When Document Used as a Combined Transport Bill of Lading.</td></tr>
<tr><td colspan="2"></td></tr>
<tr><td>Combined Transport *
Pre-carriage by</td><td>Combined Transport *
Place of Receipt</td></tr>
<tr><td></td><td></td></tr>
<tr><td>Ocean Vessel Voy. No.</td><td>Port of Loading</td></tr>
<tr><td></td><td></td></tr>
<tr><td>Port of Discharge</td><td>Combined Transport *
Place of Delivery</td></tr>
<tr><td></td><td></td></tr>
</table>

<table>
<tr><td>Marks & Nos.
Container/Seal No.</td><td>No. of Packages & Description of Goods</td><td>Gross Weight Kgs</td><td>Measurement</td></tr>
<tr><td></td><td></td><td></td><td></td></tr>
<tr><td></td><td colspan="3">Description of Contents for Shipper's Use Only (Not part of This B/L Contract)</td></tr>
<tr><td colspan="4">Total Number of containers and/or packages (in words)</td></tr>
<tr><td colspan="4">Subject to Clause 7 Limitation</td></tr>
</table>

续表

<table>
<tr><td colspan="3">Freight & Charges</td><td>Revenue Tons</td><td>Rate</td><td>Per</td><td>Prepaid</td><td>Collect</td></tr>
<tr><td colspan="3"></td><td rowspan="3"></td><td rowspan="3"></td><td rowspan="3"></td><td rowspan="3"></td><td rowspan="3"></td></tr>
<tr><td colspan="3">Declared Value Charge</td></tr>
<tr><td colspan="3"></td></tr>
<tr><td>Ex. Rate:</td><td>Prepaid at</td><td>Payable at</td><td colspan="5">Place and date of issue</td></tr>
<tr><td rowspan="3"></td><td></td><td></td><td colspan="5"></td></tr>
<tr><td>Total Prepaid</td><td>No. of Original B(s)/L</td><td colspan="5">Signed for the Carrier,
COSCO CONTAINER LINES</td></tr>
<tr><td></td><td></td><td colspan="5"></td></tr>
<tr><td colspan="8">LADEN ON BOARD THE VESSEL</td></tr>
<tr><td>DATE</td><td></td><td>BY</td><td colspan="5"></td></tr>
</table>

表 2-1-9 出口货物报关单

中华人民共和国海关出口货物报关单

预录入编号： 海关编号： （××海关） 页码/页数：

<table>
<tr><td colspan="2">境内发货人</td><td colspan="2">出境关别</td><td colspan="3">出口日期</td><td colspan="2">申报日期</td><td colspan="2">备案号</td></tr>
<tr><td colspan="2">境外收货人</td><td colspan="2">运输方式</td><td colspan="3">运输工具名称及航次号</td><td colspan="4">提运单号</td></tr>
<tr><td colspan="2">生产销售单位</td><td colspan="2">监管方式</td><td colspan="3">征免性质</td><td colspan="4">许可证号</td></tr>
<tr><td colspan="2">合同协议号</td><td colspan="2">贸易国(地区)</td><td colspan="3">运抵国(地区)</td><td colspan="2">指运港</td><td colspan="2">离境口岸</td></tr>
<tr><td colspan="2">包装种类</td><td>件数</td><td>毛重(千克)</td><td>净重(千克)</td><td colspan="2">成交方式</td><td>运费</td><td colspan="2">保费</td><td>杂费</td></tr>
<tr><td colspan="11">随附单证及编号</td></tr>
<tr><td colspan="11">标记唛码及备注</td></tr>
<tr><td>项号</td><td>商品编号</td><td colspan="2">商品名称及规格型号</td><td>数量及单位</td><td>单价/总价/币制</td><td>原产国(地区)</td><td>最终目的国(地区)</td><td colspan="2">境内货源地</td><td>征免</td></tr>
<tr><td></td><td></td><td colspan="2"></td><td></td><td></td><td></td><td></td><td colspan="2"></td><td></td></tr>
<tr><td></td><td></td><td colspan="2"></td><td></td><td></td><td></td><td></td><td colspan="2"></td><td></td></tr>
<tr><td></td><td></td><td colspan="2"></td><td></td><td></td><td></td><td></td><td colspan="2"></td><td></td></tr>
<tr><td></td><td></td><td colspan="2"></td><td></td><td></td><td></td><td></td><td colspan="2"></td><td></td></tr>
<tr><td></td><td></td><td colspan="2"></td><td></td><td></td><td></td><td></td><td colspan="2"></td><td></td></tr>
<tr><td></td><td></td><td colspan="2"></td><td></td><td></td><td></td><td></td><td colspan="2"></td><td></td></tr>
<tr><td colspan="11"></td></tr>
<tr><td colspan="7">报关人员 报关人员证号 电话
兹申明对以上内容承担如实申报、依法纳税之责任
申报单位 申报单位(签章)</td><td colspan="4">海关批注及签章</td></tr>
</table>

实训二　托收方式下出口单据缮制

一、实训资料

1. 销售合同(见表 2-2-1)。

表 2-2-1　销售合同

苏州华润纺织品有限公司
SUZHOU HUARUN TEXTILE CO.,LTD.
销售合同
SALES CONTRACT

致：　　　　　　　　　　　　　　　　编号：
TO:DORIS TEXTILE CO.,LTD.　　　　　NO.: YD-18-173
INA MARKET DELHI 110006　　　　　　日期：
IEC CODE 0507013786　　　　　　　　DATE: MAY 27,2018

买卖双方确认合同的条款如下：
Both the seller and the buyer confirm the terms and conditions as below:

品名及规格 Commodity and Specification	数量 Quantity	单价及条款 Price & Terms	金额 Amount
TEXTILE PIECE GOODS		CIF	
	2,432MTS	USD3.40/MT	US$8,268.80
	2,407.7MTS	USD3.50/MT	US$8,426.95
	总金额(Total Amount)		US$16,695.75

付款方式：
Payment Terms: D/P AT SIGHT
溢短装
More of less: □允许±10% Allowed
包装
Packing: □纸箱/Carton
装柜要求：
Loading: □整箱/FCL　　□拼箱/LCL
交货期：收到30%订金后交货
Delivery: After receiving the 30% deposit
装运港：任何中国港口　　　　　　目的港及国别：TUGHLAKABAD
Loading Port: Any Chinese port　　Destination & Country: TUGHLAKABAD,INDIA
合同有效期：合同后60天内
特约条款：

(1) 买方须于＿＿年＿＿月＿＿日前开到本批交易的信用证(或通知卖方进出口许可证号码)，否则卖方有权不经通知取消本合同，或接受买方对本约未执行的全部或一部分，或对因此遭受的损失提出索赔。

续表

The buyer shall have the covering Letter of Credit the Seller(or notify the Import License Number) be for failing which the seller reserves the right to rescind without further notice, or to accept whole of any part of this Sales Contract not fulfilled by the Buyer, or to lodge claim for losses thus sustained if any.

(2) 凡以 CIF 条件的业务，保额为发票的 110%，投保险别以本售货确认书中所开列的为限，买方如果要求增加保额或保险范围，应于装船前经卖方同意，因此增加的保险费由买方负责。

For transactions concluded on CIF basis, it is understood that the insurance amount will be for 110% of the invoice value against the risks specified in the Sales Confirmation If additional insurance amount or coverage is required, the buyer must have the consent of the Seller before shipment, and the additional premium is to be borne by the buyer.

(3) 品质/数量异议：如买方提出索赔，凡属品质异议须于货到目的地口岸之日起 3 个月内提出，数量异议须于货到目的地口岸之日起 15 天内提出，对所装货物所提任何异议属于保险公司、轮船公司、其他有关运输机构或邮递机构所负责者，卖方不负任何责任。

QUALITY/QUANTITY DISCREPANCY: In case of quality discrepancy, claim should be filed buy the buyer within 3 months after the arrival of the goods at port of destination, while for quantity discrepancy, claim should be filed by the buyer within 15 days after the arrival of the goods at port of destination. It is understood that seller shall not be liable for any discrepancy of the goods shipped due to causes for which the Insurance Company, shipping Company, other transportation organization or Post office are liable.

(4) 本合同内所述全部或部分商品，如因人力不可抗拒的原因，以致不能履约或延迟交货，售方概不负责。

The seller shall not be held for failure of delay in delivery of the entire lot or a portion of the goods under this Sales Contract in consequence of any Force Majeure inside.

吴亦凡
卖方(The Seller)

Susan
买方(The Buyer)

2. 补充资料。

(1) 资料 1

INVOICE NO.: YD-18-174

INVOICE DATE: JUN. 10, 2018

Shipping Marks: N/M

GOODS:

2432 MTS OF TEXTILE PIECEC GOODS

UNIT PRICE: USD3.40/MT

涤棉色织布 H. S. CODE: 5513.3920.00

CTNS: 55BALES

GROSS WEIGHT: 555KGS

NET WEIGHT: 540KGS

MEASUREMENT: 2.2CBMS

申报要素如下。

织造方法：梭织；染整方法：色织；组织结构：斜纹；成分含量：65％T，35％C；幅宽：148CM；平方米克重：150G/M^2；品牌：无；生产厂商名称：苏州华润纺织品有限公司。

(2) 资料 2

2407.7MTS OF TEXTILE PIECEC GOODS

UNIT PRICE：USD3.50/MT

涤棉色织布 H.S.CODE：5407.5300.91

CTNS：52 BALES

GROSS WEIGHT：525KGS

NET WEIGHT：510KGS

MEASUREMENT：2CBMS

申报要素如下。

织造方法：梭织；染整方法：色织；组织结构：斜纹；成分含量：100％T；幅宽：148CM；平方米克重：143G/M^2；品牌：无；生产厂商名称：苏州华润纺织品有限公司。

(3) 资料 3

装运港口：上海

卸货港口：PIPAVAV

目的地：ICD TUGHLAKABAD

CERTIFICATE NO.：16C3205A3543/00001

签发产地证日：JUN.30，2018

B/L NO.：CNCT224535

B/L DATE：JUN.22，2018

VESSEL'S NAME：CAP ARNAUTI

贸易方式：一般贸易

货源产地：苏州 32059

十位海关编码：32059609MU

报检单编号：007812345

海关编号：0262K5124

预录入编号：222920160777000713

境内货源地：苏州

报关员：李芳　　电话：0512-8881 2567

随附单据：出口货物通关单

该货物是完全自产品，发货单位与经营单位相同，2018 年 6 月 15 日由上海天原报关有限公司向上海吴淞海关(2202)申报出口。

COLLECTING BANK：THE BANK OF INDIA，LTD.

DATE OF NEGOTIATION：JUN.30，2018

二、实训要求

请以“单证员”的工作角色，根据以上资料缮制商业发票(见表 2-2-2)、装箱单(见表 2-2-3)、汇票(见表 2-2-4)、原产地证书申请书(见表 2-2-5)、原产地证书(见表 2-2-6)、出境货物报检单(见表 2-2-7)、投保单(见表 2-2-8)、保险单(见表 2-2-9)、海运出口托运单(表 2-2-10)、海运提单(见表 2-2-11)、出口货物报关单(见表 2-2-12)。

表 2-2-2 商业发票

<table>
<tr><td colspan="5">苏州华润纺织品有限公司
SUZHOU HUARUN TEXTILE CO. ,LTD.
MUDU VILLAGE SHANTANG STREET,SUZHOU JIANGSU PROVINCE,CHINA
TEL:+86-512-8881 2567 FAX:+86-512-8881 2567</td></tr>
<tr><td colspan="5">商业发票
COMMERCIAL INVOICE</td></tr>
<tr><td colspan="5">Messrs:</td></tr>
<tr><td colspan="2" rowspan="3"></td><td colspan="2">Invoice No. :</td><td></td></tr>
<tr><td colspan="2">Invoice Date:</td><td></td></tr>
<tr><td colspan="2">Terms of Payment:</td><td></td></tr>
<tr><td colspan="5">Exporter:</td></tr>
<tr><td colspan="2" rowspan="2"></td><td colspan="3">Transport details:</td></tr>
<tr><td colspan="3"></td></tr>
<tr><td>Marks & Nos.</td><td>Description of Goods</td><td>Quantity</td><td>Unit Price</td><td>Amount</td></tr>
<tr><td></td><td></td><td></td><td colspan="2"></td></tr>
<tr><td></td><td></td><td></td><td></td><td></td></tr>
<tr><td></td><td></td><td></td><td></td><td></td></tr>
<tr><td></td><td></td><td></td><td></td><td></td></tr>
<tr><td></td><td></td><td></td><td></td><td></td></tr>
<tr><td></td><td></td><td></td><td></td><td></td></tr>
<tr><td colspan="5">苏州华润纺织品有限公司
(章)
SUZHOU HUARUN TEXTILE CO. ,LTD.
吴亦凡(章)</td></tr>
</table>

表 2-2-3　装箱单

<table>
<tr><td colspan="8">苏州华润纺织品有限公司
SUZHOU HUARUN TEXTILE CO. ,LTD.
MUDU VILLAGE SHANTANG STREET,SUZHOU JIANGSU PROVINCE,CHINA
TEL：+86-512-8881 2567　FAX：+86-512-8881 2567</td></tr>
<tr><td colspan="8">装箱单
PACKING LIST</td></tr>
<tr><td colspan="8">To：</td></tr>
<tr><td colspan="4" rowspan="2"></td><td colspan="2">Inv. No. :</td><td colspan="2"></td></tr>
<tr><td colspan="2">Inv. Date：</td><td colspan="2"></td></tr>
<tr><td>From：</td><td colspan="2"></td><td>To：</td><td colspan="2"></td><td>By vessel</td><td></td></tr>
<tr><td>Marks & Nos.</td><td>Description of goods</td><td>Quantity (PCS)</td><td colspan="2">CARTON (CTNS)</td><td>G. Weight (KGS)</td><td>N. Weight (KGS)</td><td>Measurement (CBM)</td></tr>
<tr><td></td><td></td><td></td><td colspan="2"></td><td></td><td></td><td></td></tr>
<tr><td colspan="8"></td></tr>
<tr><td colspan="8">苏州华润纺织品有限公司
（章）
SUZHOU HUARUN TEXTILE CO. ,LTD.
吴亦凡（章）</td></tr>
</table>

表 2-2-4　汇票

BILL OF EXCHANGE

NO.　　　　Date：

EXCHANGE FOR

At　　　　Sight of THIS SECOND BILL of EXCHANGE

(First of the tenor and date being unpaid)

Pay to　　　　or order the sum of

Drawn under

TO.

表 2-2-5 原产地证书申请书

中华人民共和国出口货物

一般原产地证明书/加工装配证明书申请书

企业名称：________________ 证书号：________________

申请人郑重声明：

本人被正式授权代表本企业办理和签署本申请书。

本申请书及中华人民共和国出口货物原产地证明书/加工装配证明书所列内容正确无误，如发现弄虚作假，冒充证书所列货物，擅改证书，本人愿按《中华人民共和国出口货物原产地条例》的有关规定接受处罚并承担法律责任，现将有关情况申报如下：

<table>
<tr><td colspan="2">商品名称(中英文)</td><td></td><td>H. S. 编码
(八位数)</td><td colspan="4"></td></tr>
<tr><td colspan="2">商品 FOB 总值(以美元计)</td><td></td><td>最终目的
国/地区</td><td colspan="4"></td></tr>
<tr><td>转口国/地区</td><td></td><td>拟出运日期</td><td></td><td colspan="2">发票号</td><td colspan="2"></td></tr>
<tr><td colspan="8">贸易方式和企业性质(请在适用处画“√”)</td></tr>
<tr><td colspan="2">一般贸易</td><td colspan="2">灵活贸易</td><td colspan="4">其他贸易</td></tr>
<tr><td>中资企业</td><td>外资企业</td><td>中资企业</td><td colspan="2">外资企业</td><td colspan="2">中资企业</td><td>外资企业</td></tr>
<tr><td></td><td></td><td></td><td colspan="2"></td><td colspan="2"></td><td></td></tr>
<tr><td colspan="2">数量或重量</td><td colspan="2"></td><td colspan="4">是否含有进口成分：是(　　) 否(　　)</td></tr>
<tr><td>证书种类(画“√”)</td><td colspan="2">一般原产地</td><td colspan="2"></td><td colspan="2">加工装配证</td><td></td></tr>
<tr><td colspan="3">该批货物实际生产企业</td><td colspan="5"></td></tr>
</table>

现提交中国出口货物商业发票副本一本，中华人民共和国出口货物原产地证明书/加工装配证明书一正三副，以及其他附件________份，请予以审核签证。

申请单位盖章：

申领人(签名)：

电话：

日期：　　年　　月　　日

注：1. 灵活贸易：包括来料加工、补偿贸易、进料加工贸易。

2. 外资企业指所有含有外资的企业。

3. 其他贸易指一般贸易和灵活贸易以外的贸易，如展卖、易货、租赁等贸易方式。

表 2-2-6 原产地证书

<table>
<tr><td colspan="2">1. Exporter</td><td colspan="3" rowspan="2">Certificate No.

CERTIFICATE OF ORIGIN
OF
THE PEOPLE'S REPUBLIC OF CHINA</td></tr>
<tr><td colspan="2">2. Consignee</td></tr>
<tr><td colspan="2">3. Means of transport and route</td><td colspan="3" rowspan="2">5. For certifying authority use only</td></tr>
<tr><td colspan="2">4. Country/region of destination</td></tr>
<tr><td>6. Marks and numbers</td><td>7. Number and kind of packages; description of goods</td><td>8. H. S. code</td><td>9. Quantity</td><td>10. Number and date of invoices</td></tr>
<tr><td colspan="2">11. Declaration by the exporter
The undersigned hereby declares that the above details and statements are correct; that all the goods were produced in China and that they comply with the Rules of Origin of the People's Republic of China.

……………………………………
Place and date, signature and stamp of authorized signatory</td><td colspan="3">12. Certification
It is hereby certified that the declaration by the exporter is correct.

……………………………………
Place and date, signature and stamp of certifying authority</td></tr>
</table>

表 2-2-7 出境货物报检单

中华人民共和国出入境检验检疫

出境货物报检单

报检单位(加盖公章)： *编 号：________

报检单位登记号： 联系人： 电话： 报检日期： 年 月 日

发货人	(中文)	
	(外文)	
收货人	(中文)	
	(外文)	

货物名称(中/外文)	H.S.编码	产地	数/重量	货物总值	包装种类及数量

运输工具名称号码		贸易方式		货物存放地点	
合同号		信用证号		用途	
发货日期		输往国家(地区)		许可证/审批号	
启运地		到达口岸		生产单位注册号	
集装箱规格、数量及号码					

合同、信用证订立的检验检疫条款或特殊要求	标记及号码	随附单据(划"√"或补填)	
		□合同 □信用证 □发票 □换证凭单 □装箱单 □厂检单	□包装性能结果单 □许可/审批文件 □ □ □ □

需要证单名称(划"√"或补填)		*检验检疫费	
□品质证书 _正_副 □重量证书 _正_副 □数量证书 _正_副 □兽医卫生证书 _正_副 □健康证书 _正_副 □卫生证书 _正_副 □动物卫生证书 _正_副	□植物检疫证书 _正_副 □熏蒸/消毒证书 _正_副 □出境货物换证凭单 _正_副 □ □ □ □	总金额(人民币元)	
		计费人	
		收费人	

报检人郑重声明：	领取证单	
1. 本人被授权报检。 2. 上列填写内容正确属实，货物无伪造或冒用他人的厂名、标志、认证标志，并承担货物质量责任。	日期	
签名：________	签名	

注：有"*"号栏由出入境检验检疫机关填写。

◆国家出入境检验检疫局制

[1-2(2000.1.1)]

表 2-2-8 投保单

中国太平洋财产保险股份有限公司

CHINA PACIFIC PROPERTY INSURANCE CO.,LTD.

货物运输保险投保单

APPLICATION FOR TRANSPORTATION INSURANCE

投保人
Applicant

被保险人
Insured

行业性质(Business)

合同号(Contract No.)YD-18-173

发票号 (Invoice No.) YD-18-174

信用证号 (L/C No.)

提单号 (B/L No.)

兹有下列物品向中国太平洋财产保险股份有限公司投保(Insurance is required on the following commodity)

标记 marks & Nos.	包装及数量 Packing & quantity	保险货物项目(中、英文) Description of Goods (Both in Chinese & in English)	1. 发票金额 Invoice Value 2. 加成 Invoice Value Plus 10% 3. 保险金额 Amount Insured 4. 费率 Rate of Premium 5. 保险费 Premium 6. 币种 Currency 7. 免赔率/额 Deductible

货物类别	货物特性(请划√)	□易燃 □易爆 □易碎 □易腐易蛀 □易挥发 □易锈 ☑一般货物

运输方式 per conveyance S. S.	航行区域	装载运输工具名称 AS PER B/L	航(班)次

起运日期 Sailing on/about AS PER B/L	赔款偿付地: Claims Payable at: SPAIN IN USD	理赔代理地:

航行路线:自(起运地) Rout:From	经(转运地) Via	到达(目的地) To(destination):

承保险别 Conditions	主险:
	附加险:

特别约定(Special Coverage):

投保人兹声明:上述所填各项均属事实,同意按本投保单所列内容和货物运输保险条款及其附加险条款以及特别约定向贵公司投保货物运输保险。投保人对货物运输保险条款及其附加保险条款的内容,其中特别是责任免除条款和被保险人义务条款的内容已向投保人做出了明确说明,投保人确认对上述所有条款内容及特别约定已完全了解,同意以此订立保险合同。保险合同自保险单签发之日起成立。

投保人地址:
Applicant Add:
电话
Tel No.:
传真:
Fax No.:
联系人:
Correspondent:

投保人签章
Applicant Signature

投保日期 Contract Date:
年 月 日

表 2-2-9 保险单

中国太平洋财产保险股份有限公司

CHINA PACIFIC PROPERTY INSURANCE CO. ,LTD.

货物运输保险单 保险单号(Policy No.)：

CARGO TRANSPORTATION INSURANCE POLICY 576859430

中国太平洋财产保险股份有限公司(以下称承保人)根据被保险人的要求，在被保险人向承保人缴付约定的保险费后，按照本保险单承保险别和背面所载条款与下列特款承保下述货物运输险，特立本保险单。

This Policy of Insurance witnesses that China Pacific Property Insurance Company Limited(herein after called"The Underwriter")at the request of the Insured named hereunder and in consideration of the agreed premium paid to the Underwriter by Insured, undertakes to insure the undermentioned goods in transportation subject to the conditions of this Policy as per the Clauses printed overleaf and other special clauses attache herein.

被保险人(Insured)：

标记 Marks & Nos.	包装及数量 Quantity	保险货物项目 Description of Goods	保险金额 Amount

总保险金额：
Total Amount Insured：

费率：AS ARRANGED Rate	保费：AS ARRANGED Premium	免赔额/率： Deductible/Franchise
开航日期 AS PER B/L Slg. on or abt.	装载运输工具 AS PER B/L Per conveyance S. S.	
运输路线：自 Route：From	经 By	至 To

承保险别：
Conditions COVERING ALL RISKS AND WAR RISKS AS PER OCEAN MARINE CARGO CLAUSES(1/1/1981)(WAREHOUSE TO WAREHOUSE CLAUSE IS INCLUDED)AND OCEAN MARINE CARGO WAR RISKS CLAUSES(1/1/1981)OF THE PICC.

所保货物，如遇出险，本公司凭第一正本保险单及其他有关证件给付赔款；如发生本保险单项下负责赔偿的损失或事故，应立即通知下述代理人查勘。

Claims, if any, payable on surrender of the first original of the policy together with other relevant documents. In the event of accident whereby loss or damage may result in a claim under this policy, immediate notice applying for survey must be given to Agent as mentioned hereunder.

中国太平洋财产保险股份有限公司
CHINA PACIFIC PROPERTY INSURANCE CO. ,LTD.

NO. S OF ORIGINAL：THREE(3)

授权签发 AUTHORIZED SIGNATURE 张丹枫
地址 Address：
电话 Tel：34-3-4444 4444 传真 Fax：34-3-2455 5555

赔款偿付地点 Claim Payable at： 签单日期 Date：

表 2-2-10 海运出口托运单

SHIPPER(发货人)	B/L No.
CONSIGNEE(收货人)	中远集装箱运输有限公司 COSCO CONTAINER LINES 集装箱货物托运单
NOTIFY PARTY(通知人)	
Pre-carriage by(前程承运人) Place of Receipt(收货地点)	装货单 SHIPPING ORDER

Ocean Vessel(船名)	Voy. No.(航次)	Port of Loading(装货港)	Date(日期)

Port of Discharge(卸货港)	Place of Delivery(交货地点)	Final Destination for the Merchant's Reference(目的地)

Container No.(集装箱号)	Seal No.(铅封号) Marks & Nos.(标记与号码)	No. of container or packages(箱数或件数)	Kind of Package; Description of Goods(包装种类与货名)	Gross Weight 毛重(千克)	Measurement 尺码(立方米)

TOTAL NUMBER OF CONTINERS OR PACKAGES(JIN WORDS) 集装箱数或件数合计(大写)	

FREIGHT & CHARGES(运费与附加费)	Revenue Tons(运费吨)	Rate(运费率)	Per(每)	Prepaid(运费预付)	Collect(运费到付)

Service Type on Receiving □—CY □—CFS □—DOOR	Service Type on Delivery □—CY □—CFS □—DOOR	Reefer Temperature Required(冷藏温度)	℉	℃

TYPE OF GOODS(货类)	□Ordinary(普通) □Reefer(冷藏) □Dangerous(危险品) □Auto(裸装车辆)	危险品	IMCO Class: UN No.:
	□Liquid(液体) □Live Animal(活动物) □Bulk(散货)		IMDG Code Page: Property:

可否转船:	可否分批:	装期:	Received by the Carrier the total number of containers or other packages or units stated above to be transported subject to the terms and conditions of the Carrier's regular form of Bill of Lading(for combined Transport to Port shipment) which shall be deemed to be incorporated herein
货价:	信用证号码:	No. of original B(S)/L:	
特约事项:	合同号码:	托运人盖章:	Date: as Agent only

表 2-2-11 海运提单

<table>
<tr><td colspan="2">Shipper Insert Name, Address and Phone</td><td rowspan="4">B/L No.

中远集装箱运输有限公司
COSCO CONTAINER LINES
TLX：33057 COSCO CN
FAX：+86(021) 6545 8984
ORIGINAL</td></tr>
<tr><td colspan="2"></td></tr>
<tr><td colspan="2">Consignee Insert Name, Address and Phone</td></tr>
<tr><td colspan="2"></td></tr>
<tr><td colspan="2">Notify Party Insert Name, Address and Phone
(It is agreed that no responsibility shall attach to the Carrier or his agents for failure to notify)</td><td rowspan="8">Port-to-Port or Combined Transport
BILL OF LADING
RECEIVED in external apparent good order and condition except as other-Wise noted. The total number of packages or unites stuffed in the container, the description of the goods and the weights shown in this Bill of Lading are furnished by the Merchants, and which the carrier has no reasonable means of checking and is not a part of this Bill of Lading contract. The carrier has Issued the number of Bills of Lading stated below, all of this tenor and date, One of the original Bills of Lading must be surrendered and endorsed or signed against the delivery of the shipment and whereupon any other original Bills of Lading shall be void. The Merchants agree to be bound by the terms and conditions of this Bill of Lading as if each had personally signed this Bill of Lading.
SEE clause 4 on the back of this Bill of Lading (Terms continued on the back hereof, please read carefully).
* Applicable Only When Document Used as a Combined Transport Bill of Lading.</td></tr>
<tr><td colspan="2"></td></tr>
<tr><td>Combined Transport *
Pre-carriage by</td><td>Combined Transport *
Place of Receipt</td></tr>
<tr><td>Ocean Vessel Voy. No.</td><td>Port of Loading</td></tr>
<tr><td></td><td></td></tr>
<tr><td>Port of Discharge</td><td>Combined Transport *
Place of Delivery</td></tr>
<tr><td></td><td></td></tr>
</table>

<table>
<tr><td>Marks & Nos.
Container/Seal No.</td><td>No. of Packages & Description of Goods</td><td>Gross Weight Kgs</td><td>Measurement</td></tr>
<tr><td></td><td></td><td></td><td></td></tr>
<tr><td></td><td colspan="3">Description of Contents for Shipper's Use Only (Not part of This B/L Contract)</td></tr>
<tr><td colspan="4">Total Number of containers and/or packages (in words)</td></tr>
<tr><td colspan="4">Subject to Clause 7 Limitation</td></tr>
</table>

续表

<table>
<tr><td colspan="2">Freight & Charges</td><td>Revenue Tons</td><td>Rate</td><td>Per</td><td>Prepaid</td><td>Collect</td></tr>
<tr><td colspan="2"></td><td rowspan="3"></td><td rowspan="3"></td><td rowspan="3"></td><td rowspan="3"></td><td rowspan="3"></td></tr>
<tr><td colspan="2">Declared Value Charge</td></tr>
<tr><td colspan="2"></td></tr>
<tr><td>Ex. Rate:</td><td>Prepaid at</td><td colspan="2">Payable at</td><td colspan="3">Place and date of issue</td></tr>
<tr><td rowspan="3"></td><td></td><td colspan="2"></td><td colspan="3"></td></tr>
<tr><td>Total Prepaid</td><td colspan="2">No. of Original B(s)/L</td><td colspan="3">Signed for the Carrier,
COSCO CONTAINER LINES</td></tr>
<tr><td></td><td colspan="2"></td><td colspan="3"></td></tr>
<tr><td colspan="7">LADEN ON BOARD THE VESSEL</td></tr>
<tr><td>DATE</td><td></td><td>BY</td><td colspan="4"></td></tr>
</table>

表 2-2-12　出口货物报关单

中华人民共和国海关出口货物报关单

预录入编号：　　　　海关编号：　　　　（××海关）　　　　页码/页数：

<table>
<tr><td colspan="2">境内发货人</td><td colspan="2">出境关别</td><td colspan="2">出口日期</td><td colspan="2">申报日期</td><td colspan="2">备案号</td></tr>
<tr><td colspan="2">境外收货人</td><td colspan="2">运输方式</td><td colspan="2">运输工具名称及航次号</td><td colspan="4">提运单号</td></tr>
<tr><td colspan="2">生产销售单位</td><td colspan="2">监管方式</td><td colspan="2">征免性质</td><td colspan="4">许可证号</td></tr>
<tr><td colspan="2">合同协议号</td><td colspan="2">贸易国(地区)</td><td colspan="2">运抵国(地区)</td><td colspan="2">指运港</td><td colspan="2">离境口岸</td></tr>
<tr><td colspan="2">包装种类</td><td>件数</td><td>毛重(千克)</td><td>净重(千克)</td><td>成交方式</td><td>运费</td><td colspan="2">保费</td><td>杂费</td></tr>
<tr><td colspan="10">随附单证及编号</td></tr>
<tr><td colspan="10">标记唛码及备注</td></tr>
<tr><td>项号</td><td>商品编号</td><td>商品名称及规格型号</td><td>数量及单位</td><td>单价/总价/币制</td><td>原产国(地区)</td><td>最终目的国(地区)</td><td colspan="2">境内货源地</td><td>征免</td></tr>
<tr><td colspan="10"></td></tr>
<tr><td colspan="10"></td></tr>
<tr><td colspan="10"></td></tr>
<tr><td colspan="10"></td></tr>
<tr><td colspan="10"></td></tr>
<tr><td colspan="10"></td></tr>
<tr><td colspan="6">报关人员　　报关人员证号　　电话
兹申明对以上内容承担如实申报、依法纳税之责任
申报单位　　　　　　申报单位(签章)</td><td colspan="4">海关批注及签章</td></tr>
</table>

实训三　信用证方式下 FOB 贸易术语（延期付款）出口单据缮制

一、实训资料

1. 信用证（见表 2-3-1）。

表 2-3-1　信用证

Message Type：FIN 700 ISSUEOF A DOCUMENTARI CREDIT
MUR：BTRA010210000467
SENDER：BSCHESMMAXXX BANCO SANTANDER S. A. MADRID
OUTPUT DATE/TIME：21-03-2018 16:05
SES-ISN：3256 218930
PRIORIDAD：N
RECEPTOR：BSCHHKHHXXXX BANCO SANTANDER，S. A. HONG KONG
APLICACION：F
27:SEQUENCEOF TOTAL：1/1
40A：FORM OF DOCUMENT CREDIT：IRREVOCABLE
20：NUMBER CREDIT DOCUMEN：5494WH171868
31C：DATE OF ISSUE：21-03-18
40E：APPLICABLE RULES：UCP LATEST VERSION
31D：DATE AND PLACE OF EXPIRY：25-05-18 SPAIN
50：APPLICANT：
　ELECTRODOMESTICOS TAURUS S. L.
　AV BARCELONA S/N
　25790 OLIANA (LLEIDA)
　SPAIN
59：BENEFICIARY-NAME & ADDRESS：
　SUZHOU WENHAI INDUSTRIES CO.，LTD. NO. 159 TONGYUAN ROAD，SUZHOU CITY，CHINA
32B:CURRENCY CODE，AMUOUNT：USD21，740
39B：MAX. CREDIT AMOUNT：NOT EXCEEDING DISPONIBLE CON...
41A：Available with...By...BIC：BSCHESMMXXX
　* BANCO SANTANDER S. A.
　* MADRID
　BY DEF PAYMENT
42P：DEFERRED PAYMENT DETAILS：30 DAYS AFTER DOCUMENTS APPROVAL，PAYMENT WILL BE EFFECTED THE FOLLOWING DAY 10 OR 20.
43P：PARTIAL SHIPMENTS：PROHIBITED
43T：TRANSHIPMEN：ALLOWED

续表

44E: PORT OF LOADING: SHANGHAI PORT, CHINA
44F: PORT OF DISCHARGE: TAMPICO PORT, MEXICO
44C: LATEST DATE OF SHIPMENT: 18-05-16
45A: DESCRIPTION OF GOODS:
SLOW COOKER A 1200PC USD9.45/PC 11,340
SLOW COOKER B 1600PC USD6.50/PC 10,400
TOTAL AMOUNT: USD21,740
+AS PER ORDER. NO.: 4500048798
+DELIVERY TERMS: FOB SHANGHAI PORT, CHINA.
46A: DOCUMENTS REQUIRED:
1. ORIGINAL COMMERCIAL INVOICE, SIGNED AND STAMPED: IN 3 ORIGINALS + 3 COPIES.
2. ORIGINAL PACKING LIST: 3 ORIGINALS+3 COPIES
3. BILL OF LADING OR SEA WAYBILL PRESENTED IN ONE SET OF 3 ORIGINALS PLUS COPIES, SHOWING TO ORDER OF CONSIGNEE AND NOTIFY TO "TAURUS ESPANA, S. A. DE C. V. ROSAS MORENO NO. 4-202, COLONIA SAN RAFAEL DELEGACI ON CUAUHTEMOC MEXICO, D. F. C. P 06470 R. F. C TGE060628QD6". UNIT PRICES AND TOTAL AMOUNT MUST NOT TO BE SHOWN ON THIS DOCUMENT.
4. ONE ORIGINAL QUALITY CONTROL REPORT (DOCUMENT Q-49), MARKED ACCEPTED, FOR EACH TYPE OF GOODS DESCRIBED IN THIS DOCUMENTARY CREDIT. THIS DOCUMENT MUST BE STAMPED BY ELECTRODOMESTICOS TAURUS S. L. AND MANUFACTURER. IF PENALTY SECTION IS MARKED: 200 USD MUST BE DEDUCTED FROM L/C PAYMENT.
5. ORIGINAL CERTIFICATE OF ORIGIN, CONSIGNEE "TAURUS - ESPANA, S. A. DE C. V. ROSAS MORENO NO. 4-202, COLONIA SAN RAFAEL, DELEGACION CUAUHTEMOC, MEXICO, D. F. C. P. 06470 R. F. C TGE060628QD6".
47A: ADDITIONAL CONDITIONS:
+A DISCREPANCY FEE OF EUR100,00 WILL BE DEDUCTED FROM THE PROCEEDS ON EACH SET OF DOCUMENTS PRESENTED WITH DISCREPANCY/IES.
+L/C AMENDMENTS MUST BE CHARGED ON THE SIDE WHO MUST BE RESPONSIBLE FOR THEIR FAIL TO KEEP THE AGREEMENT ACCOUNT.
+ORDER NO. 4500048798 MUST BE WRITTEN IN ALL DOCUMENTS REQUIRED.
+THIRD PARTY DOCUMENTS ACCEPTABLE.
71B: DETAILS OF CHARGES: ALL BANK COMMISSIONS AND CHARGES OUTSIDE SPAIN ARE FOR THE BENEFICIARY ACCOUNT.
48: PRESENTATION PERIOD:
DOCUMENTS MUST BE PRESENTED WITHIN 15 DAYS AFTER SHIPMENT DATE AND WITHIN VALIDITY TERMS OF THIS DOCUMENTARY CREDIT
49: CONFIRMA INSTRUCTIONS: WITHOUT
78: INSTRUCTIONS:
BANCO SANTANDER S. A., HONG KONG HOLDS SPECIAL REIMBURSEMENT INSTRUCTIONS. ALL DOCUMENTS DRAWN UNDER THIS LETTER OF CREDIT MUST BE PRESENTED TO U. S. THROUGH THEM AT: RM 1501, ONE EXCHANGE SQUARE, 8 CONNAUGHT PLACE, CENTRAL, HONG KONG BY COURIER SERVICES. PRESENTING BANK

续表

WILL BE FULLY RESPONSIBLE FOR THE CONSEQUENCES SENDING DOCUMENTS TO THE WRONG ADDRESS. ONCE ALL L/C TERMS DULY COMPLIED WITH: WE WILL REIMBURSE YOU AS PER YOUR INSTRUCTIONS AT MATURITY DATE. 57D: "ADVISE THROUGH"BANK-NAME&ADDR: BANK OF CHINA SUZHOU BRANCH 72: SENDER TO RECEIVER INFORMATION: PLEASE,SEND DIRECTLY TO THE ADDRESS BELOW:BANCO SANTANDER,S. A. AVDA. FRANCESC MACIA,21-1A PLANTA 25007 LLEIDA (SPAIN) T R A I L E R

2. 补充资料。

INV. NO.: WH1181611　　INV. DATE:MAY 6,2018

B/L. NO.: SHWHD20079　　B/L. DATE:MAY 12,2018

C/O NO.: 208250070508　　S/C NO.:4500048798

NAME OF STEAMER: Weida V. 007N

CONTAINER&SEAL NO.: 1×40′ EMCU4688556/EMCCWG5370

SHIPPING MARKS: ET INC.

LA PAZ

4500048798

NO. 1-700

H. S. NO.: 8516. 6090. 00

GOODS: WEIGHT:G. W.:4. 25KGS/PC　N. W.:3. 75KGS/PC 0. 024CBM/PC

PACKED IN 700 CARTONS,@4PCS/CTN

SLOW COOKER A　1200PC　USD9. 45/PC　11,340

SLOW COOKER B　1600PC　USD6. 50/PC　10,400

该货物是完全自产品，报检单位登记号：3202001516，联系人：苑媛，电话：0512-6676 5660。

货物存放地点：公司仓库，生产单位：苏州苑之海电器有限公司，用途：其他。

报检日期：2018 年 5 月 9 日。

报检时提交的随附单据：合同、信用证、发票、装箱单、报检委托书。

二、实训要求

请以"单证员"的工作角色，根据以上资料缮制商业发票(见表 2-3-2)、装箱单(见表 2-3-3)、原产地证书(见表 2-3-4)、出境货物报检单(见表 2-3-5)、提单(见表 2-3-6)。

表 2-3-2 商业发票

<table>
<tr><td colspan="6">苏州文海工业有限公司
SUZHOU WENHAI INDUSTRIES CO. ,LTD.
NO. 159 TONGYUAN ROAD SUZHOU CHINA</td></tr>
<tr><td colspan="6">商业发票
COMMERCIAL INVOICE</td></tr>
<tr><td colspan="3" rowspan="4">To:</td><td colspan="2">Invoice No. :</td><td></td></tr>
<tr><td colspan="2">Invoice Date:</td><td></td></tr>
<tr><td colspan="2">L/C No. :</td><td></td></tr>
<tr><td colspan="2">L/C Date:</td><td></td></tr>
<tr><td colspan="6">Transport details</td></tr>
<tr><td>From:</td><td></td><td>To:</td><td colspan="3"></td></tr>
<tr><td>Marks & Nos.</td><td>Description of goods</td><td>Quantity</td><td>U. price</td><td colspan="2">Amount</td></tr>
<tr><td></td><td></td><td></td><td></td><td colspan="2"></td></tr>
<tr><td colspan="2">Total:</td><td colspan="4"></td></tr>
<tr><td colspan="6"></td></tr>
<tr><td colspan="6">苏州文海工业有限公司(章)
SUZHOU WENHAI INDUSTRIES CO. ,LTD.
孙越(章)</td></tr>
</table>

表 2-3-3 装箱单

苏州文海工业有限公司
SUZHOU WENHAI INDUSTRIES CO. ,LTD.
NO. 159 TONGYUAN ROAD SUZHOU CHINA

装箱单
PACKING LIST

To:	Invoice No. :	
	Invoice Date:	
	L/C No. :	

Transport details

From:		To:		

Marks & Nos.	C/No. , Packages	Quantity Description of goods	G. Weight	N. Weight	Measurement

苏州文海工业有限公司(章)
SUZHOU WENHAI INDUSTRIES CO. ,LTD.
孙越(章)

表 2-3-4 原产地证书

<table>
<tr><td colspan="2">1. Exporter</td><td colspan="3" rowspan="2">Certificate No.

CERTIFICATE OF ORIGIN
OF
THE PEOPLE'S REPUBLIC OF CHINA</td></tr>
<tr><td colspan="2">2. Consignee</td></tr>
<tr><td colspan="2">3. Means of transport and route</td><td colspan="3" rowspan="2">5. For certifying authority use only</td></tr>
<tr><td colspan="2">4. Country/region of destination</td></tr>
<tr><td>6. Marks and numbers</td><td>7. Number and kind of packages; description of goods</td><td>8. H. S. code</td><td>9. Quantity</td><td>10. Number and date of invoices</td></tr>
<tr><td colspan="2">11. Declaration by the exporter
The undersigned hereby declares that the above details and statements correct, that all the goods were produced in China and that they comply with the Rules of Origin of the People's Republic of China.

....
Place and date, signature and stamp of authorized signatory</td><td colspan="3">12. Certification
It is hereby certified that the declaration by the exporter is correct.

....
Place and date, signature and stamp of certifying authority</td></tr>
</table>

表 2-3-5 出境货物报检单

中华人民共和国出入境检验检疫

出境货物报检单

报检单位(加盖公章)： *编 号：____________

报检单位登记号： 联系人： 电话： 报检日期： 年 月 日

发货人	(中文)	
	(外文)	
收货人	(中文)	
	(外文)	

货物名称(中/外文)	H.S.编码	产地	数/重量	货物总值	包装种类及数量

运输工具名称号码		贸易方式		货物存放地点	
合同号		信用证号		用途	
发货日期		输往国家(地区)		许可证/审批号	
启运地		到达口岸		生产单位注册号	
集装箱规格、数量及号码					

合同、信用证订立的检验检疫条款或特殊要求	标记及号码	随附单据(划"√"或补填)	
		□合同	□包装性能结果单
		□信用证	□许可/审批文件
		□发票	□
		□换证凭单	□
		□装箱单	□
		□厂检单	□

需要证单名称(划"√"或补填)				*检验检疫费	
□品质证书	_正_副	□植物检疫证书	_正_副	总金额(人民币元)	
□重量证书	_正_副	□熏蒸/消毒证书	_正_副		
□数量证书	_正_副	□出境货物换证凭单	_正_副		
□兽医卫生证书	_正_副	□		计费人	
□健康证书	_正_副	□			
□卫生证书	_正_副	□		收费人	
□动物卫生证书	_正_副	□			

报检人郑重声明：	领取证单	
1. 本人被授权报检。	日期	
2. 上列填写内容正确属实，货物无伪造或冒用他人的厂名、标志、认证标志，并承担货物质量责任。		
签名：____________	签名	

注：有"*"号栏由出入境检验检疫机关填写。

◆国家出入境检验检疫局制

[1-2(2000.1.1)]

表 2-3-6　提单

<table>
<tr><td colspan="2">Shipper</td><td colspan="2" rowspan="4">B/L No.
伟达航运有限公司
WENDA SHIPPING CO. ,LTD.
BILL OF LADING
ORIGINAL
RECEIVED in external apparent good order and condition except as otherwise noted. The total number of packages or units stuffed in the container. The weight, measure, marks, numbers, quality, contents and value mentioned in this Bill of Lading are to be considered unknown unless the contrary has expressly acknowledged and agreed to. The signing of this Bill of Loading is not to be considered as such an agreement. On presentation of this Bill of Lading duly endorsed to the Carrier by or on behalf of the Holder of Bill of Lading.</td></tr>
<tr><td colspan="2">Consignee</td></tr>
<tr><td colspan="2">Notify party</td></tr>
<tr><td>Pre-carriage by</td><td>Ocean Vessel Voy. No.</td></tr>
<tr><td>Port of loading</td><td>Port of transshipment</td><td>Port of Discharge</td><td>Place of delivery</td></tr>
<tr><td colspan="4">Marks & Nos. Container No.　|　No. & kind of Packages　|　Description of goods　|　Gross weight　|　Measurement</td></tr>
<tr><td colspan="2">Total No. of container or other pkgs or units (in words)</td><td colspan="2"></td></tr>
<tr><td colspan="2">For delivery of goods please apply to:</td><td colspan="2">Freight & charges</td></tr>
<tr><td rowspan="2">Ex rate</td><td>Prepaid at</td><td>Payable at</td><td>Place and date of issue:</td></tr>
<tr><td>Total prepaid</td><td>No. of B(s)/L
THREE</td><td rowspan="2">Signed by　WENDA SHIPPING CO. ,LTD.
SHANGHAI BRANCH
As agent for the carrier　杨柳
WenDa Shipping Co. ,Ltd.</td></tr>
<tr><td colspan="3">Laden on board the Vessel:
Date:
By:</td></tr>
</table>

实训四　信用证方式下 CFR 贸易术语出口单据缮制

一、实训资料

1. 信用证(见表 2-4-1)。

表 2-4-1　信用证

MSG. NO.: MSG0010087　MT 700-ISSUE OF A DOCUMENTARY CREDIT RECEIVER: ABOCCNBJ103 AGRICULTURAL BANK OF CHINA, THE (SUZHOU BRANCH) SUZHOU 27: SEQUENCE OF TOTAL: 1/1 40A: FORM OF DOCUMENTARY CREDIT: IRREVOCABLE 20: DOCUMENTARY CREDIT NUMBER: HBZKN/0010020 31C: DATE OF ISSUE: 05-01-2018 40E: APPLICABLE RULES: UCP LATEST VERSION 31D: DATE AND PLACE OF EXPIRY: 13-02-2018 CHINA 51A: APPLICANT BANK: HFLIHKHHKNX HBZ FINANCE LIMITED (KOW LOON BRANCH) HONG KONG 50: APPLICANT: MULTI LINES INTERNATIONAL CO., LTD. 1208, 12/F, FOOK HONG UNDUSTRIAL BUILDING, 29 SHEUNG YUET ROAD, KOWLOON BAY, KOWLOON, HONG KONG. 59: BENEFICIARY: NANJING HUAMAO IMP & EXP TRADING CO., LTD. NO. 33 RENMIN ROAD, WUZHOU ECONOMIC DEVELOPMENT ZONE, NANJING, CHINA. TEL: 86-512-8228 2200　CONTACT: LUCY 32B: CURRENCY CODE, AMOUNT: CURRENCY: USD U. S. DOLLARS AMOUNT: 10,729.60 41D: AVAILABLE WITH...BY...: ANY BANK BY NEGOTIATION 42C: DRAFT AT...: SIGHT 42A: DRAWEE: HFLIHKHHKNX HBZ FINANCE LIMITED (KOW LOON BRANCH) HONG KONG

续表

43P：PARTIAL SHIPMENTS：ALLOWED IN FULL CONTAINER ONLY 43T：TRANSHIPMENT：ALLOWED 44E：PORT OF LOADING/AIRPORT OF DEPARTURE：SHANGHAI，CHINA 44F：PORT OF DISCHARGE/AIRPORT OF DESTINATION：LONDON U. K. PORT 44C：LATEST DATE OF SHIPMENT：30-01-2018 45A：DESCRIPTION OF GOODS AND/ORSERVICES： 100% ACRYLIC SCARF @USD2. 8 QUANTITY：3832PCS PACKED IN 39CTNS ALL OTHER DETAILS AS PER APPLICANT'S PURCHASE ORDER NO. MLI-11895/10 DATED 19TH DECEMBER 2017. TERM：CFR LONDON，U. K. 46A：DOCUMENTS REQUIRED： 1) BENEFICIARY'S SIGNED INVOICES IN 1 COPY. 2) PACKING LIST IN 1 COPY. 3) FULL SET OF ORIGINAL CLEAN"SHIPPED ON BOARD"OCEAN BILLS OF LADING PLUS TWO NON-NEGOTIABLE COPIES MADE OUT "TO ORDER" AND BLANK ENDORSED MARKED"FREIGHT PREPAID"AND NOTIFY "B AND M RETAIL LTD. UNIT 1G, SQUIRES GATE INDUSTRIAL ESTATE SQUIRES GATE LANE, UNITED KINGDOM"SHOWING"MULTI LINES INTERNATIONAL CO. ,LTD. "AS SHIPPER. B/L ISSUED PRIOR TO THE L/C OPENING DATE NOT ACCEPTABLE. B/L MUST SHOW THE FULL NAME, ADDRESS, TELEPHONE AND FAX NUMBERS OF THE SHIPPING COMPANY/ISSUER AND OF DELIVERY AGENT AT THE PORT OF DESTINATION. 4) BENEFICIARY'S CERTIFICATE CERTIFYING THAT ONE FULL SET OF NON-NEGOTIABLE DOCUMENTS HAS BEEN FAXED TO L/C APPLICANT WITHIN 5 DAYS AFTER SHIPMENT. 5) COPY OF SHIPMENT ADVICE SENT BY FAX TO APPLICANT BEFORE SHIPMENT DATE, SPECIFYING：ORDER N. , SHIPMENT DATE, QUANTITY, DESCRIPTION OF GOODS, AND VESSEL NAME. 6) ORIGINAL CERTIFICATE OF ORIGIN FORM A, CONSIGNEE B AND M RETAIL LTD. UNIT 1G, SQUIRES GATE INDUSTRIAL ESTATE SQUIRES GATE LANE, UNITED KINGDOM. 47A：ADDITIONAL CONDITIONS： A) FOR DISCREPANT DOCUMENTS, A DISCREPANT FEE OF USD75. 00 AND SWIFT CHARGES OF USD 30. 00 WILL BE CHARGED TO THE BENEFICIARY FOR ITS PROCESSING. HOWEVER PAYMENT UNDER THIS L/C IS SUBJECT TO ACCEPTANCE OF DISCREPANT DOCUMENTS. B) DOCUMENTS SHOWING A DATE OF ISSUANCE PRIOR TO THE DATE OF THIS CERDIT ARE NOT ALLOWED. C) IF LV IS EXPIRED AND SUCH DISCREPANCY IS ACCEPTED, LC EXPIRED COMMISSION AT 1/4 PERCENT(MINIMUM USD75. 00)IS FOR THE A/C OF BENEFICIARY AND WILL BE DEDUCTED FROM THE PROCEEDS. D) WE UNDERSTAND THAT INSURANCE IS TO BE COVERED BY ULTIMATE BUYER. E) INSPECTION CERTIFICATE STATING THAT"THE GOODS HAVE BEEN INSPECTED" TO BE ISSUED BY THE L/C APPLICANT (MULTI LINES INTERNATIONAL CO. , LTD.). (FAX COPY OF INSPECTION CERTIFICATE IS ALSO ACCEPTABLE)

续表

<table><tr><td>
F) LATE SHIPMENT PENALTIES:
7-10 DAYS LATE: 3 PERCENT PENALTY ON INVOICE AMOUNT
11-15 DAYS LATE: 5 PERCENT PENALTY ON INVOICE AMOUNT
16 DAYS OR MORE LATE: 10 PERCENT PENALTY ON INVOICE AMOUNT
71B: CHARGES:
ALL BANKING CHARGES EXCEPT L/C OPENING CHARGES ARE FOR BENEFICIARY'S ACCOUNT.
48: PRESENTATION PERIOD:
ALL DOCUMENTS TO BE PRESENTED WITHIN 15 DAYS FROM DATE OF SHIPMENT BUT WITHIN THE VALIDITY OF THE CREDIT.
49: CONFIRMA INSTRUCTIONS: WITHOUT
78: INSTRUCTIONS:
FOR DOCUMENTS NEGOTIATED STRICTLY IN COMPLIANCE WITH THE TERMS OF THIS DOCUMENTARY CREDIT, WE HEREBY UNDERTAKE TO REIMBURSE THE NEGOTIATING BANK LESS USD50.00 REIMBURSEMENT CHARGES ACCORDING TO THEIR INSTRUCTIONS ON RECEIPT OF THE DOCUMENTS ALONGWITH THEIR CERTIFICATE OF STRICT COMPLIANCE OF ALL L/C TERMS. THE NEGOTIATING BANK MUST ENDORSE THE AMOUNT OF EACH DRAWING UNDER THE CREDIT ON REVERSE OF THIS ORIGINAL LETTER OF CREDIT AND DESPATCH DOCUMENT TO US IN ONE LOT BY RECOGNISED COURIER AT FLG ADDRESS: YUE HWA INT'L BLDG.,12/FL.,1, KOWLOON PARK DRIVE TST,KOWLOON,HONG KONG.
57A: ADVICE THROUGH BANK:
ABOCCNBJ103
AGRICULTURAL BANK OF CHINA,THE (SUZHOU BRANCH)SUZHOU
72: SENDER TO RECEIVER INFORMATION:
THIS DOCUMENTARY CREDIT IS SUBJECT TO UNIFORM CUSTOMS AND PRACTICE FOR DOCUMENTARY CREDITS (2007 REVISION), INTERNATIONAL CHAMBER OF COMMERCE PUBLICATION NO. 600.
</td></tr></table>

2. 补充资料。

INV. NO.:HM1181712　　INV. DATE:JAN. 20,2018

B/L. NO.:SHHMD20080　　B/L. DATE:JAN. 26,2018

FORM A NO:G214313212741167　　S/C NO.: MLI-11895/10

NAME OF STEAMER:DONGFANG V. 957W

CONTAINER&SEAL NO.:TELU4688556/WG53706(20')/2300

SHIPPING MARKS: MLI HONG KONG.
11895/10
NO. 1-39
MADE IN CHINA

H. S. NO.: 6214.3000.00

GOODS:

PACKING: CTN NO.	QTY	QTY/CTN	G. W. /CTN	N. W. /CTN	MEA/CTN
1-8	800PCS	100PCS	@15.0KGS	@13.0KGS	60CM×40CM×40CM
9	77PCS	77PCS	@12.0KGS	@10.0KGS	60CM×40CM×40CM
10-17	800PCS	100PCS	@15.0KGS	@13.0KGS	60CM×40CM×40CM
18	86PCS	86PCS	@13.0KGS	@11.0KGS	60CM×40CM×40CM
19-27	900PCS	100PCS	@15.0KGS	@13.0KGS	60CM×40CM×40CM
28-38	1100PCS	100PCS	@15.0KGS	@13.0KGS	60CM×40CM×40CM
39	69PCS	69PCS	@11.0KGS	@9.0KGS	60CM×40CM×40CM

PACKED IN 39 CARTONS, TOTAL QUANTITY: 3,832PCS

CARRIER: DONGFANG FRIGHT SYSTEM CO., LTD. NO. 200 ZHONGSHAN ROAD, XIANNING ZONE NANJING, CHINA TEL: 025-8834 5678. FAX NO.: 025-8834 5677.

DELIVERY AGENT: JAMES SHIPPING CO.
TEL: 0044-181-8123 1234; FAX NO.: 0044-181-8834 5678.

该货物是完全自产品。

经营单位海关注册号：4205960647

运费：USD300

发货单位与经营单位相同，2018 年 1 月 24 日由上海航联报关公司向上海浦江海关(2201)申报，当月 26 日装运出口。

二、实训要求

请以"单证员"的工作角色，根据以上资料缮制汇票(见表 2-4-2)、商业发票(见表 2-4-3)、装箱单(见表 2-4-4)、普惠制原产地证书(见表 2-4-5)、出口货物报关单(见表 2-4-6)、装船通知(见表 2-4-7)、提单(见表 2-4-8)、受益人证明(见表 2-4-9)。

表 2-4-2 汇票

BILL OF EXCHANGE

凭 **Drawn under** 信用证第 号 **L/C No.**

日期 **Dated** 支取 Payable with interest @ %per annum 按年息 付款

号码 **No.** 汇票金额 **Exchange for** 南京 年 月 日 **Nanjing**

见票 **At** 日后(本汇票之副本未付)付交 sight of this **FIRST** of Exchange (Second of exchange being unpaid) **Pay to the order of** 金额 **The sum**

款已收讫 Value received

此致

To:

南京华贸进出口贸易有限公司(章)
NANJING HUAMAO IMP. & EXP. TRADING CO., LTD.

表 2-4-3　商业发票

<table>
<tr><td colspan="5">南京华贸进出口贸易有限公司
NANJING HUAMAO IMP. & EXP. TRADING CO. ,LTD.
NO. 33 RENMIN ROAD, WUZHOU ECONOMIC DEVELOPMENT ZONE, NANJING, CHINA.</td></tr>
<tr><td colspan="5">商业发票
COMMERCIAL INVOICE</td></tr>
<tr><td colspan="2">Messrs：</td><td colspan="2">Invoice No. ：</td><td></td></tr>
<tr><td colspan="2" rowspan="5"></td><td colspan="2">Invoice date：</td><td></td></tr>
<tr><td colspan="2">S/C No. ：</td><td></td></tr>
<tr><td colspan="2">S/C date：</td><td></td></tr>
<tr><td colspan="2">L/C No. ：</td><td></td></tr>
<tr><td colspan="2">L/C date：</td><td></td></tr>
<tr><td colspan="2">Exporter：</td><td colspan="3" rowspan="2">Name of issuing bank：</td></tr>
<tr><td colspan="2"></td></tr>
<tr><td colspan="2">Transport details：</td><td colspan="3">Terms of Payment：</td></tr>
<tr><td colspan="2"></td><td colspan="3"></td></tr>
<tr><td>Marks & Nos.</td><td>Description of Goods</td><td>Quantity</td><td>Unit Price</td><td>Amount</td></tr>
<tr><td rowspan="2"></td><td rowspan="2"></td><td rowspan="2"></td><td colspan="2"></td></tr>
<tr><td></td><td></td></tr>
<tr><td colspan="5"></td></tr>
<tr><td colspan="5">南京华贸进出口贸易有限公司(章)
NANJING HUAMAO IMP. & EXP. TRADING CO. ,LTD.
谢芸(章)</td></tr>
</table>

表 2-4-4 装箱单

<table>
<tr><td colspan="7">南京华贸进出口贸易有限公司
NANJING HUAMAO IMP. & EXP. TRADING CO. ,LTD.
NO. 33 RENMIN ROAD, WUZHOU ECONOMIC DEVELOPMENT ZONE, NANJING, CHINA.</td></tr>
<tr><td colspan="7">装箱单
PACKING LIST</td></tr>
<tr><td colspan="4">To:</td><td colspan="2">Invoice No. :</td><td></td></tr>
<tr><td colspan="4" rowspan="3"></td><td colspan="2">Invoice date:</td><td></td></tr>
<tr><td colspan="2">S/C No. :</td><td></td></tr>
<tr><td colspan="3"></td></tr>
<tr><td colspan="4">Transport details:</td><td colspan="3">Description of goods</td></tr>
<tr><td colspan="4"></td><td colspan="3"></td></tr>
<tr><td>Marks & Nos.</td><td>CTN NO.</td><td>Quantity</td><td>Qty per CTN</td><td>G. Weight</td><td>N. Weight</td><td>Measurement</td></tr>
<tr><td></td><td></td><td></td><td></td><td></td><td></td><td></td></tr>
<tr><td colspan="7"></td></tr>
<tr><td colspan="7">南京华贸进出口贸易有限公司(章)
NANJING HUAMAO IMP. & EXP. TRADING CO. ,LTD.
谢芸(章)</td></tr>
</table>

表 2-4-5 普惠制原产地证书

<table>
<tr><td colspan="3">1. Goods consigned from (Exporter's business name address country)

2. Goods consigned to (Consignee's name, address, country)</td><td colspan="3">Reference No.
GENERALIZED SYSTEM OF PREFERENCES
CERTIFICATE OF ORIGIN
(Combined declaration and certificate)
FORM A
issued in THE PEOPLE'S REPUBLIC OF CHINA
(country)</td></tr>
<tr><td colspan="3">3. Means of transport and route</td><td colspan="3">4. For official use</td></tr>
<tr><td>5. Item number</td><td>6. Marks & numbers of packages</td><td>7. Number of kind of packages; Description of goods</td><td>8. Origin Criterion</td><td>9. Gross weight & other Quantity</td><td>10. Number and date of Invoices</td></tr>
<tr><td></td><td></td><td></td><td></td><td></td><td></td></tr>
<tr><td colspan="3">11. Certification
It is hereby certified, on the basis of control carried out, that the declaration by the exporter is correct.

Place and date, signature and stamp of certifying authority</td><td colspan="3">12. Declaration by the exporter
The undersigned hereby declares that the above details and statements are correct; that all goods were produced in
CHINA
(country)
and that they comply with the origin requirements specified for those goods in the Generalized System of Preferences for goods exported to

(importing country)
南京华贸进出口贸易有限公司(章)
NANJING HUAMAO IMP. & EXP. TRADING CO., LTD.
朱莹(手签)
Place and date, signature of authorized signatory</td></tr>
</table>

表 2-4-6 出口货物报关单

中华人民共和国海关出口货物报关单

预录入编号：　　　　海关编号：　（××海关）　　　　页码/页数：

<table>
<tr><td colspan="2">境内发货人</td><td colspan="2">出境关别</td><td colspan="2">出口日期</td><td colspan="2">申报日期</td><td>备案号</td></tr>
<tr><td colspan="2">境外收货人</td><td colspan="2">运输方式</td><td colspan="2">运输工具名称及航次号</td><td colspan="3">提运单号</td></tr>
<tr><td colspan="2">生产销售单位</td><td colspan="2">监管方式</td><td colspan="2">征免性质</td><td colspan="3">许可证号</td></tr>
<tr><td colspan="2">合同协议号</td><td colspan="2">贸易国(地区)</td><td colspan="2">运抵国(地区)</td><td colspan="2">指运港</td><td>离境口岸</td></tr>
<tr><td>包装种类</td><td>件数</td><td>毛重(千克)</td><td>净重(千克)</td><td>成交方式</td><td>运费</td><td colspan="2">保费</td><td>杂费</td></tr>
<tr><td colspan="9">随附单证及编号</td></tr>
<tr><td colspan="9">标记唛码及备注</td></tr>
<tr><td>项号</td><td>商品编号</td><td>商品名称及规格型号</td><td>数量及单位</td><td>单价/总价/币制</td><td>原产国(地区)</td><td>最终目的国(地区)</td><td>境内货源地</td><td>征免</td></tr>
<tr><td colspan="9"></td></tr>
<tr><td colspan="9"></td></tr>
<tr><td colspan="9"></td></tr>
<tr><td colspan="9"></td></tr>
<tr><td colspan="9"></td></tr>
<tr><td colspan="9"></td></tr>
<tr><td colspan="6">报关人员　　报关人员证号　　电话
兹申明对以上内容承担如实申报、依法纳税之责任
申报单位　　　　申报单位(签章)</td><td colspan="3">海关批注及签章</td></tr>
</table>

表 2-4-7 装船通知

南京华贸进出口贸易有限公司

NANJING HUAMAO IMP. & EXP. TRADING CO. ,LTD.

NO. 33 RENMIN ROAD, WUZHOU ECONOMIC DEVELOPMENT ZONE, NANJING, CHINA.

装船通知

SHIPPING ADVICE

To:

L/C No.

L/C Date:

ORDER NO. :

To whom it may concern:

We hereby state that the goods under the Open Policy No. 08-236147 have been shipped. The shipping details are as follow:

Description of goods:

Number of packages:

Quantity:

Goods value:

Container & Seal No. :

Port of loading:

Port of discharge:

Bill of Lading No. :

Vessel Name & Voy. :

南京华贸进出口贸易有限公司(章)

NANJING HUAMAO IMP. & EXP. TRADING CO. ,LTD.

谢芸(章)

表 2-4-8 提单

<table>
<tr><td colspan="2">Shipper</td><td colspan="3" rowspan="4">B/L No.
东方航运有限公司
DONGFANG FRIGHT SYSTEM CO. ,LTD.
BILL OF LADING
ORIGINAL
RECEIVED in external apparent good order and condition except as otherwise noted. The total number of packages or units stuffed in the container. The weight, measure, marks, numbers, quality, contents and value mentioned in this Bill of Lading are to be considered unknown unless the contrary has expressly acknowledged and agreed to. The signing of this Bill of Loading is not to be considered as such an agreement. On presentation of this Bill of Lading duly endorsed to the *Carrier* by or on behalf of the Holder of Bill of Lading.</td></tr>
<tr><td colspan="2">Consignee</td></tr>
<tr><td colspan="2">Notify party</td></tr>
<tr><td>Pre-carriage by</td><td>Ocean Vessel Voy. No.</td></tr>
<tr><td>Port of loading</td><td>Port of transshipment</td><td>Port of Discharge</td><td colspan="2">Place of delivery</td></tr>
<tr><td>Marks & Nos.
Container No.</td><td>No. & kind of
Packages</td><td>Description of goods</td><td>Gross weight</td><td>Measurement</td></tr>
<tr><td colspan="2">Total No. of container or other pkgs or units (in words)</td><td colspan="3"></td></tr>
<tr><td colspan="2">For delivery of goods please apply to:</td><td colspan="3">Freight & charges</td></tr>
<tr><td rowspan="2">Ex rate</td><td>Prepaid at</td><td>Payable at</td><td colspan="2">Place and date of issue:</td></tr>
<tr><td>Total prepaid</td><td>No. of B(s)/L
THREE</td><td colspan="2" rowspan="2">Signed
by DONGFANG FRIGHT SYSTEM CO. ,LTD.
NANJING BRANCH
As agent for the carrier
WenDa Shipping Co. ,Ltd. **JAMES**</td></tr>
<tr><td colspan="3">Laden on board the Vessel:
Date:
By:</td></tr>
</table>

表 2-4-9 受益人证明

南京华贸进出口贸易有限公司

NANJINGHUAMAO IMP. & EXP. TRADING CO. ,LTD.

NO. 33 RENMIN ROAD, WUZHOU ECONOMIC DEVELOPMENT ZONE, NANJING, CHINA.

实训五　信用证方式下 CIF 贸易术语出口单据缮制

一、实训资料

1. 信用证(见表 2-5-1)。

表 2-5-1　信用证

Message Tarih：26-04-18 09：22 AM Sender LT：YAPITRISAFEX YAPI VE KREDI BANKASI A. S. (FX/MM OPERATIONS) YAPI KREDI PLAZA BUYUKDERE CADDESILEVENT ISTANBUL Receiver LT： BKCHCNBJX300 BANK OF CHINA (SHANGHAI BRANCH) 103 ZHONGSHAN SOUTH 1 ROAD 27：Sequence of Total：1/1 40A：Form of Documentary Credit：IRREVOCABLE 20：Documentary Credit Number：960 1110 1006 31C：Date of Issue：180426 40E：Applicable Rules：UCPURR LATEST VERSION 31D：Date and Place of Expiry：180705 AT YOUR COUNTERS 50：Applicant： GAMA IPLIK VE DOKUMA SAN. A. S. 2. ORGANIZE SAN. BOLGESI BASPINAR GAZIANTEP 59：Beneficiary： SHANGHAI HUASHENG TRADING CO. , LTD. 12F NO. 219 LANE 888 DONGDAMIN RD. SHANGHAI CHINA 200082 32B：Currency Code/Amount：USD125,000 39B：Maximum Credit Amount：NOT EXCEEDING 41A：Available With... By ...：BKCHCNBJX300 BANK OF CHINA (SHANGHAI BRANCH) 103 ZHONGSHAN SOUTH 1 ROAD BY PAYMENT 43P：Partial Shipments：ALLOWED 43T：Transshipment：ALLOWED 44E：Port of Loading/Airport of Departure：SHANGHAI,CHINA BY VESSEL

续表

44F：Port of Discharge/Airport of Destination：IZMIT，TURKIYE

44C：Latest Date of Shipment：180615

45A：Description of Goods and/or Services：

POLYESTER STAPLE FIBER BLACK RECYCLED

1.5DX38MM

QUANTITY：100 MT

UNIT PRICE：1,250USD/MT

TERMS OF DELIVERY：CIF，IZMIT TURKIYE(INCOTERMS 2010)

46A：Documents Required：

+3 ORIGINAL PLUS 3 COPIES OF COMMERCIAL INVOICE DULY SIGNED BY THE BENEFICIARY INDICATING CIF VALUE TOTALLY(FOB，FREIGHT AND INSURANCE VALUES SEPARATELY) AND THE ORIGIN OF THE GOODSSHIPPED. INVOICE CERTIFYING THE GOODS HAVE BEEN SHIPPED AS PER PROFORMA INVOICE NO.：BS-WBA110 DATE：180415.

+3/3 ORIGINAL PLUS 3NN COPIES OF CLEAN ON BOARD B/L ISSUED OR ENDORSED TO THE ORDER OF YAPI ve KREDI BANKASI A. S. MARKED FREIGHT PREPAID AND NOTIFY APPLICANT'S FULL NAME AND ADDRESS.

+1 ORIGINAL PLUS 3 COPIES OF CERTIFICATE OF ORIGIN ISSUED OR LEGALIZED BY THE CHAMBER OF COMMERCE INDICATING ORIGIN OF THE GOODS.

+3 ORIGINAL PLUS 3 COPIES OF PACKING LIST.

+FULL SET AT LEAST IN 2 ORIGINAL，3 COPIES OF INSURANCE POLICY BLANK ENDORSED FOR THE CIF INVOICE VALUE PLUS 10 PERCENT COVERING ALL RISKS，INSTITUTE CARGO CLAUSES (A) WAR RISKS INSTITUTE WAR CLAUSES (CARGO) S. R. AND C. C. AND N. D. AND T. P. FROM WAREHOUSE TO WAREHOUSE INDICATING CLAIMS PAYABLE IN ISTANBUL IN THE CURRENCY OF THE CREDIT AND SHOWING THE PREMIUM PAID.

+1 ORIGINAL PLUS 1 COPY OF INSPECTION CERTIFICATE ISSUED BY SGS.

47A：Additional Conditions：

+ALL DOCS WILL BE SENT TO OUR BANK'S ADDRESS：YAPI ve KREDI BANKASI A. S. H/O BANKACILIK USSU，INVENTUS 1 DIS ISLEMLER MERKEZI，AKSE MAH. SEHIT ILHAN KUCUKSOLAK CAD. 241435，CAYIROVA，KOCAELI TURKIYE BY ANY SPECIAL COURIER SERVICE.

+ALL DOCUMENTS SHOULD BEAR OUR DOCUMENTARY CREDIT NUMBER.

+USD100 DISCREPANCY FEE FOR EACH SET OF DOCS WILL BE DEDUCTED FROM PROCEEDS，IF DOCUMENTS PRESENTED WITH THE DISCREPANCIES.

+ALL DOCUMENTS MUST BE ISSUED IN ENGLISH EXCEPT PREPRINTED FORMS.

+IF THE DUE DATE COINCIDES WITH A NATIONAL HOLIDAY AND NON-BANKING DAY IN TURKIYE AND/OR IN THE COUNTRY OF THE REIMBURSEMENT BANK DUE DATE WILL BE POSTPONED TO THE NEXT.

续表

+DOCUMENTS ISSUED OR DATED PRIOR TO THIS DOCUMENTARY CREDIT ISSUANCE DATE NOT ACCEPTABLE. 71B：Charges： ALL BANKING COMMISSIONS AND CHARGES OUTSIDE OF TURKIYE INCLUDING REIMBURSMENT CHARGES ARE FOR BENEF'S ACCOUNT. 48：Period for Presentation：10 DAYS AFTER B/L DATE 49：Confirmation Instructions：WITHOUT 78：Instructions to the Paying/Accepting/Negotiating Bank： UPON PRESENTATION OF CREDIT CONFORM DOCS TO YOUR BANK, YOU ARE AUTHORIZED TO CLAIM REIMBURSMENT FROM REIMBURSING BANK FOR DOCUMENTS AMOUNT ONLY THREE WORKING DAYS BEFORE THE VALUE DATE UNDER ADVICE TO US BY TESTED MSG QUOTING OUR REFERENCE. 72：Sender to Receiver Information：PLS ACK RECEIPT

2. 补充资料。

INV. NO.：HS1151231

INV. DATE：MAY 28,2018

B/L. NO.：MASA20079

B/L. DATE：JUNE 10,2018

S/C NO.：BS-WBA110

S/C DATE：180415

NAME OF STEAMER：MASA V. 007W

CONTAINER&SEAL NO.：AEMU24485971/AEMG4374508

SHIPPING MARKS：GAMA/IZMIT

POLICY NO.：WEH3457392

FOB VALUE：USD124,100

FREIGHT CHARGES：USD700. 00

INSURANCE PRMIUM：USD200. 00

GOODS：

TOTAL WEIGHT：G. W.：101. 2MT N. W.：100MT MEA：98. 744CBMS

PACKED IN 10 BAGS

H. S. NO.：5506. 900. 000

二、实训要求

请以"单证员"的工作角色，根据以上资料缮制商业发票(见表 2-5-2)、装箱单(见表 2-5-3)、原产地证书(见表 2-5-4)、保险单(见表 2-5-5)、提单(见表 2-5-6)。

表 2-5-2　商业发票

<table>
<tr><td colspan="5">上海华盛贸易有限公司
SHANGHAI HUASHENG TRADING CO. ,LTD.
12F NO. 219 LANE 888 DONGDAMIN RD. Shanghai China 200082</td></tr>
<tr><td colspan="5">商业发票
COMMERCIAL INVOICE</td></tr>
<tr><td colspan="5">To：</td></tr>
<tr><td colspan="2" rowspan="4"></td><td colspan="2">Inv. No.：</td><td></td></tr>
<tr><td colspan="2">Inv. Date：</td><td></td></tr>
<tr><td colspan="2">S/C No.：</td><td></td></tr>
<tr><td colspan="2">S/C Date：</td><td></td></tr>
<tr><td>Credit No.：</td><td></td><td>Dated：</td><td colspan="2"></td></tr>
<tr><td>Issued by：</td><td colspan="4"></td></tr>
<tr><td>Marks & No.</td><td>Description of goods</td><td>Quantity</td><td>Unit Price</td><td>Amount</td></tr>
<tr><td rowspan="2"></td><td rowspan="2"></td><td rowspan="2"></td><td colspan="2"></td></tr>
<tr><td></td><td></td></tr>
<tr><td colspan="5"></td></tr>
<tr><td colspan="5"></td></tr>
<tr><td colspan="5">上海华盛贸易有限公司(章)
SHANGHAI HUASHENG TRADING CO. ,LTD.
汪海平(章)</td></tr>
</table>

表 2-5-3 装箱单

<table>
<tr><td colspan="7">上海华盛贸易有限公司
SHANGHAI HUASHENG TRADING CO. ,LTD.
12F NO. 219 LANE 888 DONGDAMIN RD. Shanghai China 200082</td></tr>
<tr><td colspan="7">装箱单
PACKING LIST</td></tr>
<tr><td colspan="7">To:</td></tr>
<tr><td colspan="4" rowspan="2"></td><td colspan="2">Inv. No.:</td><td></td></tr>
<tr><td colspan="2">Inv. Date:</td><td></td></tr>
<tr><td>From:</td><td colspan="2"></td><td>To:</td><td></td><td colspan="2">By vessel</td></tr>
<tr><td>Marks & Nos.</td><td>Nos. and kind of pkgs</td><td>Description of goods and Quantity</td><td>G. Weight</td><td>N. Weight</td><td colspan="2">Measurement</td></tr>
<tr><td></td><td></td><td></td><td></td><td></td><td colspan="2"></td></tr>
<tr><td colspan="7"></td></tr>
<tr><td colspan="7">上海华盛贸易有限公司(章)
SHANGHAI HUASHENG TRADING CO. ,LTD.
汪海平(章)</td></tr>
</table>

表 2-5-4 原产地证书

<table>
<tr><td colspan="2">1. Exporter:</td><td colspan="3" rowspan="2">Certificate No.

CERTIFICATE OF ORIGIN
OF
THE PEOPLE'S REPUBLIC OF CHINA</td></tr>
<tr><td colspan="2">2. Consignee:</td></tr>
<tr><td colspan="2">3. Means of transport and route</td><td colspan="3" rowspan="2">5. For certifying authority use only</td></tr>
<tr><td colspan="2">4. Country/region of destination</td></tr>
<tr><td>6. Marks & Nos.</td><td>7. Number and kind of packages; Description of goods</td><td>8. H. S. Code</td><td>9. Quantity</td><td>10. Numbers and Date of Invoice</td></tr>
<tr><td></td><td></td><td></td><td></td><td></td></tr>
<tr><td colspan="2">11. Declaration by the exporter
The undersigned hereby declares that the above details and statements correct, that all the goods were produced in China and that they comply with the Rules of Origin of the People's Republic of China.</td><td colspan="3">12. Certification
It is hereby certified that the declaration by the exporter is correct.</td></tr>
<tr><td colspan="2">Place and date, signature and stamp of authorized signatory</td><td colspan="3">Place and date, signature and stamp of certifying authority</td></tr>
</table>

表 2-5-5 保险单

PICC

中国人保财险股份有限公司
PICC Property & Casualty Company Limited
总公司设于北京 一九四九年创立
Head Office Beijing Established in 1949

货 物 运 输 保 险 单
CARGO TRANSPORTATION INSURANCE POLICY

发票号码 Invoice No.			
合同号码 Contract No.		保单号次 Policy No.	
信用证号 Credit No.			
被保险人 Insured：			

中保财产保险有限公司(以下简称本公司)根据被保险人的要求，及其所缴付约定的保险费，按照本保险单承担险别和背面所载条款与下列特别条款承保下列货物运输保险，特签发本保险单。

This policy of Insurance witnesses that The People Insurance (Property) Company of China, Ltd. (hereinafter called the Company) at the request of the Insured and in consideration of the agreed premium paid by the Insured, under takes to in sure the under mentioned goods in transportation subject to the conditions of this Policy as per the Clauses printed overleaf and other special clauses attached hereon.

标记 Marks & No.	包装及数量 Quantity	保险货物项目 Description of goods	保险金额 Amount Insured

总保险金额
Total Amount Insured：

保险费 Premium	启运日期 Date of commencement	装载运输工具 Per conveyance

自 From	经 Via	至 To

承保险别 Conditions：

所保货物，如发生本保险单项下可能引起索赔的损失或损坏，应立即通知本公司下述代理人查勘。如有索赔，应向本公司提交保险单正本(本保险单共有 2 份正本)及有关文件。如一份正本已用于索赔，其余正本则自动失效。

In the event of damage which may result in a claim under this Policy, immediate notice be given to the Company Agent as mentioned here under. Claims, if any, one of the Original Policy which has been issued in **TWO** Original(s) together with the relevant documents shall be surrendered to be Company, if one of the Original Policy has been accomplished, the others to be void.

Insurance agent at destination：

TURKIYE INSURANCE COMPANY
85 GANDY STREET, NHAVA SHEVA TURKIYE

续表

<table>
<tr><td>赔款偿付地点
Claim payable at</td><td rowspan="3">中国人保财险股份有限公司上海市分公司
PICC Property & Casualty Co.,Ltd.,Shanghai Branch
张岚
Authorized Signature</td></tr>
<tr><td>出单日期
Issuing date</td></tr>
<tr><td>地址：中国上海市中山东一路 321 号
Address: 321 Zhongshan Road One (E) Shanghai China</td></tr>
</table>

表 2-5-6 提单

<table>
<tr><td colspan="3">Shipper</td><td colspan="4" rowspan="4">B/L No.
泛亚航运有限公司
PAN-ASIA SHIPPING CO.,LTD.
BILL OF LADING
ORIGINAL
RECEIVED in external apparent good order and condition except as otherwise noted. The total of packages or units stuffed in the container. The weight, measure, marks, numbers, quality, contents and value mentioned in this Bill of Lading are to be considered unknown unless the contrary has expressly acknowledged and agreed to. The signing of this Bill of Loading is not to be considered as such an agreement. On presentation of this Bill of Lading duly endorsed to the Carrier by or on behalf of the Holder of Bill of Lading.</td></tr>
<tr><td colspan="3">Consignee</td></tr>
<tr><td colspan="3">Notify party</td></tr>
<tr><td>Pre-carriage by</td><td colspan="2">Ocean Vessel Voy. No.</td></tr>
<tr><td colspan="2">Port of loading</td><td colspan="2">Port of transshipment</td><td colspan="2">Port of Discharge</td><td>Place of delivery</td></tr>
<tr><td colspan="2">Marks & Nos.
Container No.</td><td colspan="2">No. & kind of packages</td><td>Description of goods</td><td>Gross weight</td><td>Measurement</td></tr>
<tr><td colspan="2">Total No. of container or other pkgs or units (in words)</td><td colspan="5"></td></tr>
<tr><td colspan="3">For delivery of goods please apply to:</td><td colspan="4">Freight & charges</td></tr>
<tr><td rowspan="2">Ex rate</td><td>Prepaid at</td><td colspan="2">Payable at</td><td colspan="3">Place and date of issue:</td></tr>
<tr><td>Total prepaid</td><td colspan="2">No. of B(s)/L</td><td colspan="3" rowspan="2">Signed by PAN-ASIASHIPPING CO.,LTD.
SHANGHAI BRANCH
As agent for the carrier
Pan-Asia Shipping Co.,Ltd. 杨柳</td></tr>
<tr><td colspan="4">Laden on board the Vessel:
Date:
By:</td></tr>
</table>

实训六　信用证方式下 FOB 贸易术语出口单据缮制

一、实训资料

1. 信用证(见表 2-6-1)。

表 2-6-1　信用证

MANDANT：50321-BRAUKMANN,BRAUKMANN GMBH KONZERN：50321-BRAUKMAN VR-DOKTRADE AUSDRUCK VON NACHRICHT MT700/ IMPORT-AKKREDITIV SEITE1 Trade Connect Message Type：MT：700 Status report：issue of a documentary credit Client Reference：M1：GENO40221AT00211 Issuing Media：M2：By Swift Contact Person：M4：Iris HauK Execution date：M9：10.06.2018 Issuing Bank：WGZ BANK GERMANY Advising Bank：M14：Bank of China Shanghai Branch 200 Yin Cheng Rd (C) 200120 Shanghai,P. R. China 20：Documentary Credit Number：GENOAI04036D5 40A：Form of Documentary Credit：IRREVOCABLE TRANSFERABLE 31C：Date of Issue：10.06.2018 40E：Applicable Rules：UCP LATEST VERSION 31D：Date and Place of Expiry：31.07.2018 China 50：Applicant：Braukmann GmbH Raiffeisenstr. 858757 Arnsberg I. R. Germany 59：Beneficiary：Shanghai FAFA Electrical Equipment Co. ,Ltd. WenYuan Road,NiKou Industrial Zone NanHui,ShangHai 32B：Currency Code and Amount：USD213,280.00 41D：Available with ... By ...：Any Bank in China BY NEGOTIATION 42C：DRAFT AT...：SIGHT 42A：DRAWEE：WGZ BANK GERMANY 43P：Partial Shipments：ALLOWED 43T：Transhipment：ALLOWED 44E：Port of Loading/Airport of Departure：Shanghai Port 44F：Port of Discharge/Airport of Destination：Hamburg Port 44C：Latest Date of Shipment：10.07.2018

续表

45A：Description of Goods and/or Services： VACUUM CLEANER TUBES VACUUM CLEANER TUBES NO. 540.0000 GREY-4,100PCS VACUUM CLEANER TUBES NO. 540.0000 BLACK-800PCS VACUUM CLEANER TUBES NO. 550.0000 GREY-3,900PCS VACUUM CLEANER TUBES NO. 550.0000 BLACK-600PCS VACUUM CLEANER TUBES NO. 560.0000 GREY-2,500PCS VACUUM CLEANER TUBES NO. 560.0000 BLACK-500PCS AT USD 17.2/PC as per Proforma Invoice 201111700179 DD. 24.05.2018 FOB SHANGHAI IN CHINA 46A：Documents Required： 1. SIGNED COMMERCIAL INVOICE,4-FOLD 2. FULL SET OF CLEAN ON BOARD OCEAN BILLS OF LADING MADE OUT TO ORDER AND BLANK ENDORSED IN DICATING NAME AND ADDRESS OF APPLICANT AS NOTIFY ADDRESS AND "FREIGHT COLLECT" 3. PACKING LIST,4-FOLD 4. GSP CERTIFICATE OF ORIGIN FORM A, 2-FOLD, STATING THAT GOODS WERE PRODUCED IN CHINA STAMPED AND MANUALLY SIGNED BY COMPETENT AUTHORITY/PERSON 5. INSPECTION CERTIFICATE ISSUED BY SGS SHOWING THAT SAMPLES WERE INSPECTED 47A：Additional Conditions： 1. ALL DOCUMENTS MUST SHOW THE DOC. CREDIT NUMBER. 2. ALL DOCUMENTS MUST BE ISSUED IN ENGLISH LANGUAGE. 3. DOCUMENTS MUST BE PRESENTED TO WGZ BANK THROUGH A BANK ONLY. 4. BANK OF CHINA, SHANGHAI BRANCH, IS AUTHORIZED TO TRANSFER THE CREDIT. 5. THE TRANSFERRING BANK MUST INFORM THE ISSUING BANK VIAS WIFT ABOUT ANY TRANSFER. PRESENTATION OF DOCUMENTS BY OR ON BEHALF OF THE SECONDB ENEFICIARY MUST BE MADE TO THE TRANSFERRING BANK (SUB-ARTICLE 38 K,UCP 600) BUT HONOUR OR NEGOTIATION MAY NOT BE EFFECTED TO A SECOND BENEFICIARY AT A PLACE OTHER THAN STATED IN THE CREDIT ART. 38J,UCP 600 IS NOT APPLICABLE 71B：Details of charges： ALL CHARGES OUTSIDE WGZ BANK (INCLREIMBURSING BANKS CHARGES) AND OUR DISCREPANCY FEE EUR7,500 OR EQUIVALENT FOR EACH SET OF DOCS. NOTTO BE IN COMPLIANCE WITH THIS DOC. CREDIT ARE FOR BENEFICIARY'S ACC. 48：Period for Presentation： DOCUMENTS MUST BE PRESENTED NOT LATER THAN 21 DAYS AFTER THE DATE OF SHIPMENT. 49：Confirmation Instructions：WITHOUT 78：Bank Instructions： + PLEASE SEND DOCUMENTS VIA COURIER TO：WGZ BANK AG WESTDEUTSCHE GENOSSENSCHAFTS-ZENTRALBANK LUDWIG-ERHARD-ALLEE 2040227 DUESSELDORF/F. R. GERMANY +HAVING RECEIVED CREDITCONFORM DOCUMENTS WE WILL COVER ANY NEGOTIATING BANK ACCORDING TO THEIR INSTRUCTIONS

2. 补充资料。

INV. NO.：BG91014R

INV. DATE：JUNE 22，2018

B/L. NO.：FAFA83500

B/L. DATE：JULY 05，2018

NAME OF STEAMER：LANJING V. 908

CONTAINER & SEAL NO.：TEXU34785082/LMS5314102

SHIPPING MARKS：N/M

FORM A NO.：G102243101620078

GOODS：WEIGHT：@G. W.：110kgs @N. W.：94kgs @MEA. 20CM×20CM×23CM

PACKED IN 12，400 CARTONS

该货物是完全自产品。

二、实训要求

请以"单证员"的工作角色，根据以上资料缮制汇票（见表 2-6-2）、商业发票（见表 2-6-3）、装箱单（见表 2-6-4）、提单（见表 2-6-5）、普惠制产地证书（见表 2-6-6）。

表 2-6-2 汇票

BILL OF EXCHANGE

凭 **Drawn under** 信用证 第 号 **L/C No.**

日期 **Dated** 支取 Payable with interest @ %per annum 按年息 付款

号码 **No.** 汇票金额 **Exchange for** 上海 年 月 日 **ShangHai**

见票 **At** 日后（本汇票之副本未付）付交 sight of this **FIRST** of Exchange (Second of exchange Being unpaid) **Pay to the order of** 金额 **The sum**

款已收讫

Value received

此致

To：

上海发发电器有限公司（章）

SHANGHAI FAFA ELECTRICAL EQUIPMENT CO.，LTD.

表 2-6-3 商业发票

<table>
<tr><td colspan="2">Issuer：</td><td colspan="3" rowspan="2">上海发发电器有限公司
SHANGHAI FAFA ELECTRICAL EQUIPMENT CO. ,LTD.
WENYUAN ROAD. NIKOU INDUSTRIAL ZONE NANHUI,Shanghai
发 票
INVOICE</td></tr>
<tr><td colspan="2" rowspan="2">To：</td></tr>
<tr><td>No.</td><td colspan="2">Date</td></tr>
<tr><td colspan="2" rowspan="2">Transport details：
From：
To：
By Vessel</td><td>Terms of Payment</td><td colspan="2">L/C No.</td></tr>
<tr><td colspan="3">Country of Origin</td></tr>
<tr><td>Marks & Nos.</td><td>Description of Goods</td><td>Quantity</td><td>Unit Price</td><td>Amount</td></tr>
<tr><td rowspan="2"></td><td></td><td colspan="3"></td></tr>
<tr><td></td><td></td><td></td><td></td></tr>
<tr><td colspan="5">上海发发电器有限公司(章)
SHANGHAI FAFA ELECTRICAL EQUIPMENT CO. ,LTD.
李玉霞(章)</td></tr>
</table>

表 2-6-4 装箱单

Issuer:

上海发发电器有限公司

SHANGHAI FAFA ELECTRICAL EQUIPMENT CO. ,LTD.

WENYUAN ROAD. NIKOU INDUSTRIAL ZONE NANHUI, Shanghai

装箱单

PACKING LIST

To:

No.

Date

Transport details:

From: To:

Marks & Nos.	No. & Kinds of Pkgs; Description of Goods	Gross Wt. Kilos	Net Wt. Kilos	Measurement M^3

上海发发电器有限公司(章)

SHANGHAI FAFA ELECTRICAL EQUIPMENT CO. ,LTD.

李玉霞(章)

表 2-6-5　提单

<table>
<tr><td colspan="3">Shipper</td><td colspan="4" rowspan="6">B/L No.
承运人
CARRIER
中远集装箱运输有限公司
COSCO CONTAINER LINES
Port-to-Port or Combined Transport
BILL OF LADING
ORIGINAL
RECEIVED in external apparent good order and condition except as otherwise noted. The total number of packages or units stuffed in the container. The weight, measure, marks, numbers, quality, contents and value mentioned in this Bill of Lading are to be acknowledged and agreed to. The signing of this Bill of Loading is not to be considered as such an agreement. On presentation of this Bill of Lading duly endorsed to the Carrier by or on behalf of the Holder of Bill of Lading, the rights (Terms of Bill of Lading continued on the back hereof)</td></tr>
<tr><td colspan="3">Consignee</td></tr>
<tr><td colspan="3">Notify party</td></tr>
<tr><td colspan="2">Pre-carriage by</td><td>Place of Receipt</td></tr>
<tr><td colspan="2">Ocean Vessel Voy. No.</td><td>Port of Loading</td></tr>
<tr><td colspan="2">Port of Discharge</td><td>Place of Delivery</td></tr>
<tr><td>Marks & Nos.
Container No.</td><td colspan="2">No. & kind of pkgs</td><td>Description of goods</td><td colspan="2">Gross weight</td><td>Measurement</td></tr>
<tr><td></td><td colspan="2"></td><td></td><td colspan="2"></td><td></td></tr>
<tr><td colspan="2">Total No. of container or other pkgs or units (in words)</td><td colspan="5"></td></tr>
<tr><td colspan="2">Freight & charges</td><td>Revenue Tons</td><td>Rate</td><td>Per</td><td>Prepaid</td><td>Collect</td></tr>
<tr><td colspan="2"></td><td></td><td></td><td></td><td></td><td></td></tr>
<tr><td rowspan="2">Ex rate</td><td>Prepaid at</td><td>Payable at</td><td colspan="4">Place and date of issue:</td></tr>
<tr><td>Total prepaid</td><td>No. of B(s)/L</td><td colspan="4" rowspan="2">Signed by　COSCO CONTAINER LINES SHANGHAI BRANCH
As agent for the carrier named above 李四</td></tr>
<tr><td colspan="3">Laden on board the Vessel:
Date:
By:</td></tr>
</table>

表 2-6-6 普惠制产地证书

<table>
<tr><td colspan="3">1. Goods consigned from (Exporter's business name address country)</td><td colspan="3" rowspan="2">Reference No.

GENERALIZED SYSTEM OF PREFERENCES
CERTIFICATE OF ORIGIN
(Combined declaration and certificate)

FORM A

Issued in THE PEOPLE'S REPUBLIC OF CHINA
(country)</td></tr>
<tr><td colspan="3">2. Goods consigned to (Consignee's name, address, country)</td></tr>
<tr><td colspan="3">3. Means of transport and route</td><td colspan="3">4. For official use</td></tr>
<tr><td>5. Item Number</td><td>6. Marks & Nos. of packages</td><td>7. Number of kind of packages; Description of goods</td><td>8. Origin Criterion</td><td>9. Gross weight & Other Quantity</td><td>10. Number and date of Invoice</td></tr>
<tr><td colspan="3">11. Certification
It is hereby certified, on the basis of control carried out, that the declaration by the exporter is correct.

....
Place and date, signature and stamp of certifying authority</td><td colspan="3">12. Declaration by the exporter
The undersigned hereby declares that the above details and statements are correct; that all goods were produced in

CHINA
....
(country)
and that they comply with the origin requirements specified for those goods in the Generalized System of Preferences for goods exported to
....
(importing country)

上海发发电器有限公司(章)
SHANGHAI FAFA ELECTRICAL EQUIPMENT CO.,LTD.

李玉霞(手签)
....
Place and date, signature of authorized signatory</td></tr>
</table>

实训七　信用证方式下出口单据审核

一、实训资料

1. 信用证。

进口国开来的信用证见表 2-7-1。

表 2-7-1　信用证

FROM：BANK OF BRAZIL RIO DE JANEIRO
TO：SHANGHAI PUDONG DEVELOPMENT BANK
27：SEQUENCE OF TOTAL：1/1
40A：FORM OF DOCUMENTARY CREDIT：IRREVOCABLE
20：DOCUMENTARY CREDIT NUMBER：HJQ234
31C：DATE OF ISSUE：180723
40E：APPLICABLE RULES：UCP LATEST VERSION
31D：DATE AND PLACE OF EXPIRY：180926 CHINA
50：APPLICANT：
COMPANHIA BRASILEIRA DE DISTRIBUICAO ROD. ANHANGUERA，KM 17，8 OSASCO SP BRASIL
59：BENEFICIARY：
MJ TRADE CO.，LTD.
12F 7 BLDG SHATOUJIAO FREE TRADE ZONE，YANTIAN，SHENZHEN，CHINA 416061
32B：CURRENCY CODE，AMOUNT：USD25，756.00
39A：PERCENTAGE CREDIT AMOUNT TOLERANCE：5/5
41D：AVAILABLE WITH...BY...：ANY BANK BY NEGOTIATION
42C：DRAFTS AT...：AT SIGHT
42D：DRAWEE：OURSELVES
43P：PARTIAL SHIPMENTS：PARTIAL SHIPMENTS ARE PERMITTED
43T：TRANSSHIPMENT：TRANSSHIPMENT ARE PERMITTED
44E：PORT OF LOADING/AIRPORT OF DEPARTURE：SHANGHAI PORT
44F：PORT OF DISCHARGE/AIRPORT OF DESTINATION：SANTOS
44C：LATEST DATE OF SHIPMENT：180912
45A：DESCRIPTION OF GOODS AND/OR SERVICES：
PENGUIM HUMIDIFIER(BLACK BODY-WHITE DETAIL)-127V
PENGUIM HUMIDIFIER(BLACK BODY-WHITE DETAIL)-220V
AS PER DESCRIBED ON S/C NO. TR100566 DATED JULY 16，2018.
CIFSANTOS PORT　**DRAFT**
AS PER INCOTERMS 2010 OF ICC PARIS.

续表

46A：DOCUMENTS REQUIRED：

1) 03 ORIGINALS PLUS 01 COPY OF SIGNED BY HAND AND STAMPED COMMERCIAL INVOICE WITH COMPLETE DESCRIPTION OF GOODS，SHOWING CIF AMOUNT IN FIGURES.
2) 3/3 ORIGINALS PLUS 03 COPIES OF CLEAN ON BOARD BILL OF LADIN CONSIGNED TO ORDER，NOTIFY PARTY SAME AS CONSIGNEE，FREIGHT PREPAID COVERING SHIPMENT FROM SHANGHAI TO SANTOS - BRAZIL. BILL OF LADING MUST SHOS：PO NUMBER，NUMBER OF CARTONS.
3) 03 ORIGINALS PLUS 01 COPY OF SIGNED BY HAND AND STAMPED PACKING LIST WITH FULL DESCRIPTION OF GOODS.
4) 01 ORIGINAL PLUS 01 COPY OF CERTIFICATE OF ORIGIN.
5) FULL SET OF NEGOTIABLE INSURANCE POLICY OR CERTIFICATE BLANK ENDORSED FOR 110% OF INVOICE VALUE COVERING ALL RISKS AND WAR RISK OF **Institute Cargo Clause (A)**.

47A：ADDITIONAL CONDITIONS：

1) ALL DISCREPANCIES DUE TO TYPOGRAPHICAL MISTAKES ARE WAIVED.
2) NUMBER OF THIS LETTER OF CREDIT AND THE REFERENC TR100566 MUST BE STATED ON ALL DOCUMENTS.
3) WILL BE REFUSED SHIPPING DOCUMENTS SHOWING SHIPMENT DATE PRIOR OF ISSUANCE OF THIS LETTER OF CREDIT.

71B：DETAILS CHARGES：

BANKING CHARGES OUTSIDE OF BRASIL ARE FOR BENEFICIARY'S ACCOUNT.

48：PRESENTATION PERIOD：

DOCUMENTS MUST BE PRESENTED WITHIN 14 DAYS AFTER ISSUANCE OF THE TRANSPORT DOCUMENT BUT WITHIN THE VALIDITY OF THIS CREDIT.

49： CONFIRMA INSTRUCTIONS：WITHOUT

53A：REIMBURSEMENT BANK：SCBLUS33

78：INSTRUCTIONS：

1) WHETHER ALL TERMS AND CONDITIONS ARE COMPLIED WITH，PLEASE CLAIM REIMBURSE，ON THE 5TH WORKING DAY AFTER YOUR IMMEDIATE TESTED MESSAGE TO US INFORMING AMOUNT OF DOCS.，SHIPMENT AND NEGOTIATION DATES，AWB AND COMM. INVOICE NRS，DEPATURE PLACE，DESTINATION AND CONFIRMING THAT SHIPPING DOCUMENTS ARE BEING REMITTED TO OUR OFFICE.
2) PLEASE ADVISE BENEFICIARY URGENTLY UNDER ADVISE TO US.

2. 补充资料。

INV. NO.：S2000307　　INV. DATE：AUG. 14，2018

B/L. NO.：ZHY20180　　B/L. DATE：SEP. 01，2018

REFERENCE NO.：G114303101620078　　S/C NO.：MLI-11895/10

NAME OF STEAMER：FANYA W. 102

CONTAINER & SEAL NO.：TEXU47683001/WG9006

SHIPPING MARKS：MJ HONGKONG.
100566
SANTOS
1-470

H. S. NO.：5802. 4060

POLICY NO.：SH089921

FREIGHT FEE：USD1,100

INSURANCE FEE：USD1,000

报检单编号：985614322

报检单位登记号：347698580

GOODS：

PENGUIM HUMIDIFIER(BLACK BODY-WHITE DETAIL)-127V：
@USD13. 70/PCS 1,280PCS

PENGUIM HUMIDIFIER(BLACK BODY-WHITE DETAIL)-220V：
@USD13. 70/PCS 600PCS

PACKED IN 470 CARTONS,TOTAL QUANTITY：1,880PCS

TOTAL WEIGHT：N. W.：3,525. 00KGS G. W.：3,995. 00KGS MEAS.：59. 40CBM

该货物是完全自产品。

二、实训要求

请以"单证员"的工作角色，根据以上资料审核下列单证(见表 2-7-2～表 2-7-7)，并改正单证中的错误。

表 2-7-2 汇票

BILL OF EXCHANGE

凭 信用证第 号
Drawn under BANK OF BRAZIL RIO DE JANEIRO **L/C No.** H××××××

日期
Dated JULY 23,2018 支取 Payable with interest @ %per annum 按年息 付款

号码 汇票金额 上海 年 月 日
No. S2000307 **Exchange for** USD25,136.00 **ShangHai** Sep. 15,2018

见票 日后(本汇票之副本未付)付交
At 30 days sight of this **FIRST** of Exchange (Second of exchange being unpaid) **Pay to the order of** SHANGHAI PUDONG DEVELOPMENT BANK 金额 **The sum**

SAY U. S. DOLLARS TWENTY FIVE THOUSAND ONE HUNDRED AND THIRTY SIX ONLY.

款已收讫
Value received
此致
To：
COMPANHIA BRASILEIRA DE
DISTRIBUICAO ROD. ANHANGUERA,KM 17,8
OSASCO-SP-BRASIL

明基贸易有限公司(章)
MJ TRADE CO.,LTD.
刘德福(章)

表 2-7-3 商业发票

<table>
<tr><td colspan="2">Issuer:
MJ TRADE CO. ,LTD.
12F 7 BLDG SHATOUJIAO FREE TRADE ZONE,
YANTIAN,SHENZHEN,CHINA 416061</td><td colspan="3" rowspan="2">明基贸易有限公司
MJ TRADE CO. ,LTD.
12F 7 BLDG SHATOUJIAO FREE TRADE ZONE,
YANTIAN,SHENZHEN,CHINA 416061

发 票
INVOICE</td></tr>
<tr><td colspan="2" rowspan="2">To:
COMPANHIA BRASILEIRA DE DISTRIBUICAO ROD. ANHANGUERA, KM 17,8
OSASCO-SP-BRASIL</td></tr>
<tr><td>No.
S2000307</td><td colspan="2">Date
APR. 14,2018</td></tr>
<tr><td colspan="2" rowspan="2">Transport details:
From: YANTIAN
To: SANTOS
By Vessel</td><td>Terms of Payment
BY L/C</td><td colspan="2">L/C No.
H×××××</td></tr>
<tr><td colspan="3">Country of Origin
CHINA</td></tr>
<tr><td>Marks & Nos.</td><td>Description of Goods</td><td>Quantity</td><td>Unit Price</td><td>Amount</td></tr>
<tr><td rowspan="2">MJ
HONGKONG
100566
SANTOS
1-470</td><td rowspan="2">PENGUIM HUMIDIFIER
(BLACK BODY-WHITE DETAIL)
127V

220V
AS PER DESCRIBED ON S/C NO. TR100566 DATED JULY 16,2011</td><td rowspan="2">

1,280PCS

600PCS</td><td colspan="2">CFR SANTOS PORT</td></tr>
<tr><td>USD13.7/PCS</td><td>USD17,536

USD8,220</td></tr>
<tr><td colspan="2">TOTAL:</td><td colspan="2">1,800PCS</td><td>USD25,756</td></tr>
<tr><td colspan="5">SAY U.S. DOLLARS TWENTY FIVE THOUSAND SEVEN HUNDRED AND FIFTY SIX ONLY.
TOTAL PACKED IN 470CTNS.</td></tr>
<tr><td colspan="5">明基贸易有限公司(章)
MJ TRADE CO. ,LTD.
刘德福(章)</td></tr>
</table>

表 2-7-4　装箱单

Issuer:
MJ TRADE CO. ,LTD.
12F 7 BLDG SHATOUJIAO FREE TRADE ZONE,
YANTIAN,SHENZHEN,CHINA 416061

明基贸易有限公司
MJ TRADE CO. ,LTD.
12F 7 BLDG SHATOUJIAO FREE TRADE ZONE,
YANTIAN,SHENZHEN,CHINA 416061

装 箱 单
PACKING LIST

To:
COMPANHIA BRASILEIRA DE
DISTRIBUICAO ROD. ANHANGUERA, KM
17,8
OSASCO-SP-BRASIL

No.	Date
S2000307	APR. 14,2018

Transport details:
From: SHANGHAI　　To: SANTOS　　BY SEA FREIGHT

Marks & Nos.	No. & kinds of pkgs; Description of Goods	Gross Wt. Kilos	Net Wt. Kilos	Measurement M³
MJ HONGKONG 100566 SANTOS 1-470	PENGUIM HUMIDIFIER (BLACK BODY-WHITE DETAIL) 127V 1,280PCS 320CTNS 4PCS/CTN 220V 600PCS 150CTNS 4PCS/CTN AS PER DESCRIBED ON S/C NO. TR100566 DATED JULY 16,2018 L/C NO:H×××××	3,525KGS	3,995KGS	59.40CBM
TOTAL:	1,800PCS 470CTNS	3,525KGS	3,995KGS	59.40CBM

TOTAL FOUR HUNDRED AND SEVENTY CARTONS ONLY.

明基贸易有限公司(章)
MJ TRADE CO. ,LTD.
刘德福(章)

表 2-7-5 原产地证书

<table>
<tr><td colspan="2">1. Exporter:
MJ TRADE CO. ,LTD.
12F 7 BLDG SHATOUJIAO FREE TRADE ZONE, YANTIAN, SHENZHEN,
CHINA 416061</td><td colspan="3" rowspan="2">Certificate No. G114303101620078

CERTIFICATE OF ORIGIN
OF
THE PEOPLE'S REPUBLIC OF CHINA</td></tr>
<tr><td colspan="2">2. Consignee:
COMPANHIA BRASILEIRA DE DISTRIBUICAO ROD. ANHANGUERA, KM 17,8
OSASCO-SP-BRASIL</td></tr>
<tr><td colspan="2">3. Means of transport and route
From SHANGHAI To ANY PORT IN BRASIL BY SEA FREIGHT</td><td colspan="3" rowspan="2">5. For certifying authority use only</td></tr>
<tr><td colspan="2">4. Country/region of destination
BRAZIL</td></tr>
<tr><td>6. Marks & Nos.</td><td>7. Number and kind of packages; Description of goods</td><td>8. H. S. Code</td><td>9. Quantity</td><td>10. Numbers and Date of Invoice</td></tr>
<tr><td>MJ
HONGKONG
100566
SANTOS
1-470</td><td>FOUR HUNDRED AND SEVENTY (470) CARTONS OF PENGUIM HUMIDIFIER (BLACK BODY-WHITE DETAIL)</td><td>5,802.4060</td><td>1,880PCS</td><td>S2000307
APR. 14,2018</td></tr>
<tr><td colspan="2">11. Declaration by the exporter
The undersigned hereby declares that the above details and statements correct, that all the goods were produced in China and that they comply with the Rules of Origin of the people's Republic of China

明基贸易有限公司(章)
MJ TRADE CO. ,LTD.
文清(手签)
SHANGHAI APR. 18,2018
……………………………………
Place and date, signature and stamp of authorized signatory</td><td colspan="3">12. Certification
It is hereby certified that the declaration by the exporter is correct.

上海市
贸促会（商会）
（章）
刘元(手签)
SHANGHAI APR. 20,2018
……………………………………
Place and date, signature and stamp of certifying authority</td></tr>
</table>

表 2-7-6 保险单

<table>
<tr><td colspan="4">PICC
中国人保财险股份有限公司
PICC Property & Casualty Company Limited
总公司设于北京 一九四九年创立
Head Office Beijing Established in 1949</td></tr>
<tr><td colspan="4">货 物 运 输 保 险 单
CARGO TRANSPORTATION INSURANCE POLICY</td></tr>
<tr><td>发票号码 Invoice No.</td><td colspan="3">S2000307</td></tr>
<tr><td>合同号码 Contract No.</td><td>TR100566</td><td>保单号次 Policy No.</td><td>SH089921</td></tr>
<tr><td>信用证号 Credit No.</td><td colspan="3">H×××××</td></tr>
<tr><td>被保险人 Insured：</td><td colspan="3">COMPANHIA BRASILEIRA DE
DISTRIBUICAO ROD. ANHANGUERA，KM 17，8
OSASCO-SP-BRASIL</td></tr>
<tr><td colspan="4">中保财产保险有限公司(以下简称本公司)根据被保险人的要求，及其所缴付约定的保险费，按照本保险单承担险别和背面所载条款与下列特别条款承保下列货物运输保险，特签发本保险单。
This policy of Insurance witnesses that The People Insurance (Property) Company of China，Ltd. (hereinafter called the Company) at the request of the Insured and in consideration of the agreed premium paid by the Insured，undertakes to insure the under mentioned goods in transportation subject to the conditions of this Policy as per the Clauses printed overleaf and other special clauses attached hereon.</td></tr>
<tr><td>标记
Marks & No.</td><td>包装及数量
Quantity</td><td>保险货物项目
Description of goods</td><td>保险金额
Amount Insured</td></tr>
<tr><td>MJ HONGKONG
100566
SANTOS
1-470</td><td>1，880PCS
IN 470 CTNS</td><td>PENGUIM HUMIDIFIER
(BLACK BODY-WHITE DETAIL)</td><td>USD25，136.00</td></tr>
<tr><td colspan="4">总保险金额
Total Amount Insured：SAY U. S. DOLLARS TWENTY FIVE THOUSAND ONE HUNDRED AND THIRTY SIX ONLY.</td></tr>
<tr><td>保险费
Premium</td><td>启运日期
Date of commencement SEP. 12. 2018</td><td colspan="2">装载运输工具
Per conveyance FANYAW. 102</td></tr>
<tr><td>自
From SHANGHAI</td><td>经
Via</td><td colspan="2">至
To SANTOS</td></tr>
<tr><td colspan="4">承保险别 Conditions：</td></tr>
<tr><td colspan="4">covering all risks and war risk of Institute Cargo Clause (A)</td></tr>
<tr><td colspan="4">所保货物，如发生本保险单项下可能引起索赔的损失或损坏，应立即通知本公司下述代理人查勘。如有索赔，应向本公司提交保险单正本(本保险单共有 2 份正本)及有关文件。如一份正本已用于索赔，其余正本则自动失效。</td></tr>
</table>

续表

In the event of damage which may result in a claim under this Policy, immediate notice be given to the Company Agent as mentioned here under. Claims, if any, one of the Original Policy which has been issued in **TWO** Original(s) together with the relevant documents shall be surrendered to be Company, if one of the Original Policy has been accomplished, the others to be void.	
Insurance agent at destination:	
BRAIIL INSURANCE COMPANY 85 GANDY STREET, NHAVA SHEVA BRAIIL	
赔款偿付地点 Claim payable at SANTOS IN BRAIIL	中国人保财险股份有限公司上海市分公司 PICC Property & Casualty Co., Ltd., Shanghai Branch 谢丹 Authorized Signature
出单日期 Issuing date SEP. 12. 2018 SHANGHAI	
地址：中国上海市中山东一路 321 号 Address: 321 Zhongshan Road One (E) Shanghai China	

表 2-7-7 提单

Shipper MJ TRADE CO., LTD. 12F 7 BLDG SHATOUJIAO FREE TRADE ZONE, YANTIAN, SHENZHEN, CHINA 416061		B/L No. 承运人 *CARRIER* 中远集装箱运输有限公司 COSCO CONTAINER LINES Port-to-Port or Combined Transport BILL OF LADING
Consignee COMPANHIA BRASILEIRA DE DISTRIBUICAO ROD. ANHANGUERA, KM 17,8 OSASCO-SP-BRASIL		
Notify party COMPANHIA BRASILEIRA DE DISTRIBUICAO ROD. ANHANGUERA, KM 17,8 OSASCO-SP-BRASIL		ORIGINAL RECEIVED in external apparent good order and condition except as otherwise noted. The total number of packages or units stuffed in the container. The weight, measure, marks, numbers, quality, contents and value mentioned in this Bill of Lading are to be acknowledged and agreed to. The signing of this Bill of Loading is not to be considered as such an agreement. On presentation of this Bill of Lading duly endorsed to the *Carrier* by or on behalf of the Holder of Bill of Lading, the rights (Terms of Bill of Lading continued on the back hereof)
Pre-carriage by	Place of Receipt	
Ocean Vessel Voy. No. FANYA W. 102	Port of loading SHANGHAI	
Port of Discharge SANTOS BRAZIL	Place of delivery	

Marks & Nos. Container No.	No. & kind of pkgs	Description of goods	Gross weight	Measurement
MJ HONGKONG 100566 SANTOS 1-470	470CTNS	PENGUIM HUMIDIFIER (BLACK BODY-WHITE DETAIL)	1,880PCS	59.40CBM

续表

<table>
<tr><td colspan="8">CNO. :TEXU47683001
SNO. :WG9006

S/C NO. : TR100566
L/C NO. : H×××××</td></tr>
<tr><td colspan="3">Total No. of container or other pkgs or units (in words)</td><td colspan="5">SAY FOUR HUNDRED AND SEVENTY CARTONS ONLY.</td></tr>
<tr><td colspan="3">Freight & charges
FREIGHT COLLECT</td><td>Revenue Tons</td><td>Rate</td><td>Per</td><td>Prepaid</td><td>Collect</td></tr>
<tr><td rowspan="2">Ex rate</td><td>Prepaid at</td><td colspan="2">Payable at</td><td colspan="4">Place and date of issue:
SHANGHAI SEP. 12. 2018</td></tr>
<tr><td>Total prepaid</td><td colspan="2">No. of B(s)/L
THREE</td><td colspan="4" rowspan="2">Signed by COSCO CONTAINER LINES SHANGHAI BRANCH
As agent for the carrier named above 李四</td></tr>
<tr><td colspan="4">Laden on board the Vessel:
Date: SEP. 12,2018
By: C. C. L. SHANGHAI</td></tr>
</table>

实训八　信用证方式下进口单据缮制

一、实训资料

1. 购货合同(见表 2-8-1)。

表 2-8-1　购货合同

ZWY TRADING(SHANGHAI)CO. ,LTD.
ROOM 916,NO. 500 BINGKE ROAD,WAIGAOQIAO
FREE TRADE ZONE,SHANGHAI,P. R. C. 201631

TEL：86-512-6251 8881
FAX：86-512-6715 3385

Purchase Order
ZWY P/O LIG16031402T
Date：2018-03-29
Ship Via：DHL
Terms：FOB
DHL ACC：951087040

TO：COORSTEK
4544 McGrath Street Ventura California 93003 U. S. A.
Attn：Debra Pierpoint
Tel：(805)644-5583
Fax：(805)644-2016

Delivery：See Below
Payment：Net 105 Days
Currency：USD

ITEM	Q'ty	Description	U/P(US$)	TOTAL(US$)	Delivery date	RFQ#	JOB#
1	5665	Capillary	3.627	20,549.91	03/29/18		

Total amount(US$)：20,549.91

INVOICE TO：ZWY TRADING(SHANGHAI)CO. ,LTD.
ROOM 916, NO. 500 BINGKE ROAD, WAIGAOQIAO FREE TRADE ZONE, SHANGHAI, P. R. C. 201631
SHIP TO：ZWY TRADING(SHANGHAI)CO. ,LTD. SUZHOU BRANCH
C203. INTERNATIONAL SCIENCE & TECHNOLOGY PARK,SUZHOU INDUSTRIAL PARK,JIANGSU
Contact Person：Fenny zhou
TEL：+86-512-6251 9725
FAX：86-512-6715 3385
Instructions for shipping documents：
* Type on inv/pck slip：Cust P/N
* Show on inv/pck slip：
"Automatic Die-Adhering Machine Capillary"after the part number
Manufacture from USA
Weight,size of each carton
Total q'ty and total weight of carton
* Pls show customer's name and customer's PO number

续表

* Send "Declaration of No Wood Packaging Material" with shipment * Send original invoice & 3 copies with shipment * Original signature & date must be no all copies in blue ink Fax all shipping documents to Fenny at ZWY  PREPARED  SIGNATURE

2. 发票(见表 2-8-2)。

表 2-8-2 发票

<table>
<tr><td colspan="2">**COORSTEK**
Amazing solutions.
4544 McGrath St.
VENTURA, CA 93003
United States
SEE REMIT-TO ADDRESS INFORMATION BELOW</td><td>**INVOICE**
--ORIGINAL--</td><td>INVOICE NO. :2282611
CUSTOMER PO:LIG16031402T
INVOICE DATE:03/29/18
CREDIT TERMS:105 Days</td><td>Page:1 of 1</td></tr>
<tr><td colspan="2">ZWY TRADING(SHANGHAI)CO. ,LTD.
ROOM 204,2F XINYI BUILDING
NO. 2005 YANGGAO NORTH ROAD
WAIGAOQIAO FREE TRADE ZONE
SHANGHAI,P. R. ,...201631 China

BILL TO:64728002 TAX ID:</td><td colspan="3"><table><tr><td colspan="2">COORSTEK ORDER #:1005451</td></tr><tr><td>SHIP DATE:
03/29/18</td><td>SHIP TO: 64727-07</td></tr><tr><td>SHIP VIA:
FEDEX</td><td rowspan="4">ZWY TRADING COMPANY,LTD.
C203 INTL SCIENCE $ TECH PARK
JIANGSU PROVINCE,P. R. ,...215021
CHINA</td></tr><tr><td>FREIGHT TERMS:
FOB</td></tr><tr><td>SHIP POINT:
VENTURA,CA</td></tr><tr><td>BOL:</td></tr></table></td></tr>
<tr><td colspan="2">SALES PERSON: Debra Pier point</td><td colspan="3">PHONE:905-644-5593-113</td></tr>
<tr><td colspan="2">NUMBER OF CARTONS:</td><td colspan="2">NUMBER OF PALLETS:</td><td>TOTAL WEIGHT:</td></tr>
</table>

续表

<table>
<tr><th>LN</th><th>ITEM NUMBER/DESCRIPTION</th><th>S/C</th><th>UOM</th><th>QTY SHIPPED</th><th>NET PRICE</th><th>EXTENDED PRICE</th></tr>
<tr><td>1</td><td colspan="6">*
THIS IS AN EXPORT ORDER. PRICES STATED ARE IN U. S. DOLLARS.
COUNTRY OF ORIGIN U. S. A.
*
THESE ITEMS WERE SOLD WITH EXPRESSED CONSIDERATION THAT THE BUYER AGREES TO
COMPLY WITH ALL APPLICABLE UNITED STATES EXPORT CONTROL LAWS. THESE COMMODITIES, TECHNOLOGIES OR SOFTWARE WERE EXPORTED FROM THE UNITED STATES
IN ACCORDANCE WITH THE EXPORT ADMINISTRATION REGULATIONS. DIVERSION CONTRARY
TO U. S. LAW PROHIBITED.
*
FOR ULTIMATE DESTINATION:CHINA
*
LICENSE:NLR
*
ROUTED(Y/N):Y
*
AUTOMATIC DIE ADHERING MACHINE CAPILLARIES
MANUFACTURE FROM USA
THERE IS ONE CARTON BOX ONLY
SHIPMENT MADE WITH ONLY PAPER CARTON
DOES NOT CONTAIN ANY WOODEN PACKAGING
*
* 03/29/18
____
COORSTEK INC. DATE</td></tr>
<tr><td></td><td>Class Description:
Capillary</td><td>0650</td><td>EA</td><td>5,665PCS</td><td>$ 3.627</td><td>$ 20,549.91</td></tr>
</table>

<table>
<tr><td colspan="2">Please make sure your advising bank references CoorsTek Invoice # 2282611 ensure proper credit. Notice is hereby given that CoorTek Terms and Conditions of Sale, Revision 060106, shall apply to this Order and can be found at http://www.coorstek.com/resources/85101426 Terms & Conditions SALE.pdf. Please contact your Customer Service Representative if you are experiencing any problems accessing this link.</td><td colspan="2">LINE TOTAL: 5,665 PCS $ 20,549.91
PLEASE PAY: 20,549.91USD</td></tr>
<tr><td>USA
Remittance:
CoorsTek, Inc.
Dept, # 1515
Denver,
CO80291-1515</td><td>USA Electronic Remittance:
CoorsTek, Inc., ABA
#:121000248
Wells Fargo Swift
#:WFBIUS6S
Acct#:4945080380</td><td>Canadian Funds Remittance:
CoorsTek, Inc.
P. O. Box 9122
Station M
Calgary, Alberta
T3C0J2 Canada</td><td>Euro Funds Remittance;
Bayerische landesbank Girozcntralc, Munich Germany
SWIFT ID: BYLADEMM ACCT: 8/8/19401
BENEE: (WFBIU86S) Wells Fargo Bank Na San Francisco, CA FURTHER CREDIT: CoorsTek. Inc. 110897EUR</td></tr>
<tr><td colspan="4">COORSTEK accepts VISA, MASTERCARD and AMERICAN EXPRESS!</td></tr>
</table>

3. 补充资料。

最迟开证日期：2018 年 3 月 28 日

开户行及账号：ZWY TRADING(SHANGHAI)CO.,LTD. SUZHOU BRANCH,4945080380

法人代表：杜媄

CONTAINER NO.:1×40′COSU829234-2　　自重：3 960 千克

货物存放地点：黄源仓库

入境口岸：浦江海关(2201)　　买方报检单位登记号：3101460789

用途：其他　　产地：美国加州　　报检人：李月

报检日期：2018 年 4 月 2 日

运输工具：XIJ V.432　　运单号：CUDMN040690024

报验时提交的随附单据：合同、信用证、发票、装箱单

需要的证单：品质证书(1 正 2 副)，出境货物换证凭单(1 正 1 副)

贸易方式：一般贸易　　进口货物申报日期：2018 年 6 月 2 日

毛重(千克)：580　　净重(千克)：512

运费：350 美元　　保费：75 美元

报关随附单证：入境货物通关单，原产地证书

二、实训要求

请以"单证员"的工作角色，根据以上资料缮制下列单据。

(1) 根据合同及相关资料用英文缮制开证申请书(见表 2-8-3)。

表 2-8-3　开证申请书

IRREVOCABLE DOCUMENTARY CREDIT APPLICATION

To:　　　　　　　　　　Date:

<table>
<tr><td colspan="2" rowspan="3">Beneficiary(full name and address)</td><td>L/C No.

Ex-Card No.
Contract No.</td></tr>
<tr><td>Date and place of expiry of the credit</td></tr>
<tr><td></td></tr>
<tr><td>Partial shipment
□allowed
□not allowed</td><td>Transshipment
□allowed
□not allowed</td><td rowspan="2">□Issued by airmail
□With brief advice by teletransmission
□Issued by express delivery
□Issued by teletransmission (which shall be the operative instrument)</td></tr>
<tr><td colspan="2" rowspan="2">Loading on board/dispatch/taking in charge at/from

Not late than
For transportation to</td></tr>
<tr><td>Amount (both in figures and words)</td></tr>
</table>

续表

Description of goods:	Credit available with □by sight payment □by acceptance □by negotiation □by deferred payment at against the documents detailed herein □and beneficiary's drafts for ____% of the invoice value at on
Packing:	□FOB □CFR □CIF □or other terms

Documents required: (marked with ×)

1. ( ) Signed Commercial invoice in ________ copies indication.
2. ( ) Full set of clean on board ocean Bill of Lading made out ________ and ( ) blank endorsed, marked"freight" ( ) collect/( ) prepaid Notify.
3. ( ) Air Waybill showing "freight( ) to collect/( ) prepaid ( ) indicating freight amount" and consigned to ________.
4. ( ) Memovandum issued by ________ consigned to ________.
5. ( ) Insurance Policy/Certificate in ________ copies for 110% of the invoice value showing claims payable in China in currency of the draft, blank endorsed, covering ( ) Ocean Marine Transportation/( ) Air Transportation/( ) Over Land transportation ( ) All risks, war risk.
6. ( ) Packing List in ________ copies indication gross and net weights for each package and packing conditions as called for by the L/C.
7. ( ) Certificate of Quantity/Weight in ________ copies issued by an independent surveyor at the loading port, indicating the actual surveyed quantity/weight of shipped goods as well as the packing condition.
8. ( ) Certificate of Quality in ________ copies issued by ( ) manufacturer/( ) public recognized surveyor/( ).
9. ( ) Beneficiary's Certified copy of cable/telex dispatched to the accountees within ________ hours after shipment advising ( ) name of vessel/( ) flight No. /( ) wagon No. , date, quantity, weight and value of shipment.
10. ( ) Beneficiary's Certificate certifying that extra copies of the documents have been dispatched according to the contract terms.
11. ( ) Shipping Co's certificate attesting that the carrying vessel is chartered or booked by accountee or their shipping agents.
12. ( ) Other documents, if any:

Additional Instructions:

1. ( ) All banking charges outside opening bank are for beneficiary's account.
2. ( ) Documents must be presented within ________ days after the date of issuance of the transport documents but within the validity of this credit.
3. ( ) Third party as shipper is not acceptable. Short form/Blank back B/L is not acceptable.
4. ( ) Both quantity and amount ________% more or less are allowed.
5. ( ) Prepaid freight drawn in excess of L/C amount is acceptable against presentation of original charges voucher issued by( ) Shipping Co./Air Line/or it's agent.
6. ( ) All documents to be forwarded in one cover, unless otherwise stated above.
7. ( ) Other terms, if any:

Account No.: with ____________________ (name of bank)

Transacted by: (Applicant: name signature of authorized person)

Telephone No.: (with seal)

（2）缮制入境货物报检单（见表 2-8-4）。

表 2-8-4　入境货物报检单

中华人民共和国出入境检验检疫
入境货物报检单

报检单位（加盖公章）：　　　　　　　　　　　　　　　编　　号：________

报检单位登记号：　　　　　联系人：　　　电话：　　　报检日期：　　年　　月　　日

发货人	（中文）	企业性质（划"√"）	□合资 □外资 □合作
	（外文）		
收货人	（中文）		
	（外文）		

货物名称（中/外文）	H. S. 编码	产地	数/重量	货物总值	包装种类及数量
运输工具名称号码				合同号	

贸易方式		贸易国别（地区）		提单/运单号	
到货日期		起运国家（地区）		许可证/审批号	
卸货日期		起运口岸		入境口岸	
索赔有效期至		经停口岸		目的地	
集装箱规格、数量及号码					
合同、信用证订立的检验检疫条款或特殊要求				货物存放地点	
				用途	

随附单据（划"√"或补填）		标记及号码	＊外商投资企业（划"√"）	□是　□否
□合同 □信用证 □发票 □提/运单 □兽医卫生证书 □植物检疫证书 □动物检疫证书 □卫生证书 □原产地证 □许可/审批文件	□到货通知 □装箱单 □质保书 □理货清单 □磅码单 □验收报告 □提货单		＊检验检疫费	
			总金额（人民币元）	
			计费人	
			收费人	
报检人郑重声明： 1. 本人被授权报检。 2. 上列填写内容正确属实。 签名：________			领取证单	
			日期	
			签名	

注：有"＊"号栏由出入境检验检疫机关填写。　　　　◆国家出入境检验检疫局制

（3）缮制进口货物报关单（见表 2-8-5）。

表 2-8-5　进口货物报关单

中华人民共和国海关进口货物报关单

预录人编号：　　　　海关编号：　　　（××海关）　　　　　　　　页码/页数：

<table>
<tr><td>境内发货人</td><td colspan="2">进境关别</td><td colspan="2">进口日期</td><td colspan="2">申报日期</td><td colspan="2">备案号</td></tr>
<tr><td>境外发货人</td><td colspan="2">运输方式</td><td colspan="2">运输工具名称及航次号</td><td colspan="2">提运单号</td><td colspan="2">货物存放地点</td></tr>
<tr><td>消费使用单位</td><td colspan="2">监管方式</td><td colspan="2">征免性质</td><td colspan="2">许可证号</td><td colspan="2">启运港</td></tr>
<tr><td>合同协议号</td><td colspan="2">贸易国（地区）</td><td colspan="2">启运国（地区）</td><td colspan="2">经停港</td><td colspan="2">入境口岸</td></tr>
<tr><td>包装种类</td><td>件数</td><td>毛重（千克）</td><td>净重（千克）</td><td>成交方式</td><td>运费</td><td colspan="2">保费</td><td>杂费</td></tr>
<tr><td colspan="9">随附单证及编号</td></tr>
<tr><td colspan="9">标记唛码及备注</td></tr>
<tr><td colspan="9">项号　商品编号　商品名称及规格型号　数量及单位　单价/总价/币制　原产国（地区）　最终目的国（地区）　境内货源地　征免</td></tr>
<tr><td colspan="9"></td></tr>
<tr><td colspan="9"></td></tr>
<tr><td colspan="9"></td></tr>
<tr><td colspan="9"></td></tr>
<tr><td colspan="9"></td></tr>
<tr><td colspan="9"></td></tr>
<tr><td colspan="6">报关人员　　报关人员证号　　电话
兹申明对以上内容承担如实申报、依法纳税之责任
申报单位　　　　　　　　申报单位（签章）</td><td colspan="3">海关批注及签章</td></tr>
</table>

第三部分

基础理论与知识综合训练

综合训练一

一、单项选择题

1. 以下关于汇付的陈述正确的是(　　)。

　A. 由于汇出汇款申请书是汇款人和汇出行之间的一种契约，所以由于汇款申请书的错漏引起的延误、差错等，汇款人应自负后果

　B. 汇付属于顺汇性质

　C. 汇付的基本当事人包括汇款人和收款人

　D. 汇付方式比托收方式更安全、更迅速

2. 在托运、报检和报关的单证中，由出口商出具的单证有(　　)。

　A. 发票、报关单、报检单和提单

　B. 发票、装箱单、报检单和通关单

　C. 发票、报关单、装箱单和提单

　D. 发票、装箱单、报检单和托运单

3. 我国某公司与美国某公司以 CFR Ex ship's hold New York 的条件成交了一笔出口生意，按照一般惯例，这批货物在纽约港的卸货费用应由(　　)承担。

　A. 美国公司　　B. 我国公司　　C. 承运人　　D. 保险公司

4. 我方以每箱 100 美元 CIF 纽约价出口货物 100 箱，合同允许 5%的数量增减，实际交货 105 箱，我方应收款(　　)。

　A. 10 000 美元　　B. 10 500 美元　　C. 9 500 美元　　D. 双方再协议

5. 一般情况下，按 CFR 贸易术语成交的合同中，不应计入货物价格的是(　　)。

　A. 货物成本　　B. 海运费　　C. 保险费　　D. 各项出口税费

6. 根据出入境检验检疫局的规定，出境货物最迟应于报关或装运前(　　)天报验。

　A. 3　　B. 7　　C. 10　　D. 15

7. 关于各种单据的出单日期，下列表述正确的是(　　)。

　A. 保险单的出单期可以晚于已装船提单的出单期

　B. 提单签发日可迟于信用证或合同规定的装运期限

　C. 汇票的日期可以比发票早

　D. 议付单据中，发票日期一般比其他单据早

8. 在以 CIF 和 CFR 术语成交的条件下，货物运输保险分别由卖方和买方办理，运输途中货物灭失和损失的风险描述正确的是(　　)。

　A. 前者由卖方承担，后者由买方承担

　B. 均由卖方承担

　C. 均由买方承担

　D. 前者由买方承担，后者由卖方承担

9. 卖方在货物交付运输前不必预先通知买方交运时间的贸易术语是(　　)。

A. FOB　B. CFR　C. CPT　D. DDU

10. 商业汇票是指汇票的(　　)为商业企业的汇票。

A. 受票人　B. 受款人　C. 付款人　D. 出票人

11. 汇票的抬头做成指示样式,说明(　　)。

A. 汇票不能通过背书转让　B. 汇票无须通过背书即可转让

C. 仅能由银行转让　D. 须经过背书方能转让

12. 根据 UCP 600 的规定,若信用证没有特别说明,则信用证(　　)。

A. 未注明“Transferable”字样或条款,即为可转让信用证

B. 未注明“Irrevocable”字样,即为可撤销信用证

C. 未注明“Confirmed”字样,即为不保兑信用证

D. 未注明是否即期付款,即为远期付款信用证

13. 如果信用证未规定交单期限,根据 UCP 600 的规定,受益人必须在货物装船后(　　)天内交单议付,但不能超过信用证的有效期。

A. 15　B. 21　C. 3　D. 7

14. 联合国世界卫生组织向我国提供数台英国制造的医疗设备。英国受联合国委托,直接将该设备运送到我国。则进口报关单上的起运国填报________,原产地填报________。(　　)

A. 联合国　英国　B. 英国　联合国

C. 联合国　联合国　D. 英国　英国

15. 进口货物到达目的地后,进口商应及时填写(　　),随附进口合同书、进口商业发票和运输单据等有关证件,向当地出入境货物检验检疫局申请检验。

A. 入境货物报验单　B. 出境货物报验单

C. 入境货物通关单　D. 出境货物通关单

16. 托收汇票一般应在出票条款栏内加注(　　)。

A. COLLECTNG　B. FOR COLLECTION

C. COLLECTION　D. ON COLLECTION

17. CIF Ex ship's hold 属于(　　)。

A. 内陆交货类　B. 装运港船上交货类

C. 目的港交货类　D. 目的地交货类

18. 货物从上海运往纽约,根据 INCOTERMS 2000,如果采取贸易术语 CIF NEW YORK,卖方对货物所承担的风险责任界限是(　　)。

A. 货物在上海卸下卖方车辆以前　B. 货物在纽约装下买方车辆以前

C. 货物在上海装船越过船舷以前　D. 货物在纽约卸货越过船舷以前

19. 我国检验检疫管制的商品,必须向海关提交出入境检验检疫机构签发的单证是(　　)。

A. 进出口货物报关单　B. 入境货物通关单

C. 进口许可证　D. 进口收汇核销单

20. 上海甲公司向美国纽约乙公司报价,出口货物从上海运至纽约,单价的正确表示方

法应为(　　)。

A. USD100.00 PER CARTON

B. USD100.00 PER CARTON CIF NEWYORK

C. USD100.00 PER CARTON FOB NEWYORK

D. USD100.00 PER CARTON CIF SHANGHAI

21. 按照现行的国际贸易惯例解释,若以 CFR 条件成交,买卖双方风险划分是以(　　)为界。

A. 货物交给承运人保管　　B. 货物交给第一承运人保管

C. 货物在装运港越过船舷　　D. 货物到达目的港

22. 我国甲公司欲与韩国乙公司签订进口合同,进口冰箱到中国,拟采取海运方式,乙公司承担将货物运至指定目的地的运费并支付保险。根据 INCOTERMS 2010,应采用的贸易术语为(　　)。

A. EXW　　B. CIF　　C. FAS　　D. FOB

23. 汇票是由(　　)签发的,命令付款人在见票时或者在指定日期无条件支付确定金额给收款人或者持票人的票据。

A. 承兑人　　B. 收款人　　C. 出票人　　D. 付款人

24. 托收的优点不包括(　　)。

A. 进口人可免去申请开立信用证的手续,不必预付银行押金

B. 属于银行信用,出口人能安全、及时收汇

C. 有利于资金融通和周转,增强出口商品的竞争力

D. 减少费用支出

25. 信用证规定到期日为 2018 年 5 月 15 日,最迟装运日为 2018 年 4 月 30 日,如果提单出单日为 2018 年 4 月 10 日,则受益人最迟交单日应为(　　)。

A. 4 月 30 日　　B. 4 月 10 日　　C. 5 月 15 日　　D. 5 月 1 日

26. 我国某公司与外商签订一份 CIF 出口合同,以 L/C 为支付方式。国外银行开来的信用证中规定:"信用证有效期为 8 月 8 日,最迟装运期为 7 月 31 日。"我方加紧备货出运,于 7 月 21 日取得大副收据,并换回正本已装船清洁提单,我方应不迟于(　　)向银行提交单据。

A. 7 月 21 日　　B. 7 月 31 日　　C. 8 月 8 日　　D. 8 月 11 日

27. 厂商发票是厂方出具给出口商的销售货物的凭证。来证要求提供厂商发票,其目的是(　　)。

A. 检查是否有削价倾销行为,以便确定是否征收"反倾销税"

B. 按某些国家法令规定,出口商对其国输入货物时必须取得进口国在出口国或其邻近地区的领事签证的、作为装运单据一部分和货物进口报关的前提条件之一的特殊发票

C. 为进口商向其本国当局申请进口许可证或请求核批外汇之用

D. 作为国际商务单据中的基础单据,是缮制报关单、产地证、报检单、投保单等其他单据的依据

28. 出口货物的发货人或其代理人,在办理了出口申报、配合查验、缴纳税费、海关放行

后，持凭海关加盖（　　）的出口装货凭证，通知码头、机场等有关单位装运出口货物。

A. 监管章　　B. 放行章　　C. 单证章　　D. 验讫章

29. 单证缮制必须做到正确、完整、及时、简明和整洁，其中（　　）是单证工作的前提。

A. 正确　　B. 完整　　C. 及时　　D. 简明

30. 一张汇票规定见票后60天付款，而持票人于2018年9月28日提示承兑，则付款到期日为（　　）。

A. 2018年11月26日　　B. 2018年11月27日

C. 2018年11月28日　　D. 2018年11月29日

31. 本票是出票人签发的，承诺（　　）在见票时无条件支付确定的金额给收款人或持票人的票据。

A. 出票人本人　　B. 承兑人　　C. 付款人　　D. 议付行

32. （　　）是结汇单证中最重要的单据，能让有关当事人了解一笔交易的全貌，其他单据都以其为依据。

A. 装箱单　　B. 产地证书　　C. 发票　　D. 提单

33. 在进料加工和补偿贸易中常使用（　　）。

A. 循环信用证　　B. 对开信用证

C. 对背信用证　　D. 预支信用证

34. 信用证的到期日为12月31日，最迟装运期为12月16日，最迟交单日期为运输单据出单后15天，出口人备妥货物安排出运的时间是12月10日，则出口人最迟应于（　　）向银行交单议付。

A. 12月16日　　B. 12月25日　　C. 12月28日　　D. 12月31日

35. 根据UCP 600的规定，正本运输单据受益人或其代表在不迟于发运日之后的21个日历日内交单，并不得迟于信用证的截止日。若发生正本提单交银行超过提单签发日期21天，则该正本提单为（　　）。

A. 过期提单　　B. 倒签提单　　C. 不清洁提单　　D. 无效提单

36. 从2004年11月15日起，货主提供的报关单必须用有海关编号的新版通用业务单证，其中出口报关单的颜色为（　　）。

A. 进料加工报关单粉红色、来料加工报关单浅蓝色、一般贸易报关单浅绿色

B. 进料加工报关单浅蓝色、来料加工报关单粉红色、一般贸易报关单浅绿色

C. 进料加工报关单粉红色、来料加工报关单浅绿色、一般贸易报关单浅蓝色

D. 进料加工报关单浅绿色、来料加工报关单粉红色、一般贸易报关单浅蓝色

37. 对于原产地证书，如果客户要求官方提供，则应由（　　）出具。

A. 国家质检局　　B. 贸促会　　C. 商会　　D. 以上答案都不对

38. 假设提单的签发日期为“MARCH 24，2018”，那么以下保单的开航日期中，填写错误的是（　　）。

A. MARCH 24，2018　　B. AS PE RB/L

C. MARCH 30，2018　　D. MARCH 23，2018

39. 2011年12月1日起，（　　）企业逐笔业务均须到外汇局进行审核登记后方可办理结汇或付汇。

A. A类　　B. B类　　C. C类　　D. D类

40. (　　)使国际贸易节省了时间和费用,减少了单证出错的情况。

A. 网上洽谈　　B. 电子支付　　C. 单证电子化　　D. 电子合同

二、多项选择题

1. 单证缮制的具体要求包括(　　)。

A. 正确　　B. 完整　　C. 及时　　D. 简明和整洁

2. 进口合同如采用FOB条件,下面表述正确的有(　　)。

A. 一般由出口商办理保险事宜

B. 出口商提供的单据中应有发票

C. 发票中的货物描述应与买卖合同或信用证规定相符

D. 提单中应有“Freight payable at destination”字样

3. 集装箱班轮运输的优越性包括(　　)。

A. 提高了装卸效率,减轻了劳动强度,提高了港口吞吐能力

B. 提高了货物运输质量,减少了货损货差现象,并推动了货物包装的标准化

C. 加快了车船周转,缩短了货物在途时间,降低了运营成本

D. 有利于多种运输方式的灵活运用

4. 集装箱海运出口托运时,关于场站收据的表述正确的有(　　)。

A. 是堆场或货运站收货的凭证

B. 是划分承、托双方责任的重要依据

C. 是发货人凭以换取提单的唯一凭证

D. 是承运人通知装运船舶接货装船的命令

5. 商业发票是出口商在准备全套出口文件时首先缮制的单证,因为在出口货物装运前的(　　)环节中要使用它。

A. 托运订舱　　B. 办理投保　　C. 出口报关　　D. 商品报检

6. 企业审核单据的标准为“四相符”,即(　　)。

A. 单证相符　　B. 单单相符　　C. 单货相符　　D. 单同相符

7. 开证行审单时如发现不符点可拒付货物,其理由可以是(　　)。

A. 单证不符　　B. 单单不符

C. 货物不符合合同规定　　D. 货物未装运

8. 贸易术语DAP与DDP的区别有(　　)。

A. 进口报关手续的办理人不同

B. 交货地点不同

C. 风险转移地点不同

D. DAP卖方不负责卸货,DDP卖方负责卸货

9. 按照INCOTERMS 2010,以下仅适用于海洋、内河运输方式的术语有(　　)。

A. FAS　　B. CIP　　C. FCA　　D. CIF

E. DDP

10. 在装运港完成交货义务的术语有(　　)。

A. FOB　　B. DAP　　C. FAS　　D. CFR

E. DDP

11. 对票汇的概念,表述正确的有(　　)。

A. 票汇使用银行汇票,是一种银行信用

B. 票汇使用银行汇票,是一种商业信用

C. 银行开具的汇票由买方径寄卖方

D. 票汇支付方式可以通过背书转让

E. 票汇不通过银行的资金调拨

12. 采用托收方式时,应特别注意的问题有(　　)。

A. 考虑进口方的资信情况

B. 国外代收行一般不能由进口方指定

C. 应采用 CIF 或 CIP 贸易术语

D. 不宜对贸易管制和外汇管制较严的国家

13. 福费廷业务中的包买商承担收取债务的一切责任和风险,包括原本出口人应承担的(　　)。

A. 汇价风险　　B. 利率风险　　C. 信用风险　　D. 资金转移风险

14. 一般不适宜采用信用证结算方式的贸易术语为(　　)。

A. CIF　　B. DAT　　C. FOB　　D. EXW

15. 装运通知是指出口商在出口货物装运后,向收货人或其通知人发出货物装运情况的书面文件,其主要作用有(　　)。

A. 考虑进口方的资信情况

B. 国外代收行一般不能由进口方指定

C. 应采用 CIF 或 CIP 贸易术语

D. 不宜对贸易管制和外汇管制较严的国家

16. 运用电子托运单订舱是实现未来我国“无纸化贸易运输”项目的途径之一。电子托运单的优点主要有(　　)。

A. 订舱速度快　　B. 形式简单

C. 电子托运单可与纸质托运单共存　　D. 差错率降低

17. 海运提单的作用主要有(　　)。

A. Receipt for the goods　　B. Documents of title

C. Evidence of Contract of Carrier　　D. Commercial Bill

18. 所谓清洁运输单据,是指承运人未在运输单据上加注针对货物表面状况的不良批注。反之,则称作不清洁运输单据。下列属于不清洁提单的是(　　)。

A. 两袋扯破(2 bags torn)

B. “对货物或包装生锈免责(Not responsible for rusty)”或“对货物或包装破损免责(Not responsible for breakage)”

C. 提单注明货物装入开顶集装箱

D. 短装十箱(10 cases short shipped)

19. 航空运输中,托运人可以对航空货运单上除(　　)以外的其他条款向承运人提出更改。

A. 航空运费　　B. 保险金额　　C. 申明价值　　D. 货物价值

20. 以下关于报关单正确填报的选项有（ ）。

A. 裸装货物在件数栏内填报为 1

B. 毛重栏的计量单位为千克，货物不足 1 千克的填报为 1

C. 净重栏的计量单位为千克，填报的计量单位也可以为磅（折算成磅填报）

D. 数量和单位栏的计量单位按照成交数量和单位填报，不必按照海关计量单位填

21. 我国出口商可以向（ ）机构或其下属机构申领原产地证书。

A. 中华人民共和国海关

B. 中华人民共和国国家质量监督检验检疫总局

C. 中国国际贸易促进委员会

D. 中华人民共和国商务部

E. 中华人民共和国财政部

22. 下列关于普惠制产地证书的表述，正确的有（ ）。

A. 出口企业最迟应于货物装运 5 天后申请普惠制产地证书

B. 如果出口的产品含有进口成分，应提交《含进口成分受惠商品成本明细单》

C. 普惠制产地的证书申报日期不得早于发票日期，不得晚于提单日期

D. 普惠制产地证书主要有三种格式，其中“格式 A”使用范围较广

23. 对制单收汇的要求有（ ）。

A. 保险单的日期不能迟于提单日期

B. 商业发票的名称必须和信用证的一致

C. 提单的抬头应为凭卖方指示或空白抬头

D. 汇票的受票人必须做成开证行或付款行

E. 保险单的被保险人必须做成开证申请人

24. 形式发票也称预开发票或估价发票，通常在未成交之前，为进口商向其本国当局申请进口许可证或请求核批外汇之用。关于形式发票，下列表述正确的有（ ）。

A. 形式发票不是一种正式发票

B. 能用于托收和议付，正式成交后不需另外重新缮制商业发票

C. 形式发票与商业发票的关系密切，信用证在货物描述后面常有“按照某月某日之形式发票”等条款

D. 假如来证附有形式发票，则形式发票构成信用证的组成部分，制单时要按形式发票内容全部打上

25. 当信用证要求同时出具（ ），但未列明具体内容时，出口商可以将这几种单据合并缮制，分别冠以相应的单据名称，并满足信用证对各类单据的份数要求。

A. 发票　　B. 装箱单　　C. 重量单　　D. 尺码单

26. 按照 UCP 600 的规定，银行接受 7 种装运单据。除非另有约定，银行不接受卖方提交的（ ）。

A. 收货待运提单　　B. 租船提单

C. 邮局收据　　D. 不清洁提单

27. 发票是国外卖方或厂商对货物出具的明细账单，它的内容和作用包括（ ）。

A. 收货人的名称、地址、发票开具日期及具名签字

B. 提单、装箱单或磅码单、品质与重量证书、原产地证书等的号码

C. 它的作用主要是作为办理接运和结算的一种重要单证

D. 将货名、规格、件数、重量、单价、金额、H. S. 编码、唛头标记、包装件数及装载船名,根据合同和信用证的规定做较为详细的说明

28. 保险单的生效日期原则上不得迟于货物单据上的日期,这些日期包括(　　)。

A. 装货日期　　B. 发货(或在联合货运场)日期

C. 承运日期　　D. 检验日期

29. 在产地证、许可证等清关文件上,收货人的表示方法有(　　)。

A. 进口商的账户行

B. 填写实际买主

C. 当进口商有具体规定时,按要求办

D. 若进口商没有提出要求,可按提单上的通知人或其他货运单据上的收货人填

30. 按 CIFC 价格条件成交,报价中包含(　　)。

A. 包装费　　B. 国内费用　　C. 国外运费　　D. 保险费

E. 佣金

31. 采用信用证结汇时,银行要求"单证表面严格相符"。但如果出现单证不符,出口商可以采用(　　)。

A. 表提　　B. 电提　　C. 跟证托收　　D. 押汇

32. 使用制单软件制作单证的优势包括(　　)。

A. 无纸化　　B. 节省时间和费用

C. 准确度高　　D. 提高出口方的资信度

33. 中国财产保险公司《海洋运输货物保险条款》中的基本险包括(　　)。

A. 水渍险　　B. 平安险　　C. 战争险　　D. 一切险

34. 发票的抬头人应是(　　)。

A. 托收项下的卖方　　B. 托收项下的买方

C. 信用证项下的受益人　　D. 信用证项下的开证申请人

35. 海运提单中运费缴付方式填写为"FREIGHT PREPAID",如果信用证没有特别要求,那么此缴付方式一般适用于(　　)。

A. FOB　　B. CFR　　C. CIP　　D. CIF

36. 运输包装分为单件运输包装和集合运输包装,属于集合运输包装的有(　　)。

A. 托盘　　B. 箱　　C. 集装箱　　D. 包

37. 根据国家质量监督检验检疫总局的规定,出境货物报验时须提交的有关单据包括(　　)。

A. 外贸合同(确认书)　　B. 信用证

C. 提单　　D. 发票

38. 下列表述正确的有(　　)。

A. 航空运单不是物权凭证　　B. 航空运单是物权凭证

C. 航空运单不可转让　　D. 航空运单经背书后可以转让

39. (　　)可以作为经营单位进行填报。

A. 对外签订合同但并非执行合同的单位

B. 非对外签订合同但具体执行合同的单位

C. 委托外贸公司对外签订并执行进口投资设备合同的外商投资企业

D. 接受并办理进口溢卸货物报关纳税手续的单位

40. 信用证申请书中的(　　)不是由开证人填写。

A. 开证日　　B. 到期日　　C. L/C 号码　　D. 通知行

三、判断题

1. FOB、CFR 和 CIF 三种常用的贸易术语都是象征性交货。(　　)

2. 出口信用保险是各国政府普遍采用的抵御出口风险的措施。(　　)

3. 航空货运中,承运人有权选择运输路线或变更货运单上由托运人所填的运输路线,不必事先通知托运人。(　　)

4. 在 SWIFT 信用证中,数字“2584678.36”表示为“2584678,36”。(　　)

5. 信用证规定起运港为 CHINA PORTS,若信用证禁止分批,则信用证中装运港 CHINA PORTS 的实际意义与 CHINA PORT 相同。(　　)

6. 信用证没有规定有效期或装运期,则该信用证为无效信用证。(　　)

7. 信用证的性质是银行信用,因此,信用证项下使用的汇票必定是银行汇票。(　　)

8. 背对背信用证是指交易的一方开出第一张信用证,但暂不生效,须在对方开来一定金额的回头信用证经受益人表示接受时,才通知对方银行两证同时生效。(　　)

9. 对于不可撤销信用证,如果开证人提出申请,开证行可随时撤销该信用证。(　　)

10. 进口企业申请开立信用证时,须填写开证申请书,并向银行递交进口合同副本、有关附件,向银行交纳一定的押金和手续费。(　　)

11. 在审核信用证时,对信用证中的附加条款一般可以不审核。(　　)

12. 根据 UCP 600 的规定,标明“正本”(Original)字样的单据为正本单据,须经出单人签署方为有效。标明“副本”(Copy)或不标明“正本”字样的单据为副本单据,无须签署。(　　)

13. 根据《票据法》的规定,背书人对票据所负的责任与出票人相同,但对其后手没有担保责任。(　　)

14. 票据是一种流通证券,所有票据都可经过背书转让。(　　)

15. 在托收业务中,如果委托人没有指定代收行,托收行可自行选择代收行。(　　)

16. 根据 UCP 600 的规定,保兑行保兑信用证后,对随后接到的修改书可自行决定是否将保兑责任扩展至修改书。(　　)

17. 货物装船后,托运人凭船公司的装货单换取已装船提单。(　　)

18. 票据的转让必须通知债务人方为有效。(　　)

19. 提单单上载明“货于 4 月 8 日全部装完”表示的是“已装船提单”的日期。(　　)

20. “PLS OFFER 600MT GROUND NUTS 2012 CROP CIFC5 TOKYO DIRECT STEAMER INDICATING PYMT TERMS EARLIEST SHIPMENT.”上述内容是贸易磋商中的发盘环节。(　　)

四、简答题

1. 简述国际贸易单证的制作依据。

2. 简述海运提单的性质和作用。

3. 简述信用证支付方式的一般程序。

4. 我出口公司对外报价，某产品 50.00 美元/箱 FOB 上海，后外商要求改报 CIF 汉堡价，此货物按 W/M 计费，基本运费为 60.00 美元/运费吨，燃油附加费为 10%，体积每箱为 48×25×20CMS，毛重为 27 千克/箱，保险费率为 2‰，试计算我方应报的 CIF 汉堡价。（按惯例加一成，计算过程保留六位小数点，答案保留两位小数点。）

5. 日本 A 公司向我国 B 公司订购电子设备 800 台，合同规定，该电子设备的价格为 800 美元/台 CIF 长崎，2018 年 4 月 30 日，宁波港装货。货物于 2018 年 4 月 30 日装船，装船时外包装有严重破损，B 公司向船舶公司出具了货物品质的保函。船长应 B 公司的请求，出具了清洁提单，B 公司据此向银行取得了货款。货物到达长崎后，A 公司发现，货物外包装箱有严重破损，船舶公司出示了 B 公司提供的保函，认为该事应向 B 公司索赔。请问：

（1）船舶公司是否应承担责任？为什么？

（2）B 公司是否应承担责任？为什么？

（3）保险公司如何对待 A 公司的索赔？

（4）A 公司的损失如何得到补偿？

综合训练二

一、单项选择题

1. CFR 合同下，如果卖方装船后未及时向买方发出装船通知，致使买方未能办理货运保险，则运输途中的风险由（　　）。

A. 买方承担　　B. 卖方承担

C. 承运人承担　　D. 买卖双方各承担一半

2. 在国际贸易中，含佣价的计算公式是（　　）。

A. 净价÷(1－佣金率)　　B. 净价×(1＋佣金率)

C. 净价×佣金率　　D. 单价×佣金率

3. CIF 条件下交货，（　　）。

A. 装运时间先于交货时间　　B. 装运时间迟于交货时间

C. 装运时间与交货时间一致　　D. 其先后次序视运输方式而定

4. 定牌中性包装是指（　　）。

A. 有商标、牌名，无产地、厂名　　B. 无商标、牌名，无产地、厂名

C. 有商标、牌名，有产地、厂名　　D. 无商标、牌名，有产地、厂名

5. 开展（　　）是实现"门到门"运输的有效途径，它有利于简化手续，减少中间环节，快速低成本地提高运输质量。

A. 航空运输　　B. 邮包运输　　C. 铁路运输　　D. 集装箱运输

6. 按照惯例，开证行在收到国外寄来的全套单证后应进行严格审核，下列不属于审核事项的是（　　）。

A. 单据与信用证之间是否相符

B. 单据与单据之间是否相符

C. 单据与货物之间是否相符

D. 单据与《跟单信用证统一惯例》是否相符

7. 在海洋运输货物保险业务中，共同海损（　　）。

A. 是部分损失的一种

B. 是全部损失的一种

C. 有时为部分损失，有时为全部损失

D. 是推定全损

8. 货物外包装上有一只酒杯或一把雨伞，这种标志属于（　　）。

A. 危险性标志　　B. 指示性标志

C. 警告性标志　　D. 易燃性标志

9. 发生（　　），违约方可援引不可抗力条款要求免责。

A. 战争　　B. 世界市场价格上涨

C. 生产制作过程中的过失　　D. 货币贬值

10. 预约保险以(　　)代替投保单,说明投保的一方已办理了投保手续。

A. 提单　　B. 国外的装运通知

C. 大副收据　　D. 买卖合同

11. “仓至仓”条款是(　　)。

A. 承运人负责运输起讫的条款　　B. 保险人负责保险责任起讫的条款

C. 出口人负责交货责任起讫的条款　　D. 进口人负责付款责任起讫的条款

12. 某提单“已装船”日期是5月9日,表明(　　)。

A. 货于5月9日送交船公司　　B. 货于5月9日开始装船

C. 货于5月9日全部装完　　D. 货于5月9日抵达目的港

13. 出口商审核信用证的依据是(　　)。

A. 合同及UCP 600的规定　　B. 整套单据

C. 开证申请书　　D. 商业发票

14. 根据《伦敦保险协会海运保险条款》的规定,承保范围最小的险别是(　　)。

A. ICC(A)　　B. ICC (B)　　C. ICC(C)　　D. ICC War Clause

15. 国际多式联运的经营人(承运人)(　　)。

A. 对运输全程负责

B. 仅对第一程运输负责

C. 仅对第二程运输负责

D. 接受第二程运输承运人的委托并向原货主负责

16. 关于商品检验时间和地点的规定,我国进出口业务中使用较多的是(　　)。

A. 离岸品质,离岸重量

B. 到岸品质,到岸重量

C. 出口国装运港检验,进口国目的港复验

D. 离岸重量,到岸品质

17. 唛头一般不包括(　　)。

A. 收货人简称或代号　　B. 参考号

C. 件号　　D. 装运港

18. 对于价值低的商品,往往采用(　　)计算其重量。

A. 理论重量　　B. 净重　　C. 法定重量　　D. 以毛作净

19. 商业发票的抬头人一般是(　　)。

A. 受益人　　B. 开证申请人　　C. 开证银行　　D. 卖方

20. 在使用(　　)贸易术语进行交易时,卖方及时向买方发出“已装船通知”至关重要,因为它将直接影响买卖双方对运输途中的风险承担。

A. CIP　　B. DES　　C. FCA　　D. CFR

21. 根据UCP 600的规定,受益人超过提单签发日期后21天才交到银行议付的提单称为(　　)。

A. 过期提单　　B. 倒签提单　　C. 预借提单　　D. 转船提单

22. DAT意指(　　)。

A. 装运港船上交货　　　　　　　　B. 目的港船上交货

C. 装运港码头交货　　　　　　　　D. 运输终端交货

23. 根据《跟单信用证统一惯例》的规定，若信用证中对是否分批装运与转运未予规定，则受益人（　　）。

A. 可以分批装运，也可以转运　　　B. 不可以分批装运，也不可以转运

C. 可以分批装运，但不可以转运　　D. 不可以分批装运，但可以转运

24. 按照国际保险市场惯例，投保金额通常在 CIF 总值的基础上（　　）。

A. 加一成　　B. 加二成　　C. 加三成　　D. 加四成

25. CIC"特殊附加险"是指在特殊情况下，要求保险公司承保的险别，（　　）。

A. 一般可以单独投保

B. 不能单独投保

C. 可单独投保两项以上的"特殊附加险"

D. 在被保险人同意的情况下，可以单独投保

26. 各种运输单据中，同时具有货物收据、运输合同证明和物权凭证作用的是（　　）。

A. Railway Bill　　　　　　　　B. Air Waybill

C. Bill of Lading　　　　　　　D. Post Receipt

27. FCA、CPT、CIP 三种术语涉及的运费与 FOB、CFR、CIF 相比较，它们的区别是前者包括（　　）。

A. 装卸费　　B. 邮电费　　C. 预计耗损　　D. 拼箱费

28. 下列贸易术语中表示含佣价的是（　　）。

A. FOBS　　B. FOBT　　C. FOBC 5%　　D. FOBD 3%

29. 如果信用证显示"Available with any bank"，在缮制汇票时，受款人栏目（　　）。

A. 只能填写 ANY BANK　　　　　B. 可以由受益人指定

C. 只能由开证行指定　　　　　　D. 可以由进口商指定

30. 按照 INCOTERMS 2010 的规定，以 FOB 贸易术语成交，买卖双方风险划分的界限是（　　）。

A. 货交承运人　　　　　　　　　B. 货物越过装运港船上

C. 货物在目的港卸货后　　　　　D. 目的港码头

31. 我国某公司与美国某公司以 CFR Ex ship's hold New York 的条件成交了一笔出口生意，按照一般惯例，这批货物在纽约港的卸货费用应由（　　）承担。

A. 美国某公司　　B. 我国某公司　　C. 承运人　　D. 保险公司

32. 卖方不负责办理出口清关手续及支付相关费用的术语是（　　）。

A. FCA　　B. FAS　　C. FOB　　D. EXW

33. 直接接触商品并随商品进入零售网点与消费者见面的包装叫（　　）。

A. 运输包装　　B. 销售包装　　C. 中性包装　　D. 定牌包装

34. 信用证一般采用电子方式传输，它采用的是（　　）机构的协议标准。

A. SWIFT　　B. UNSM　　C. ICC　　D. MAR

35. 下列对模板式制单软件的表述中错误的是（　　）。

A. 操作简单，方便实现单证的信息化管理

B. 它是当今国内外贸易企业使用的业务运作管理系统

C. 它是一套集合了众多不同单证不同版本模板的外贸制单软件

D. 所填即所得

36. 根据 INCOTERMS 2010 的规定,CIF 和 CIP 的区别是(　　)。

A. 出口报关责任负担不同　　B. 进口报关责任负担不同

C. 保险费、海运费负担不同　　D. 风险转移界限不同

37. 海运提单日期应理解为(　　)。

A. 签订运输合同的日期　　B. 货物开始装船的日期

C. 货物装船过程中的任何一天　　D. 货物装船完毕的日期

38. 根据我国《海洋货物运输保险条款》的规定,"一切险"包括(　　)。

A. 平安险加 11 种一般附加险　　B. 一切险加 11 种一般附加险

C. 水渍险加 11 种一般附加险　　D. 特殊附加险加 11 种一般附加险

39. 各种单据的签发日期应符合逻辑性和国际惯例,通常(　　)日期是确定各单据日期的关键。

A. 发票　　B. 提单　　C. 许可证　　D. 报关单

40. 不可撤销信用证在信用证的有效期内,未经(　　)的同意,开证行或开证人不得撤销或修改。

A. 受益人　　B. 开证人

C. 开证行　　D. 受益人、开证人以及有关银行

二、多项选择题

1. FOB、CFR、CIF 和 FCA、CPT、CIP 术语的主要区别有(　　)。

A. 适用的运输方式不同　　B. 风险转移的地点不同

C. 装卸费用的负担不同　　D. 运输单据不同

2. 对于信用证与合同关系的表述正确的有(　　)。

A. 信用证的开立以买卖合同为依据

B. 信用证的履行不受买卖合同的约束

C. 有关银行只根据信用证的规定办理信用证业务

D. 合同是审核信用证的唯一依据

3. 进口货物的索赔包括向(　　)提出的索赔。

A. 出口商　　B. 银行　　C. 保险公司　　D. 承运人

4. 信用证中对装运期规定的表示方法有多种,以下各项中符合 UCP 600 规定的有(　　)。

A. Immediately　　B. on or about

C. between　　D. beginning of a month

5. 确定进出口商品的价格,除了要考虑商品的质量和档次、运输的距离、成交数量外、还要考虑(　　)。

A. 交货地点和交货条件　　B. 季节性需求的变化

C. 支付条件和汇率变动的风险　　D. 国际市场商品供求变化和价格走势

6. 信用证做了如下规定,其中属于"非单据条件"的有(　　)。

A. 载货船舶的船龄不超过 15 年

B. 载货船舶挂巴拿马国旗

C. 装船后立即通知申请人装货细节并提交传真副本

D. 提供原产地证明书

7. 假远期信用证与远期信用证的区别有(　　)。

A. 开证基础不同　　B. 信用证条款不同

C. 利息的负担者不同　　D. 收汇的时间不同

8. (　　)条款应被视为信用证的"软条款"。

A. 检验人在检验证书上的签名必须与开证行所保留的签名样本相符

B. 受益人出具的报关单、合同及商业发票必须做使馆认证

C. 必须得到开证申请人对样品的确认后,信用证方可生效

D. 货物必须经开证申请人的代表检验合格后方可装船

9. FOB、CFR、CIF 和 FCA、CPT、CIP 两组术语的价格构成都包括(　　)。

A. 保险费　　B. 进货成本　　C. 费用　　D. 净利润

10. 商业发票是国际货物买卖中的核心单据,其作用表现为(　　)。

A. 进出口报关完税必不可少的单据　　B. 是全套单据的中心

C. 是结算货款的依据　　D. 是物权凭证

11. 海运提单的性质与作用包括(　　)。

A. 它是海运单据的唯一表现形式

B. 它是承运人或其代理人出具的货物收据

C. 它是代表货物所有权的凭证

D. 它是承运人与托运人之间订立的运输契约的证明

12. 在国际贸易中,从事商品检验的机构主要有(　　)。

A. 官方机构　　B. 非官方机构

C. 生产制造商　　D. 用货单位或买方

13. 我国对外贸易货运保险可分为(　　)。

A. 海上运输保险　　B. 陆上运输保险

C. 航空运输保险　　D. 邮包运输保险

14. 我方出口商品单价写法正确的有(　　)。

A. 每打 50 港元 FOB 广州黄埔

B. 每台 5 800 日元 FOB 大连,减 2%的折扣

C. 每套 200 美元 CIFC 3%香港

D. 每桶 36 英镑 CFR 伦敦

15. 在进出口合同中,单价条款包括的内容是(　　)。

A. 计量单位　　B. 价格金额　　C. 计价货币　　D. 贸易术语

16. (　　)情况下,开证行有权拒付票款。

A. 单据内容与信用证条款不符　　B. 实际货物未装运

C. 单据与货物有出入　　D. 单据与单据相互之间不符

17. 唛头的主要内容包括(　　)。

A. 目的港(地)名称　　B. 收货人名称

C. 件号　　D. 信用证号或合同号

18. 贸易术语的性质包括(　　)。

A. 交货条件　　B. 成交价格的构成因素

C. 付款条件　　D. 运输条件

19. 如果信用证要求提单做成“空白抬头、空白背书”,则(　　)。

A. 做成指示式提单　　B. 做成凭买方指示式提单

C. 做成买方背书的提单　　D. 背书时不写明受让人名称

E. 背书时须注明受让人的名称

20. 在国际贸易中,常见的计重方法有(　　)。

A. 毛重　　B. 净重

C. 公量　　D. 理论重量和法定重量

21. 河北某外贸公司的工作人员因为在审证过程中粗心大意,未能发现合同、发票上的公司名称与公司印章上的名称不一致,合同发票上是 ABC Corporation,而印章上是 ABC Company,仅一词之差,此时又恰逢国际市场价格有变,在这种情况下,(　　)。

A. 外商有权拒绝付款　　B. 责任在外商

C. 外商应按规定如期付款　　D. 责任在河北某外贸公司

22. 属于报关基本单证的有(　　)。

A. 商业发票　　B. 贸易合同　　C. 装箱单　　D. 保险单

23. 根据我国《商检法》的规定,地方检验检疫局在进出口商品检验方面的基本任务是(　　)。

A. 对所有商品进行检验检疫　　B. 实施法定检验

C. 办理鉴定业务　　D. 对进出口商品工作实施监督管理

24. 在使用集装箱海运出口贸易中,卖方采用 CIP 术语比采用 CIF 术语更为有利的具体表现是(　　)。

A. 可以提前转移风险　　B. 可以提前取得运输单据

C. 可以提前交单结汇　　D. 可以提高资金周转率

25. 在实际业务中,凭信用证成交出口的货物,如货物出运后,发现单证不符,又由于时间的限制,无法在信用证有效期或交单期内做到单证相符,可采取的变通办法有(　　)。

A. 担保议付　　B. 采用“电提”方式征求开证行意见

C. 改成“跟证托收”　　D. 直接要求买方付款

26. 国际货物买卖合同中比较常见的装运期的规定方法有(　　)。

A. 规定在某一天装运　　B. 规定在收到信用证后若干天内装运

C. 规定一个笼统的装运期限　　D. 明确规定具体的装运期限

27. 租船运输包括(　　)。

A. 定期租船　　B. 集装箱运输　　C. 班轮运输　　D. 定程租船

28. 在我国的进出口业务中,出口结汇的方法有(　　)。

A. 收妥结汇　　B. 买单结汇　　C. 定期结汇　　D. 预付结汇

29. 根据我国《票据法》的规定,汇票上必须记载的事项包括(　　)。

A. 确定的金额　　B. 汇票日期　　C. 付款人名称　　D. 汇票编号

30. 根据我国《海运货物运输保险条款》(即CIC条款)的规定,其中的基本险可分为(　　)。
A. 平安险　B. 水渍险　C. 一切险　D. 附加险
31. 国际货款结算票据主要包括(　　)。
A. 支票　B. 汇票　C. 外币现钞　D. 本票
32. 因租船订舱和装运而产生的单据有(　　)。
A. 托运单　B. 装货单　C. 收货单　D. 海运提单
33. 以下各种贸易术语中只适用于水上运输方式的是(　　)。
A. EXW　B. FAS　C. FOB　D. DDU
34. 在国际贸易中,常用的支付方式有(　　)。
A. 预付　B. 汇付　C. 托收　D. 信用证
35. 备用信用证与一般跟单信用证的区别主要有(　　)。
A. 备用信用证属于商业信用,跟单信用证属于银行信用
B. 银行付款的条件不同
C. 适用的范围不同
D. 受款人要求银行付款时所需提供的单据不同
36. 关于形式发票,下列说法正确的有(　　)。
A. 形式发票不是一种正式发票
B. 形式发票能用于托收和议付,其正式成效后不需另外再缮制商业发票
C. 形式发票与商业发票的关系密切,信用证在货物描述后面常有"按照某月某日之形式发票"等条款
D. 假如来证附有形式发票,则形式发票构成信用证的组成部分,在制单时要按形式发票内容全部填写在商业发票上
37. 接受所必须具备的条件有(　　)。
A. 接受必须由受盘人做出
B. 接受的内容必须与发盘的内容相符
C. 接受的内容必须与还盘的内容相符
D. 必须在有效期限内接受
38. 佣金的表示方法有(　　)。
A. 在价格中表明所含佣金的百分比　B. 用字母"C"表示
C. 用字母"R"表示　D. 用字母"D"表示
39. 在国际贸易中使用EDI的现实意义有(　　)。
A. 降低经营成本及费用　B. 速度快,时效性强
C. 准确率高,差错率少　D. 节省时间,提高企业管理水平
40. 信用证支付方式的特点有(　　)。
A. 信用证是一种银行信用　B. 信用证是一种商业信用
C. 信用证是一种自足文件　D. 信用证是一种单据的买卖

三、判断题

1. 一份报关单可以填报多个许可证号。(　　)
2. 所有出口货物都需要经过法定检验后,才能报关出运。(　　)

3. 在 FOB 条件下，卖方可以接受买方委托，代办租船订舱手续。（　　）

4. 不清洁提单的不良批注是从大副收据上转注过来的。（　　）

5. 对开信用证多用于易货贸易、补偿贸易和来料加工、来件装配等业务。（　　）

6. 班轮运输的特点之一是由船方负责装卸。（　　）

7. 一项发盘如表明是不可撤销的，则意味着发盘人无权撤销该发盘。（　　）

8. 按照 UCP 600 的规定，银行接受七种运输单据，除非另有约定，否则一般银行不接受卖方提交的快递收据。（　　）

9. 如果信用证只规定最迟装运期，未列有效期，受益人应按双到期来操作。（　　）

10. 可转让信用证只能转让一次，所以，第二受益人将可转让信用证再转让给第一受益人是不被允许的。（　　）

11. 信托收据实质上是银行向进口商提供资金融通的一种方式。（　　）

12. 我国某公司按 CIF 条件出口某商品，采用信用证支付方式。买方在约定时间内未开来信用证，但约定的装运期已到，为了重合同和守信用，我方仍应按期发运货物。（　　）

13. 采用信用证收汇方式时，空运提单最好做成 TO ORDER OF ISSUING BANK，以防收汇风险。（　　）

14. 在按装运港交货的贸易术语成交时，合同中规定检验地点应以“离岸品质、离岸重量”为宜。（　　）

15. 在国际货物买卖合同中，约定包装时，“习惯包装”“适合海运包装”等是常用的、比较好的规定方法。（　　）

16. 班轮运费包括基本运费和附加费两部分。（　　）

17. 提单在法律上具有物权凭证的作用，在国际贸易中，提单可以通过背书进行转让，转让也就意味着转让货物的所有权。（　　）

18. 发盘人在其提出的订约建议中加注诸如“仅供参考”“须以发盘人的最后确认为准”或其他类似的保留条件，这样的订约建议就不是发盘，而只是发盘的邀请。（　　）

19. 一张未记载付款日期的汇票，按惯例可理解为见票后 21 天付款。（　　）

20. 开证行、保兑行或其他指定银行都有一段合理时间审核单据，但不超过收到单据次日起的 15 个银行工作日。（　　）

四、简答题

1. 简述国际贸易单证制作的基本要求。

2. 在出口业务中，与旧的三种贸易术语 FOB、CFR 和 CIF 比较，为什么应该积极推广新三种贸易术语 FCA、CPT 和 CIP?

3. 我国南方公司向澳大利亚出口一批服装，价格为 CIF SYDNEY USD70.40/DOZ，进口商要求改报含佣金 3%的出口价格，试计算该商品的 CIFC 3 价。

4. 根据资料回答问题。

托收方式	首次提示日	承兑日	付款日	银行交单日
D/P AT SIGHT	3 月 8 日	3 月 9 日	3 月 7 日	3 月 10 日
D/A AT 30DAYS	3 月 8 日	3 月 7 日	4 月 21 日	4 月 20 日

要求：根据已知资料和惯例，将你认为应改正的日期填在下面的表格中。

托收方式	首次提示日	承兑日	付款日	银行交单日
D/P AT SIGHT				
D/A AT 30DAYS				

5. UCP 600 项下某一不可撤销信用证，规定货物为羊毛毛线，共 37 000 磅，分两批装运，第一批 20 000 磅，最晚于 2018 年 4 月 22 日交货；第二批 17 000 磅，最晚于 2018 年 4 月 27 日交货。并且，L/C 金额与货物数量均有 5%的增减幅度。L/C 受益人发运货物，第一批于 2018 年 4 月 19 日发货 20 000 磅；第二批于 2018 年 4 月 24 日发货 18 000 磅。开证行拒付第二批货物的单据，拒付理由是超装。议付行认为 5%的增减幅度是针对全部提交的货物而言的，故提交单据相符。开证行称该幅度指每批货物而言，故第二批货物超装。你认为上述拒付成立吗？

综合训练三

一、单项选择题

1. 某公司与国外一家公司以 EXW 条件成交了一笔买卖，在这种情况下，其交货地点不正确的是(　　)。

A. 出口国港口　　B. 进口国港口

C. 出口商工厂　　D. 出口商仓库

2. 经过背书才能转让的提单是(　　)。

A. 指示提单　　B. 不记名提单

C. 记名提单　　D. 清洁提单

3. 下列条件中不是构成发盘的必备条件的是(　　)。

A. 发盘的内容必须十分确定　　B. 主要交易条件必须十分完整齐全

C. 向一个或一个以上特定的人发出　　D. 表明发盘人承受约束的意旨

4. 在 FOB 条件下，若采用租船运输，如买方不愿承担装货费及理舱费，则应在合同中规定(　　)。

A. FOB Liner Terms　　B. FOB Under Tackle

C. FOB Stowed　　D. FOB Trimmed

5. 根据我国《海洋货物运输保险条款》的规定，承保范围最小的基本险别是(　　)。

A. 平安险　　B. 水渍险　　C. 一切险　　D. 罢工险

6. 假设提单的签发日期为“MARCH 24,2018”，那么以下保单的开航日期中，填写错误的是(　　)。

A. MARCH 24,2018　　B. AS PER B/L

C. MARCH 30,2018　　D. MARCH 23,2018

7. 保险的赔付地点一般填写(　　)。

A. 起运港(地)　　B. 目的港(地)

C. 投保人所在地　　D. 保险公司所在地

8. 一般情况下，按 CFR 贸易术语成交的合同中，不应计入货物价格的是(　　)。

A. 货物成本　　B. 海运费　　C. 保险费　　D. 各项出口税费

9. 在以 CIF 和 CFR 术语成交的条件下，货物运输保险分别由卖方和买方办理，运输途中货物灭失和损坏的风险(　　)。

A. 前者由卖方承担，后者由买方承担

B. 均由卖方承担

C. 均由买方承担

D. 前者由买方承担，后者由卖方承担

10. 象征性交货指卖方交货义务是(　　)。

A. 不交货　　B. 既交单又实际交货

C. 凭单交货　　D. 实际交货

11. 信用证的到期日为12月31日，最迟装运期为12月16日，最迟交单日期为运输单据出单后15天，出口人备妥货物安排出运的时间是12月10日，则出口人最迟应于(　　)向银行交单议付。

A. 12月16日　　B. 12月25日　　C. 12月28日　　D. 12月31日

12. G. S. P. Form A 是一种(　　)。

A. 船公司证明信　　B. 原产地证书

C. 受益人证明信　　D. 检验检疫证明书

13. 在程租船条件下，表示船方负担装卸费的是(　　)。

A. Free In and Out　　B. Free In

C. Free Out　　D. Gross Term

14. 预约保险以(　　)代替投保单，说明投保的一方已办理了投保手续。

A. 提单　　B. 国外的装运通知

C. 大副收据　　D. 买卖合同

15. CIF 是(　　)船上交货，DAT 是(　　)船上交货。

A. 装运港　目的港　　B. 目的港　目的港

C. 目的港　装运港　　D. 装运港　装运港

16. 合同中未注明商品重量是按毛重还是按净重计价时，按照惯例以(　　)计价。

A. 毛重　　B. 净重　　C. 毛作净　　D. 公量

17. 海运提单的抬头是指提单的(　　)。

A. Shipper　　B. Consignee　　C. Notify Party　　D. Voyage No.

18. 一般情况下，在以 FOB 贸易术语成交的合同中，货物的价格构成是(　　)。

A. 货物成本　　B. 货物成本＋运费

C. 货物成本＋保险费　　D. 货物成本＋运费＋保险费

19. 在货物买卖中，通常收取佣金的是(　　)。

A. 进口商　　B. 出口商　　C. 承运人　　D. 中间商

20. 根据 UCP 600 的规定，信用证中货物的数量规定有“约”“大约”“近似”或类似意义的词语时，应理解为其有关数量增减幅度不超过(　　)%。

A. 3　　B. 5　　C. 10　　D. 15

21. 按照《国际货物销售合同公约》的规定，一项发盘在尚未送达受盘人之前，是可以阻止其生效的，这叫发盘的(　　)。

A. 撤回　　B. 撤销　　C. 还盘　　D. 接受

22. 在托收项下，单据缮制一般以(　　)为依据。如有特殊要求，应参照相应文件或资料。

A. 信用证　　B. 发票　　C. 合同　　D. 提单

23. 信用证上若未注明汇票的付款人，根据 UCP 600 的规定，汇票的付款人应是(　　)。

A. The Applicant　　B. The Issuing Bank

C. The Negotiation Bank　　D. The Beneficiary

24. 根据 URC 522 的规定,D/A 90 天远期的结算方式,代收行应在(　　)交单。

A. 收到单据后 5 个工作日内　　B. 进口商承兑汇票后

C. 货物到达目的港后　　D. 进口商付款后

25. 在租船合同中明示 Free in,主要是解决在(　　)条件下货物的装船费用问题。

A. 班轮　　B. 程租船　　C. 期租船　　D. 光船租船

26. 以下关于汇款方式的说法正确的是(　　)。

A. 汇款方式属商业信用

B. 信汇、电汇属商业信用,票汇因为使用银行汇票,所以属银行信用

C. 信汇属商业信用,电汇和票汇属银行信用

D. 汇款方式属银行信用

27. 承兑是指汇票付款人承诺对远期汇票承担到期付款责任的行为。根据我国《票据法》的规定,自收到提示承兑汇票之日起(　　)日内付款人必须做出承兑。

A. 3　　B. 4　　C. 5　　D. 6

28. 按照海运运输的业务要求,进口商办理租船订舱手续,必须由委托人填写(　　)。

A. 海运提单　　B. 海运货运委托书

C. 海运单　　D. 配舱单

29. 如信用证规定“Shipment about 15th Oct. 2018”,那么装运期可以是(　　)。

A. 10—19 日　　B. 11—20 日

C. 10—20 日　　D. 11—10 日

30. 在录入单证信息时,应首先录入的单证信息是(　　)。

A. 商业发票　　B. 原产地证　　C. 订舱委托书　　D. 商业汇票

31. 汇票的抬头人是指汇票的(　　)。

A. 受款人　　B. 受票人　　C. 付款人　　D. 出票人

32. 构成不清洁提单的批注是(　　)。

A. 旧桶装　　B. 铁条松散,货物外露

C. 发货人装箱、点数并铅封　　D. 货物状况良好

33. 以 CIF 出口时,如合同和信用证无特别规定,保险单“Insured”一栏应填(　　)。

A. 进口商名称　　B. 开证申请人名称

C. 出口商名称　　D. 开证行名称

34. 甲向乙发盘:可供贵厂一年生产所需的全部铁矿石,价格按交货时伦敦五金交易所价格计算。根据《联合国国际货物销售合同公约》,这是一项(　　)。

A. 询盘　　B. 邀请发盘　　C. 有效发盘　　D. 无效发盘

35. 在托运、报检、报关和结汇的单证中,由出口商出具的单证有(　　)。

A. 发票、报关单、提单和通关单　　B. 汇票、通关单、提单和托运单

C. 发票、通关单、提单和保险单　　D. 发票、托运单、汇票和尺码单

36. 根据《中华人民共和国海关法》,进口货物的收货人向海关申报的时限是(　　)。

A. 自运输工具申报进境之日起 7 日内

B. 自运输工具申报进境之日起 10 日内

C. 自运输工具申报进境之日起 14 日内

D. 自运输工具申报进境之日起 15 日内

37. 转让保险单时,如信用证未明确规定背书方式,应采用(　　)的方式。

A. 空白背书　B. 记名背书　C. 记名指示背书　D. 不必背书

38. 信用证和托收项下的汇票抬头一般做成(　　)。

A. to Bearer　B. pay to ×× only

C. pay to the order of ×××　D. open

39. 使用信用证、付款交单、承兑交单三种方式结算贷款,就卖方的收汇风险而言,从小到大依次排序为(　　)。

A. D/P、D/A 和 L/C　B. D/A、D/P 和 L/C

C. L/C、D/P 和 D/A　D. L/C、D/A 和 D/P

40. 在信用证方式下,(　　)是开证行付款的唯一依据。

A. 发票　B. 收汇单证　C. 提单　D. 出口许可证

二、多项选择题

1. 海运提单的性质与作用有(　　)。

A. 它是海运单据的唯一表现形式

B. 它是承运人或其代理人出具的货物收据

C. 它是代表货物所有权的凭证

D. 它是承运人与托运人之间订立的运输契约的证明

2. 在交易磋商程序中,必不可少的两个法律环节是(　　)。

A. 询盘　B. 发盘　C. 还盘　D. 接受

3. 属于包装标志的有(　　)。

A. 运输标志　B. 条形码　C. 指示性标志　D. 警告性标志

4. FOB 贸易术语的变形有(　　)。

A. FOB 班轮条件　B. FOB 包括平舱

C. FOB 包括理舱　D. FOB 吊钩下交货

5. 信用证支付方式的特点包括(　　)。

A. 信用证是一种银行信用　B. 信用证是一种商业信用

C. 信用证是一种自足文件　D. 信用证是一种单据的买卖

6. 采用托收方式时要注意的问题有(　　)。

A. 考虑进口商的资信情况　B. 此种结算方式有利于进口商

C. 不宜对贸易管制较严的国家　D. 不宜对外汇管制较严的国家

7. 在国际贸易实践中,常用的保险单据有(　　)。

A. 保险单　B. 保险凭证　C. 预约保险单　D. 保险批单

8. 银行处理信用证业务是以单证表面相符的原则来决定是否付款,而不管实际货物如何。因此出口商必须做到(　　),开证行才承担付款责任。

A. 单证一致　B. 证同一致　C. 单单一致　D. 单货一致

9. 以下对于贸易术语变形说法正确的有(　　)。

A. 不改变费用的负担　B. 不改变交货地点

C. 不改变风险划分的界限　　D. 不改变支付条件

10. 因租船订舱和装船而产生的单据是(　　)。

A. 托运单　　B. 装货单　　C. 装箱单　　D. 海运提单

11. 本票与汇票的区别是(　　)。

A. 前者是无条件的支付承诺,后者是无条件支付命令

B. 前者的当事人为两个,后者的当事人则有三个

C. 前者在使用过程中有承兑,后者则无须承兑

D. 汇票有即期与远期之分,本票则只有远期

12. 按照《国际货物销售合同公约》的规定,一项发盘的内容必须十分确定。只有具备(　　),才算十分确定。

A. 标明货物名称

B. 明示或默示货物的包装

C. 明示或默示货物的数量或规定数量的方法

D. 明示或默示货物的价格或规定价格的方法

13. 提单背书一般分为(　　)。

A. 记名背书　　B. 指示背书　　C. 空白背书　　D. 任意背书

14. 国际货物买卖中比较常见的装运港和目的港的规定方法有(　　)。

A. 笼统地规定装运港和目的港

B. 一般情况下,只规定一个装运港和一个目的港

C. 大宗商品可规定两个装运港和一个目的港

D. 在双方洽商暂无法确定装运港和目的港时,可采用选择港的方式

15. 国际上汇票的抬头通常有三种写法,即(　　)。

A. 限制性抬头　　B. 指示性抬头　　C. 持票人抬头　　D. 背书性抬头

16. 进口时若使用(　　)术语,应在开证申请书的保险单条款前的括号里打"×"。

A. CFR　　B. FOB　　C. CIF　　D. CIP

17. 提单按收货人的不同可分为(　　)。

A. Straight B/L　　B. Master B/L　　C. Blank B/L　　D. Order B/L

18. 集装箱海运出口托运时,关于装货单,下列表述正确的有(　　)。

A. 是承运人确认承运货物的证明

B. 是发货人凭以换取提单的唯一凭证

C. 是海关对出口货物进行监管的单据之一

D. 是承运人通知装运船舶接货装船的命令

19. 在我国的进出口业务中,出口结汇的方法有(　　)。

A. 收妥结汇　　B. 买单结汇　　C. 定期结汇　　D. 预付结汇

20. 装箱单的作用主要是补充发票内容的不足,通过填制包装件数、唛头、规格等,明确产品的包装情况,(　　)。

A. 便于进口商了解产品的数量与包装

B. 便于进口国海关检查与核对产品

C. 是出口商必须向进口商提交的单据

D. 是出口商必须向银行提交的单据

21. 在交易过程中,卖方的基本义务有(　　)。

A. 提交货物　　B. 提交与货物有关的单据

C. 转移货物的所有权　　D. 支付货款

22. 履行出口合同的程序可概括为(　　)。

A. 货　　B. 证　　C. 船　　D. 款

23. 进口国家要求出口商提供海关发票的目的是(　　)。

A. 作为进口估价完税的依据　　B. 作为征收差别待遇关税的依据

C. 作为征收反倾销税的依据　　D. 作为进口商付款的依据

24. 在实际业务中,凭信用证成交出口的货物,如货物出运后,发现单证不符,又因为时间的限制,无法在信用证有效期或交单期内做到单证相符,可采取的变通办法有(　　)。

A. 担保议付　　B. "电提"方式征求开证行意见

C. 改为跟证托收　　D. 直接要求买方付款

25. 在审核信用证和单据的金额与货币时,需要审核的内容包括(　　)。

A. 信用证总金额的大小写必须一致

B. 来证采用的货币与合同规定的货币必须一致

C. 发票和/或汇票的金额不能超过信用证规定的总金额

D. 若合同中订有溢短装条款,信用证金额应有相应的规定

26. 在实际的进出口业务中,接受的形式有(　　)。

A. 用口头或书面的形式表示　　B. 用缄默表示

C. 用广告表示　　D. 用行动表示

27. 我国某公司 15 日向日商发盘,限 20 日复到有效,日商于 19 日用电报表示接受我方 15 日电,我方于 21 日中午才收到对方的接受通知,此时(　　)。

A. 合同已成立

B. 若我方毫不迟延表示接受,合同成立

C. 若我方于 21 日才收到接受通知是由于电信部门的延误,则我方缄默,合同成立

D. 若我方于 21 日才收到接受通知是由于电信部门的延误,则合同一定成立

28. 国际货款结算的工具主要有(　　)。

A. 支票　　B. 汇票　　C. 外币现钞　　D. 票据

29. 在我国海洋运输货物保险业务中,下列(　　)险别均可适用"仓至仓"条款。

A. ALL RISKS　　B. WA or WPA　　C. FPA　　D. WAR RISK

30. 若买卖双方以 CFR 卸至岸上术语成交,以下答案正确的是(　　)。

A. 卖方应承担货物运至目的港以前的一切风险

B. 当货物卸至目的港后,卖方的交货完毕

C. 装运港船上是买卖双方风险划分的界限

D. 卖方在装运港船上完成交货义务

31. 信用证有关提单条款为"DOCUMENTS REQUIRED:FULL SET OF CLEAN ON BOARD MARINE BILL OF LADING,MADE OUT TO ORDER OF WIM BOSMAN BV, P. O. BOX 54064,NL-3008 JB ROTERDAM,NETHERLANDS."信用证未对提单做任何

其他规定,提单正本的签发份数(NO. OF ORIGINAL B(S)/L)应为(　　)。

A. 1份　　B. 2份

C. 3份　　D. 选项A和选项B错误

32. 在我国,签发原产地证的机构包括(　　)。

A. 海关总署及各省市海关　　B. 各省市出入境检验检疫局

C. 商务部及各省市经贸厅　　D. 各省市对外贸易促进委员会

33. 印刷在运输包装上的唛头,其作用是在运输过程中使有关人员易于辨认货物,便于核对单证,按习惯做法,唛头由(　　)提供。

A. 卖方　　B. 买方　　C. 船方　　D. 货代公司

34. 在国际贸易中,检验证书所起的作用有(　　)。

A. 公证证明

B. 买卖双方交接货物、结算货款和进行索赔和理赔的依据

C. 通关的有效凭证

D. 以信用证支付时,通常是银行议付货款的依据

35. 航空运单的托运人名称和地址栏目,一般填写(　　)。

A. 托运人的名称和地址　　B. 托运人的国家(或国家两字代号)

C. 托运人的传真、电传号码　　D. 托运人的电话号码

36. 某合资企业从韩国进口一批作为投资的机器设备,该合资企业委托A进出口公司对外签订进口合同,并代办进口手续。A进出口公司与外商订货后,随即委托B公司具体办理货物运输事宜,同时委托上海C报关公司负责办理进口报关手续。下列出现在报关单有关栏目内的单位,填写错误的是(　　)。

A. 经营单位:A进出口公司　　B. 收货单位:某合资企业

C. 申报单位:B公司　　D. 收货单位:A进出口公司

37. 若在信用证申请书中无明确规定,根据UCP 600的规定,应视为允许的有(　　)。

A. 分运　　B. 转运

C. 接受第三者装运单据　　D. 可撤销信用证

38. 制单原则中所说的"正确",其含义有(　　)。

A. 单单相符

B. 单证相符

C. 单同相符

D. 符合有关国际惯例和进口国有关法令法规

E. 符合国际统一格式

39. 程租船合同中,装卸条款的规定方法有(　　)。

A. FIO　　B. FCA　　C. FI　　D. FO

E. FIOST

40. 收汇单证的作用有(　　)。

A. 是付款依据。对进口商而言,根据出口商提供的收汇单证,了解出口商交付货物的品质及交货时间

B. 是履约证明。国际贸易中无论采用哪种方式收取货款,出口商都要提供收汇单

证,说明自己已经履行了合同中规定的义务

C. 是物权凭证。国际贸易中的买卖双方相隔遥远,交货过程中,有关单据起到了物权凭证的作用

D. 是企业经营成果的体现

三、判断题

1. 国际邮包运输具有国际多式联运和“门到门”运输的性质。 ( )

2. 签发国际多式联运提单的经营人,其责任只是对第一段运输负责。 ( )

3. 国际贸易惯例已得到各国公认,因此它对于买卖双方都具有普遍的法律约束力。 ( )

4. 合同的书面形式包括销售合同、购货确认书、备忘录、订单等形式。 ( )

5. 信用证要求海运提单,货物运抵 LATTAKIA PORT IN TRANSIT TO MAMASCUS,提单实际显示:PORT OF DISCHAGE:LA'ITAKINA,PLACE OF DELIVERY:DAMASCUS(SYRIA),因此,与信用证对海运提单的要求不符。 ( )

6. 开证申请书申明用 MTT00 格式,则表明该信用证是信开信用证格式。 ( )

7. 信用证中的保险条款规定 irrespective of percentage,则保险单中应有免赔率的条款。 ( )

8. 联合国设计推荐使用的运输标志(唛头)代码由收货人简称、合同号、目的地和件号四个部分组成。 ( )

9. 单证的完整性是指成套单证的群体的完整性。 ( )

10. 任何情况下,银行审核单据总是以 UCP 600 为依据。 ( )

11. 不使用海关发票或领事发票的国家,通常要求出口商提供原产地证明书,以确定对货物征税的税率。 ( )

12. 在进出口贸易中,我们要尽量选择对我方来说责任低、费用少和风险小的贸易术语。 ( )

13. 在象征性交货条件下,装运和交货同时发生,卖方凭单交货,买方凭单付款。 ( )

14. 航空运单的抬头一般可做成“凭指示(To order)”或“凭某人指示(To order of ABC)”的抬头。 ( )

15. 如果信用证对分批装运没有明确规定,就意味着不能分批装运。 ( )

16. 按 CIF 术语成交,卖方一般情况下只投保最低险别及战争险。 ( )

17. 汇票的“出票”就是出票人在汇票上写明有关内容并签名的行为。 ( )

18. CIF 被称作“到岸价”,如果按 CIF 价格成交,理所当然卖方承担货物到达目的港之前的风险与责任。 ( )

19. 我国国内的通过铁路运往港、澳的出口货物所使用的货运单据为承运货物收据。 ( )

20. 银行可以拒绝接受表明投保生效日期迟于装运日期的保险单。 ( )

四、简答题

1. 什么是贸易术语?选用贸易术语应考虑的因素是什么?

2. 简述合同有效成立的条件。

3. 我国某外贸公司向中东某商人 B 出口盘钢一批，支付方式为 L/C Sight Irrevocable，货物按时出运后，我国公司向银行按时交单，后接议付行通知，单据遭开证行拒付。开证行拒付的理由是：①B/L 正本仅提供了一份，不够“全套”；②提单上商品名称与 L/C 不符，只用了统称。试问开证行拒付是否有理？为什么？

4. 我国某外贸公司于 8 月 28 日接印尼客商来电洽购慈溪某公司的飞人牌抽油烟机 26 000 台。慈溪某公司恰巧有现货存于仓库，并查悉 9 月有班轮直达印尼雅加达。我方于 8 月 30 日向对方发盘：“现报即装飞人牌油烟机器 26 000 台，80 美元/台 CIF 雅加达，即期不可撤销信用证付款方式，限 9 月 10 日复到有效。”9 月 5 日对方复电称：“你 8 月 30 日发盘接受，即开信用证。”接电后，我方立即组织装运，取得 9 月 24 日的已装船清洁提单，但对方的信用证一直未到，几经催促，终于在 9 月 27 日收到对方 9 月 25 日电开出的信用证。信用证中规定：装运期为“不得迟于 10 月 15 日”，信用证的有效期为 10 月 30 日，交单期为提单日期后 15 天。请问：根据该信用证的规定，我方可否顺利收汇？为什么？

5. 我国某外贸公司出口卡拉奇小五金 100 箱，每箱净重 25 千克，毛重 28 千克，体积为 0.026 立方米，出口成本为 700.00 元/箱，外销价为 120.00 美元/箱 CFR 卡拉奇。海运费按照 W/M 计算，基本运费为 80.00 美元/运费吨，外加燃油附加费 15%。若收汇当天人民币对美元的银行换汇牌价比是 680∶100。试计算该商品出口销售换汇成本及盈亏率。（计算过程保留四位小数点，答案保留两位小数点。）

综合训练四

一、单项选择题

1. CIF Ex ship's hold 与 DAT 相比，买方承担的风险（　　）。

A. 前者大　　B. 两者相同

C. 后者大　　D. 买方不承担任何风险

2. 出口报关的时间应是（　　）。

A. 备货前　　B. 装船前　　C. 装船后　　D. 货到目的港后

3. 下列单证不属于包装单据的是（　　）

A. 重量单　　B. 尺码单　　C. 装货单　　D. 装箱单

4. 出票人签发支票时，应在付款银行存有不低于票面金额的存款。如果存款低于票面金额，则这种支票被称为（　　）。

A. 空头支票　　B. 划线支票　　C. 现金支票　　D. 转账支票

5. 汇票的抬头有三种填写方式，根据我国《票据法》的规定，签发（　　）的汇票无效。

A. 限制性抬头　　B. 指示性抬头

C. 持票人或来人抬头　　D. 记名抬头

6. 根据《国际货物销售合同公约》的规定，一项发盘必须具备的基本要素是（　　）。

A. 货名、品质、数量　　B. 货名、数量、价格

C. 货名、价格、支付方式　　D. 货名、品质、价格

7. 信用证的汇票条款注明 Drawn on us，则汇票的付款人应是（　　）。

A. 开证行　　B. 开证申请人　　C. 通知行　　D. 议付行

8. 卖方不负责办理出口手续及支付相关费用的术语是（　　）。

A. FCA　　B. CIP　　C. CPT　　D. DDP

9. 在出口业务中，国外客户往往要我国出口商提供 GSP Form A 产地证。在我国这种证书的签发机构是（　　）。

A. 商会　　B. 行业公会

C. 贸促会　　D. 出入境检验检疫局

10. 假定货物由承运人 COSCO 承运，船长为张三，提单由其代理 ABC SHIPPING CO. 签署，签发人为李四，如果提单表面已经表明了承运人的身份，则提单的签发应该是（　　）。

A. ABC SHIPPING CO. 李四 AS CARRIER

B. COSCO 张三 AS CARRIER

C. ABC SHIPPING CO. 李四 AS AGENT FOR THE CARRIER NAMED ABOVE

D. ABC SHIPPING CO. 张三 AS AGENT FOR THE CARRIER NAMED ABOVE

11. 若信用证规定货物装船后30天付款,则在信用证中的汇票付款期限栏应填写(　　)。

A. At 30 days after sight

B. At 30 days after B/L date,并在汇票上注明提单日期

C. At 30 days after drafts date

D. At ****** sight

12. 北京某贸易公司进口一批货物,从美国波士顿装运,经中国香港中转,运抵天津塘沽港报关进境。该公司填写进口报关单时,应在装货港一栏中填报(　　)。

A. 天津　　B. 塘沽港　　C. 波士顿　　D. 中国香港

13. 英国某买主向我国轻工业品进出口公司来电:"拟购奇奇牌儿童书包10,000个,请电告最低价格最快交货期。"此来电属交易磋商的(　　)环节。

A. 发盘　　B. 询盘　　C. 还盘　　D. 接受

14. 根据UCP 600的规定,银行审单时间最多为收到单据次日起的第(　　)个银行工作日。

A. 3　　B. 5　　C. 7　　D. 10

15. 开立信用证时要注意(　　)。

A. 证同一致　　B. 单证一致　　C. 单单一致　　D. 单货一致

16. 合同上货物名称是"SHIRTS",信用证上的名称误为"SKIRTS",受益人(　　)。

A. 应该修改信用证,把货物名称改正确

B. 不必修改信用证,按SHIRTS制单

C. 不必修改信用证,按SKIRTS制单

D. 不必修改信用证,按SKIRTS(SHIRTS)制单

17. 汇票上的出票日期也称汇票日期,是全套单据日期(　　)。

A. 最晚的一个,但不能晚于信用证有效期和规定的交单期

B. 最晚的一个,可以晚于信用证有效期

C. 最早的一个,但不要早于信用证开证日期

D. 最早的一个,可以早于信用证开证日期

18. 承兑是指汇票付款人承诺对远期汇票承担到期付款责任的行为。根据我国《票据法》的规定,自收到提示承兑汇票之日起(　　)天内,付款人必须做出承兑。

A. 2　　B. 3　　C. 4　　D. 5

19. 根据UCP 600的规定,开证行开立的信用证不会是(　　)。

A. 可撤销信用证　　B. 议付信用证

C. 跟单信用证　　D. 转让信用证

20.《1932年华沙-牛津规则》是国际法协会专门为解释(　　)合同而制定的。

A. FOB　　B. CFR　　C. CIF　　D. FCA

21. 我国某公司与外商签订一份CIF出口合同,以L/C为支付方式。国外银行开来的信用证中规定:"信用证有效期为8月10日,最迟装运期为7月31日。"我方加紧备货出运,于7月21日取得大副收据,并换回正本已装船清洁提单,我方应不迟于(　　)向银行提交单据。

A. 7月21日　　B. 7月31日　　C. 8月10日　　D. 8月11日

22. 根据 UCP 600 的规定，若信用证条款中未明确规定是否“允许分批装运”“允许转运”，则应将其视为(　　)。

A. 可允许分批装运，但不允许转运　　B. 可允许分批装运和转运

C. 可允许转运，但不允许分批装运　　D. 不允许分批装运和转运

23. “仓至仓”条款是(　　)。

A. 承运人负责运输起讫的条款

B. 保险人负责保险责任起讫的条款

C. 出口人负责交货责任起讫的条款

D. 进口人负责付款责任起讫的条款

24. 我某公司对外报价某商品 10 000 美元/公吨 CIF 纽约，该商品投保一切险，保险费率为 1%，现外商要求将价格改报为 CFR 纽约，我方应从原报价格中减去的保险费为(　　)

A. 1 100 美元　　B. 110 美元　　C. 1 1000 美元　　D. 9 900 美元

25. 在其他条件相同的前提下，(　　)的远期汇票对受款人最为有利。

A. 出票后 30 天付款　　B. 提单签发日后 30 天付款

C. 见票后 30 天付款　　D. 货到目的港后 30 天

26. 信用证经保兑后，保兑行(　　)。

A. 只有在开证行没有能力付款时，才能承担保证付款的责任

B. 和开证行一样，承担第一性付款责任

C. 需和开证行商议决定双方各自的责任

D. 只有在买方没有能力付款时，才承担保证付款的责任

27. 根据 UCP 600 的规定，信用证的第一付款人是(　　)。

A. 进口人　　B. 开证行　　C. 议付行　　D. 通知行

28. 国外开来的可撤销信用证规定，汇票的付款人为开证行，货物装船完毕，开证行没有撤销信用证，但出口人闻悉申请人已破产倒闭，则(　　)。

A. 由于付款人破产，货款将落空

B. 开证行获悉申请人破产后，即使货已装船，仍可撤回信用证，受益人未能取得货款

C. 只要单证相符，受益人仍可从开证行取得货款

D. 待付款人财产清算后方可收回货款

29. 承兑是(　　)对远期汇票表示承担到期付款责任的行为。

A. 付款人　　B. 收款人　　C. 出口人　　D. 议付银行

30. 我国香港某公司出售一批商品给美国 ABC Co.，美国银行开来一份不可撤销可转让信用证，我国香港某银行按香港某公司委托，将信用证转让给我国某进出口公司，如信用证内未对转让费用做明确规定，按惯例应由(　　)。

A. 我国某进出口公司负担　　B. 我国香港某公司负担

C. 美国 ABC Co. 负担　　D. 我国香港某银行负担

31. L/C 与托收相结合的支付方式，其全套货运单据应(　　)。

A. 随信用证项下的汇票

B. 随托收项下的汇票

C. 50%随信用证项下,50%随托收项下

D. 单据与票据分列在信用证和托收汇票项下

32. 检验证书的作用不包括(　　)。

A. 作为证明卖方所交货物的品质、重量(数量)、包装以及卫生条件等是否符合合同规定及索赔、理赔的依据

B. 确定检验标准和检验方法的依据

C. 作为卖方向银行议付货款的单据之一

D. 作为海关验关放行的凭证

33. 海关发票及领事发票(　　)。

A. 都由买方国家有关部门提供

B. 都由卖方国家有关部门提供

C. 前者由买方国家提供,后者由卖方国家提供

D. 前者由卖方国家提供,后者由买方国家提供

34. 根据 UCP 600 的规定,海运提单中货物的描述(　　)。

A. 必须与信用证规定完全一致

B. 必须使用货物的全称

C. 只要与信用证对货物的描述不相抵触,可使用货物的统称

D. 必须与商业发票的填写完全一致

35. 一份 CIF 合同下,合同与信用证均没有规定投保何种险别,交单时保险单上反映出投保了平安险,该出口商品为易碎品,而其他单据与信用证要求相符。因此,(　　)。

A. 银行将拒收单据　　B. 买方将拒收单据

C. 买方应接受单据　　D. 银行应接受单据

36. 信用证修改通知书的内容在两项以上者,受益人(　　)。

A. 要么全部接受,要么全部拒绝　　B. 可选择接受

C. 必须全部接受　　D. 只能部分接受

37. 商业发票的抬头人一般是(　　)。

A. 受益人　　B. 开证申请人　　C. 开证银行　　D. 卖方

38. 进口许可证自签发之日起(　　)内有效。

A. 三个月　　B. 一年　　C. 一个月　　D. 半年

39. 一般情况下,发票金额应与(　　)一致。

A. 合同金额　　B. 信用证金额　　C. 保险金额　　D. 汇票金额

40. 如来证没有申请人(或付款人)一栏,而是直接指明汇票付款人时,如"WE OPEN CREDIT NO. PS8803 AVAILABLE BY DRAFTS DRAWN ON EEC CO.,LTD.",那么发票的抬头人应写成(　　)。

A. 不填　　B. 开证行

C. DRAWN ON EEC CO.,LTD.　　D. EEC CO.,LTD.

二、多项选择题

1. FOB 贸易术语的变形有(　　)。

A. FOB班轮条件　　B. FOB包括平舱、理舱

C. FOB包括理舱　　D. FOB吊钩下交货

2. 伦敦保险协会海运货物保险条款所规定的险别中可单独投保的有(　　)。

A. ICC(A)、ICC(B)、ICC(C)　　B. 协会战争条款

C. 协会罢工条款　　D. 恶意损害险条款

3. 我方出口商品单价写法正确的有(　　)。

A. 每打50港元FOB广州黄埔

B. 每套200美元CIFC 3%香港

C. 每台5 800日元FOB大连,含2%的折扣

D. 每桶36英镑CFR伦敦

4. 下列说法中正确的是(　　)。

A. 远期本票的当事人有出票人、收款人、付款人

B. 商业本票有即期和远期之分

C. 远期本票不需承兑

D. 本票的付款人是出票人

5. 根据我国《商检法》的规定,地方检验检疫局在进出口商品检验方面的基本任务是(　　)。

A. 对所有商品进行检验检疫　　B. 实施法定检验

C. 办理鉴定业务　　D. 对进出口商品工作实施监督管理

6. 在国际贸易中,合同生效的时间主要有(　　)。

A. 接受送达发盘人时

B. 依约定签订正式书面合同时

C. 依国家法律或行政法规的规定,合同获得批准时

D. 口头合同被当即接受时

7. 在国际贸易中,合同成立的有效条件包括(　　)。

A. 当事人必须具有签订合同的行为能力

B. 合同必须有对价或约因

C. 合同的形式和内容必须符合法律的要求

D. 合同当事人的意思表示必须真实

8. 商业发票的作用主要有(　　)。

A. 进出口报关完税必不可少的单据　　B. 是全套单据的中心

C. 是结算货款的依据　　D. 是物权凭证

9. 如果货物运输的装运港为GUANGZHOU,目的港为LONDON,转运港为HONGKONG,且合同和信用证没有对提单中的转运港有特别要求,那么,海运提单对转运港的标示方式可采用(　　)。

A. 在装运港栏目填写GUANGZHOU/HONGKONG

B. 在目的港栏目填写LONDON W/T HONGKONG

C. 在目的港栏目填写LONDON VIA HONGKONG

D. 在海运提单上注明FROM GUANGZHOU TO LONDON VIA HONGKONG

10. 普惠制原产地证明书 FORM A 的申报日期(　　)。

A. 早于发票日期　　B. 不得早于发票日期

C. 与发票日期同日　　D. 与提单日期同日

11. 航空运单的作用包括(　　)。

A. 航空运单是航空运输承运人与托运人之间的运输合同

B. 航空运单是航空公司或其代理人收运货物的证明文件

C. 航空运单是承运人核收运费的依据

D. 航空运单是承运人处理货物运输过程情况的依据

12. (　　)是结汇单据,如果缮制错漏、延误等,就会影响安全结汇。

A. 汇票　　B. 发票　　C. 托运单　　D. 受益人证明书

13. 进口货物报关单有若干联,属于基本联的有(　　)。

A. 海关留存联　　B. 企业留存联　　C. 海关核销联　　D. 海关统计联

14. 我国某合资企业从英国进口一批作为投资的机器设备,该合资企业委托 A 进出口公司对外签订进口合同,并代办进口手续,A 进出口公司与外商订货后,随即委托 B 公司具体办理货物运输事宜。下列出现在报关单栏目内的单位,错误的是(　　)。

A. 经营单位:A 进出口公司　　B. 收货单位:某合资企业

C. 申报单位:B 公司　　D. 收货单位:A 进出口公司

15. 信用证申请书上常见的付款方式有(　　)。

A. 即期支付　　B. 承兑支付　　C. 议付　　D. 延期支付

16. 申请开立信用证的具体手续有(　　)。

A. 递交有关合同的副本及附件　　B. 填写开证申请书

C. 缴付保证金　　D. 递交发票

17. 单证工作主要有(　　)等方面的内容,它贯穿于进出口合同履行的全过程。

A. 审证　　B. 制单　　C. 审单　　D. 交单

18. 关于制单的"完整"原则,下列表述正确的有(　　)。

A. 单据种类的完整　　B. 单据所填内容的完整

C. 每种单据份数的完整　　D. 出单日期的完整表述

19. 按照贸易双方设计的单证划分,出口单证包括(　　)。

A. 商业发票　　B. 汇票　　C. 信用证　　D. 产地证

20. 托收的优点包括(　　)。

A. 进口人可免去申请开立信用证的手续,不必预付银行押金

B. 属于银行信用,出口人能安全、及时收汇

C. 有利于资金融通和周转,增强出口商品的竞争力

D. 减少费用支出

21. 根据 UCP 600 的规定,下列关于通知行责任的叙述,正确的有(　　)。

A. 决定通知时要检验信用证的表面真实性

B. 决定不通知时必须告知开证行以免误事

C. 对内容不全、条款不清的信用证或修改书,可以预先通知受益人仅供参考而不承担责任

D. 如果开证行授权通知行对信用证加具保兑,通知行必须根据开证行指示行事

22. 海运提单要求做成指示性抬头,CONSIGNEE一栏可以填写(　　)。

A. TO ORDER　　B. TO ORDER OF SHIPPER

C. TO CONSIGNED　　D. TO ORDER OF ISSUING BANK

23. 在使用提单的正常情况下,收货人要取得提货的权利,必须(　　)。

A. 将全套提单交回承运人　　B. 将任一份提单交回承运人

C. 在提单上正确背书　　D. 付清应支付的费用

24. 租船订舱所需要的单据有(　　)。

A. 托运单　　B. 装货单　　C. 装箱单　　D. 海运提单

25. 装箱单的作用主要是补充发票内容的不足,通过填制包装件数、唛头、规格等,明确产品的包装情况,(　　)。

A. 便于进口商了解产品的数量与包装

B. 便于进口国海关检查与核对产品

C. 是出口商必须向进口商提交的单据

D. 是出口商必须向银行提交的单据

26. 属于商业信用的结算方式有(　　)。

A. 电汇　　B. 信用证　　C. 付款交单　　D. 承兑交单

27. 商业发票是出口商在准备全套出口文件时首先缮制的单证,因为在出口货物装运前的(　　)环节中要使用它。

A. 托运订舱　　B. 办理投保　　C. 出口报关　　D. 商品报检

28. FOB、CFR、CIF和FCA、CPT、CIP两组术语的价格构成都包括(　　)。

A. 保险费　　B. 进货成本　　C. 费用　　D. 净利润

29. 提单或航空货运单中的SHIPPER可以是(　　)。

A. 销售合同中的供货商　　B. 买卖合同中的购货商

C. 将货物交给承运人的人　　D. 与承运人签订代理合同的人

30. 如果信用证中没有特别规定,原产地证可以由(　　)出具。

A. 商检局　　B. 贸促会　　C. 生产企业　　D. 出口企业

31. 报关程序按时间先后分为前期阶段、进出境阶段、后续阶段。其中对进出口货物的收发货人而言,在进出境阶段包括(　　)等环节。

A. 进出口申报　　B. 缴纳税费　　C. 备案、销案　　D. 配合查验

32. 信用证做了如下规定,其中属于"非单据条件"的有(　　)。

A. 载货船舶的船龄不超过15年

B. 载货船舶挂巴拿马国旗

C. 装船后立即通知申请人装货细节并提交传真副本

D. 提供原产地证明书

33. 唛头的主要内容包括(　　)。

A. 目的港(地)名称　　B. 收货人名称

C. 件号　　D. 信用证号或合同号

34. 进出口报关时不必在报关单随附单据栏目中填写的必备的随附单证有(　　)。

A. 商业发票　B. 通关单　C. 装箱单　D. 许可证

35. 在实际业务中,凭信用证成交出口的货物,如货物出运后,发现单证不符,又因为时间的限制,无法在信用证有效期或交单期内做到单证相符,可采取的变通办法有(　　)。

A. 担保议付　B. 采用"电提"方式征求开证行意见

C. 改成"跟证托收"　D. 直接要求买方付款

36. 被视为信用证的"软条款"的是(　　)。

A. 检验人在检验证书上的签名必须与开证行所保留的签名样本相符

B. 受益人出具的报关单、合同及商业发票必须做使馆认证

C. 必须得到开证申请人对样品的确认后,信用证方可生效

D. 货物必须经有关人员检验合格后方可装船

37. 国际货款结算票据主要包括(　　)。

A. 外币现钞　B. 汇票　C. 支票　D. 本票

38. 根据我国《票据法》,汇票上必须记载的事项包括(　　)。

A. 确定的金额　B. 汇票日期　C. 付款人名称　D. 合同编号

39. 多式联运提单的副本是不可转让的,提单上(　　)属于副本。

A. 注有"Original"字样的

B. 未签署的

C. 未注明"Original"字样的

D. 未注明"Original"字样的或"Copy"字样的

40. 一般情况下,出境货物报检时需提交的单证有(　　)。

A. 汇票　B. 发票

C. 合同　D. 包装性能结果单

三、判断题

1. 如果国外银行开来信用证中金额比买卖合同的金额多了 1 000 美元,装运期比合同规定早了 20 天,受益人可要求对装运期进行修改,信用证金额不必修改。(　　)

2. 在交易磋商过程中,对发盘的逾期接受一律无效。(　　)

3. 国际贸易惯例已得到多国的公认,因此,它对于任何买卖合同当事人具有普遍的法律上的约束。(　　)

4. 在航空运输中,收货人提货是凭航空公司的提货通知单。(　　)

5. 空白抬头、空白背书的提单是指提单收货人一栏内空白而不需要背书的提单。(　　)

6. 汇票是信用证项下的必备单证。(　　)

7. 信用证规定的装运期是 6 月 30 日,有效期是 7 月 15 日,交单期是提单日期后 21 天。若实际装船日是 6 月 25 日,受益人可以于 7 月 16 日交单。(　　)

8. 信用证关于货物的描述为"blue cotton wears",发票显示为"colored cotton wears"是可以接受的。(　　)

9. 集装箱运输是以集装箱作为运输单位进行运输的一种现代化的运输方式,适用于海洋运输、铁路运输、公路运输和国际多式联运等。(　　)

10. 一项合同的有效成立必须经过询盘、发盘、还盘、接受四个环节。(　　)

11. 我方按 CIF 伦敦出口英国一批产品，即交货地点为伦敦。（　）

12. 保险单据的签发日期应迟于提单签发日期。（　）

13. 托收支付方式是商业信用，所使用的汇票属于商业汇票；信用证支付方式是银行信用，所使用的汇票属于银行汇票。（　）

14. 出口公司在收到对方开出的不可撤销信用证后，应严格按照信用证条款进行发货、装运、制单、结汇。在任何情况下，都无权要求开证行撤销信用证。（　）

15. 没有有效到期日期的信用证，应以最后装运期限作为有效到期日期。（　）

16. 根据 UCP 600 的规定，在规定装运期时，如使用了“迅速”“立即”“尽快”或类似词句者，银行将不予置理。（　）

17. 根据 UCP 600 的规定，信用证项下单据应在信用证效期和交单期内向银行提交，如果信用证对“交单期”未做出规定，则交单期不得迟于运输单据日后的 21 天，并且不得迟于信用证的有效期。（　）

18. 对外已签合同的进口货物，在进口许可证有效期限内尚未进口的，则可到原发证机构申请进口许可证的展期，但不能超过次年的 3 月底。（　）

19. 海运提单代表货物的所有权，持单人或正当被背书人可凭它提取货物。（　）

20. 在信用证业务中，信用证的开立是以买卖合同为基础的，因此，信用证条款与买卖合同条款严格相符是开证行向受益人承担付款责任的前提条件。（　）

四、简答题

1. 简述 FOB、CFR、CIF 与 FCA、CPT、CIP 两组贸易术语的异同。

2. 简述出口业务程序。

3. 简述信用证与买卖合同的关系。

4. 简述进口货物通关的程序。

5. 我方出口货物 2 300 件，对外报价为 3 美元/件 CFR 利物浦。为避免漏报，客户来证要求我方装船前按 CIF 总值代为办理投保手续。查得该货的保险费率为 0.8%。试问，我方对该货投保时，投保金额和应缴纳的保险费是多少？（计算结果保留两位小数。）

综合训练五

一、单项选择题

1. 根据《联合国国际货物销售合同公约》的规定，合同成立的时间是(　　)。

A. 接受生效的时间　　B. 交易双方签订书面合同的时间

C. 在合同获得国家批准时　　D. 当发盘到达受盘人时

2. 有关国际贸易术语的国际贸易惯例，使用最广泛的和影响最大的是(　　)。

A. UCP 600

B.《2010 年国际贸易术语解释通则》

C.《1990 年美国对外贸易定义修正本》

D.《1932 年华沙-牛津规则》

3. 在 CFR 合同下，如果卖方装船后未及时向买方发出装船通知，致使买方未能办理货运保险，则运输途中的风险由(　　)。

A. 买方承担　　B. 卖方承担

C. 承运人承担　　D. 买卖双方各承担一半

4. 某外贸公司对外以 CFR 报价，如果该公司先将货物交到货站或使用滚装与集装箱运输时，应采用(　　)为宜。

A. FCA　　B. CIP　　C. CPT　　D. CFR

5. 上海某公司从美国某公司进口货物，货物从纽约运至上海，单价的正确表示方法为(　　)。

A. UCD9.00 EACH PIECE FOB SHANGHAI

B. UCD9.00 EACH PIECE CIF NEWYORK

C. UCD9.00 EACH PIECE CFR NEWYORK

D. UCD9.00 EACH PIECE CIP SHANGHAI

6. 汇付的三种汇款方法中，以(　　)方式付款最为快捷。

A. 电汇　　B. 信汇　　C. 票汇　　D. 信用证

7. 在托运、报检和报关的单证中，由出口商出具的有关单证是(　　)。

A. 发票、报关单、报检单和提单　　B. 发票、装箱单、报检单和通关单

C. 发票、报关单、装箱单和提单　　D. 发票、装箱单、报检单和托运单

8. CIF 条件下交货，(　　)。

A. 装运时间先于交货时间　　B. 装运时间迟于交货时间

C. 装运时间与交货时间一致　　D. 其先后次序视运输方式而定

9. 我国某公司与美国某公司以 CFR Ex ship's hold New York 的条件成交了一笔出口生意，按照一般惯例，这批货物在纽约港的卸货费用应由(　　)承担。

A. 美国某公司　　B. 我国某公司　　C. 承运人　　D. 保险公司

10. 海运提单日期应理解为(　　)。

A. 签订运输合同的日期　　B. 货物开始装船的日期

C. 货物装船过程中任何一天　　D. 货物装船完毕的日期

11. 我国某公司与国外一家公司以 EXW 条件成交了一笔买卖,在这种情况下,其交货地点不正确的是(　　)。

A. 出口国港口　　B. 商品产地　　C. 出口商工厂　　D. 出口商仓库

12. 下列条件中,不是构成发盘的必备条件的是(　　)。

A. 发盘的内容必须十分确定　　B. 主要交易条件必须十分完整齐全

C. 向一个或一个以上特定的人发出　　D. 表明发盘人承受约束的意旨

13. 我方以 100 美元/箱 CIF 纽约价出口货物 100 箱,合同允许 5%的数量增减,实际交货 105 箱,我方应收款(　　)。

A. 10 000 美元　　B. 10 500 美元　　C. 9 500 美元　　D. 双方再协议

14. 在使用(　　)贸易术语进行交易时,卖方及时向买方发出"已装船通知"至关重要,因为它将直接影响买卖双方对运输途中的风险承担。

A. CIP　　B. DAT　　C. FCA　　D. CFR

15. 我国供货商出口给英国一批货物共 10 万美元,分批交货,信用证支付。与我国供货商签订合同的是新加坡一家公司,信用证由英国进口商开立,然后新加坡的有关银行按照信用证的要求将该证转给我国供货商,则这张信用证是(　　)。

A. 可转让信用证　　B. 不可转让信用证

C. 可循环信用证　　D. 可撤销信用证

16. 按照 INCOTERMS 2010 的规定,CIF 和 CIP 的区别是(　　)。

A. 出口报关责任负担不同　　B. 进口报关责任负担不同

C. 保险费、海运费负担不同　　D. 风险转移界限不同

17. 如果信用证显示"Available with any bank",在缮制汇票时,受款人栏目(　　)。

A. 只能填写 ANY BANK　　B. 可以由受益人指定

C. 只能由开证行指定　　D. 可以由进口商指定

18. 在一般情况下,按 CFR 贸易术语成交的合同中,不应计入货物价格的是(　　)。

A. 货物成本　　B. 海运费　　C. 保险费　　D. 各项出口税费

19. 在托收项下,单据缮制一般以(　　)为依据。如有特殊要求,应参照相应文件或资料。

A. 信用证　　B. 发票　　C. 合同　　D. 提单

20. 假定货物由承运人 COSCO 承运,船长为张三,提单由其代理 ABC SHIPPING CO. 签署,签发人为李四,如果提单表面已经表明了承运人的身份,则提单的签发应该是(　　)。

A. ABC SHIPPING CO. 李四 AS CARRIER

B. COSCO 张三 AS CARRIER

C. ABC SHIPPING CO. 李四 AS AGENT FOR THE CARRIER NAMED ABOVE

D. ABC SHIPPING CO. 张三 AS AGENT FOR THE CARRIER NAMED ABOVE

21. 订舱委托书的主要作用是(　　)。

A. 承运人制作、签发提单的依据　　B. 报关单的依据

C. 目的港代理交货依据　　D. 出口商申请出口退税的依据

22. 海关凭出入境检验检疫机构填发的有关单据对进口货物办理海关通关手续，该单据是（　　）。

A. 进口许可证　　B. 进口货物报关单

C. 查验通知　　D. 入境货物通关单

23. 下面关于提单的说法正确的是（　　）。

A. 提单是代表货物所有权的物权凭证或运输契约

B. 提单辅助发票说明它的不足，并详细说明包装内容或货物数量，以及标记号

C. 提单是国外卖方或厂商对货物出具的明细账单

D. 提单又称来源证，主要对货物的产地、厂家作佐证，这有助于海关掌握国别地区，在纳税时进行参考

24. 在CIF条件下，开证申请书应标明要求卖方提交的提单有（　　）字样。

A. 运费已付　　B. 保费已付　　C. 清洁提单　　D. 运费未收

25. 进口商在开立信用证时，要注意信用证与合同保持一致，必须做到（　　）。

A. 使用“参阅第××号合同”或“第××号合同项下货物”等条款

B. 以对外签订的买卖合同（包括修改后的买卖合同）为依据，合同中规定要在信用证上明确的条款都必须列明

C. 将有关合同作为信用证附件附在信用证后

D. 标明信用证是合同的附属文件

26. 下列关于信用证的表述不正确的是（　　）。

A. 开立信用证时，进口商应向银行交付保证金

B. 开证行根据合同开立信用证

C. 开证后，银行的权利和义务只限于信用证的规定，只对信用证负责

D. 开证后，银行的权利和义务还要受到合同的约束

27. 若信用证规定“DRAWN ON US”，则汇票应该（　　）。

A. 在付款人栏目处填写“US”

B. 在受款人栏目处填写“US”

C. 在付款人栏目处填写“开证行名称”

D. 在付款人栏目处填写“开证申请人名称”

28. 结汇单证中的汇票，指用于托收和信用证收汇方式中，出口商向进口商或银行签发的，要求后者即期或在一个固定的日期或在可以确定的将来时间，对某人或其指定人或持票人支付一定金额的无条件的书面支付命令。大部分情况下使用的汇票是（　　）。

A. 光票　　B. 跟单汇票　　C. 银行汇票　　D. 商业承兑汇票

29. 信用证项下，受益人向客户收取货款的凭据是（　　）。

A. 实际货物　　B. 与信用证规定相符的全套单据

C. 买卖合同　　D. 客户保函

30. 在国际商务单证缮制的基本要求中，（　　）是单证工作的前提。

A. 正确　　B. 整洁　　C. 及时　　D. 简明

31. 关于各种单据的出单日期，下列表述正确的是（　　）。

A. 保险单的出单期可以晚于已装船提单的出单期

B. 提单签发日可迟于信用证或合同规定的最迟装运时间

C. 通常汇票是议付单据中出单时间最晚的单据

D. 议付单据中,发票日期一般比其他单据晚

32. 一般而言,对于出口商来说,采用信用证结算方式比采用即期付款交单结算方式承担的风险(　　)。

A. 更小　　B. 更大　　C. 一样　　D. 无法比较

33. 根据 UCP 600 的规定,若信用证条款未明确规定是否"允许分期发运""允许转运",则应理解为(　　)。

A. 允许分期发运,但不允许转运　　B. 允许分期发运,允许转运

C. 允许转运,但不允许分期发运　　D. 不允许分期发运,不允许转运

34. 纸质托运单一式十联单,其中,(　　)是托运单的核心。此联在海关放行后被海关盖上"放行章",船公司据此联才可以将货物装上船。

A. 第二联船代留底　　B. 第五联装货单

C. 第七联场站收据　　D. 第九联配舱回单

35. 若货物从广州运往荷兰的鹿特丹港口后,再运至德国一内陆城市 SCHORNDORF,贸易术语为 CIF ROTTERDAM,则托运单的目的港应填(　　)。

A. ROTTERDAM　　B. NETHERLAND

C. SCHORNDORF　　D. GERMANY

36. 我国 A 公司以海运 CIF 贸易术语进口一批货物,国外卖方提交的海运提单上的"运费支付"一栏应填写(　　)。

A. Freight Prepaid　　B. Freight as Arranged

C. Freight Collect　　D. Freight Payable at Destination

37. 一般出口商品应在出口报关或装运前(　　)天报检。

A. 3　　B. 5　　C. 7　　D. 9

38. 我方报价 CIF 安特卫普 USD2 000/MT,对方要求 2%的折扣,则折实售价为(　　)。

A. USD1 690　　B. USD1 960　　C. USD1 069　　D. USD40

39. 根据我国有关规定,出口企业最迟于货物出运前 3 天,持签证机构规定的正本文件,向签证机构申请办理一般原产地证书。申请一般原产地证书时不需要的文件是(　　)。

A. 一般原产地证书申请单　　B. 中华人民共和国原产地证书

C. 正本商业发票　　D. 商检证书

40. 国际上针对不符点单据的交单,规定出口商提供给议付行的额外单据是(　　)。

A. 权威机构出具的检验证书　　B. 担保书

C. 出口商的财务报表　　D. 出口商的经营情况

二、多项选择题

1. 电子报关申报方式包括(　　)。

A. 终端申报方式　　B. 录入申报方式

C. 网上申报方式　　D. EDI 申报方式

2. 下列对模板式制单软件的表述，正确的有（　　）。

A. 操作简单，方便实现单证的信息化管理

B. 它是当今国内外贸易企业使用的业务运作管理系统

C. 它是一套集合了众多不同单证不同版本模板的外贸制单软件

D. 所填即所得

3. 玉米等谷物产品实行非“一批一证”制度的出口许可证的使用规定包括（　　）。

A. 无配额管理　　B. 多次出口报关使用

C. 最多不超过12次　　D. 海关在许可证上签批

4. 国际商务单证的工作意义有（　　）。

A. 它是国际结算的工具　　B. 它是经营管理的重要环节

C. 它代表了一笔交易的本质　　D. 它是政策性很强的涉外工作

5. 外贸单证工作具有（　　）等特点，必须仔细、认真、及时地做好这项工作。

A. 工作量大　　B. 涉及面广　　C. 实践性强　　D. 要求高

6. 按照海关规定的《结汇方式代码表》，出口货物报关单中的“结汇方式”栏可以填写（　　）。

A. 信汇　　B. 信用证　　C. 汇票　　D. 电汇

7. 在我国的出口业务中，实施法定检验的范围包括（　　）。

A. 列入《商检机构实施检验的进出口商品种类表》的进口商品

B. 对有关国际条约规定须商检机构检验的进口商品

C. 进口商品的残损鉴定和海损鉴定

D. 对其他法律、行政法规规定须经商检机构检验的进口商品

8. 出口企业申请签发普惠制原产地证书应提供的单证和资料有（　　）。

A. 普惠制原产地证书申请书一份

B. 普惠制原产地证书(FORM A)一套

C. 正式的出口商业发票正本一份，装箱单一份

D. 含有进口成分的产品，应提交《含进口成分商品成本明细单》

9. 信用证审核的要点包括（　　）。

A. 是否与开证申请书一致　　B. 信用证条款与买卖合同是否一致

C. 是否加列了对卖方不利的条款　　D. 是否有境外有效期

E. 是否存在着软条款

10. 我国出口公司A公司与菲律宾进口公司B公司签订贸易合同，规定采用CIF贸易术语，采用L/C付款，则A公司应该承担的义务有（　　）。

A. 租船、发货、装船并支付运费，及时向B公司发出已经装船的通知

B. 提供进口许可证、办理货物水上运输保险以及进口清关手续

C. 承担货物运至装运港船上的一切费用并支付保险费、进口关税以及费用

D. 提供商业发票、相关货物单据和相应的电子信息

11. 按CIF术语成交的合同，卖方交货后办理交单议付，必须提交的单据包括（　　）。

A. 商业发票　　B. 保险单　　C. 提单　　D. 商检证书

E. 进口许可证

12. 根据 UCP 600 的规定，信用证项下汇票的付款人应规定为（　　）。
A. 开证行　　B. 开证行指定的银行
C. 开证申请人　　D. 开证申请人指定的银行

13. 根据 UCP 600 的规定，信用证支付方式的特点有（　　）。
A. 信用证属于银行信用，开证行负有第一性付款责任
B. 信用证一经开证行开立，即是独立于买卖合同之外的自主性文件
C. 信用证条件下由申请人直接向卖方付款
D. 信用证业务是一种单纯的单据业务，银行只处理单据，不涉及货物和合同行为

14. 对托运人而言，选择海上货物承运人时，主要考虑的因素包括（　　）。
A. 运输服务的定期性　　B. 运输时间
C. 运输费用　　D. 运输的可靠性
E. 承运人的经营状况和责任

15. 出口货物托运人缮制《国际货物托运委托书》所依据的文件有（　　）。
A. 外销出仓单　　B. 销售合同　　C. 信用证　　D. 配舱回单

16. 在海运实践中，有权签发提单的当事人有（　　）。
A. 承运人本人　　B. 货代公司
C. 载货船长　　D. 经承运人授权的代理人

17. 以下单据中，对发票起补充说明作用的有（　　）。
A. 装箱单　　B. 提单　　C. 尺码单　　D. 重量单
E. 品质证书

18. 缮制受益人证明等附属单据时，必须注意（　　）。
A. 单据名称和出具人签署应符合信用证要求
B. 单据内容应符合信用证要求，并与其他单据相关内容不矛盾
C. 应该至少提供一份正本
D. 应注明出单日

19. 采用集装箱海运出口的货物，卖方采用 FCA 比 FOB 更为有利的是（　　）。
A. 可以提前转移风险　　B. 可以提早取得运输单据
C. 可以减少卖方的风险责任　　D. 可以提早交单结汇

20. 托收业务的主要当事人有（　　）。
A. 委托人　　B. 汇出行　　C. 提示行　　D. 托收行
E. 代收行

21. 付款交单业务的主要特征有（　　）。
A. 付款交单属于商业信用
B. 付款交单业务中为融资目的也可使用远期汇票
C. 付款交单的安全性高于承兑交单
D. 付款交单属于银行信用

22. 按 FOB 价格术语成交，报价中包含（　　）。
A. 购货成本　　B. 国内费用　　C. 国外运费　　D. 保险费
E. 利润

23. 海运提单做成指示性抬头时，提单收货人一栏可以填写(　　)。

A. to order of shipper　　B. to order of issuing bank

C. to issuing bank　　D. to order

24. 产地证书是由出口国政府有关机构签发的一种证明货物原产地或制造地的证明文件，通常多用于不需要提供(　　)的国家和地区。

A. 海关发票　　B. 领事发票　　C. 形式发票　　D. 厂商发票

E. 商业发票

25. 对检验时间、地点的规定方法，符合惯例的有(　　)。

A. 出口国检验　　B. 进口国检验

C. 出口国检验，进口国复验　　D. 离岸重量，到岸品质

26. 在出口业务中，卖方可凭以结汇的运输单据有(　　)。

A. 海运提单　　B. 铁路提单正本

C. 承运货物收据　　D. 大副收据

27. 进口报检应随附的单据或证件有(　　)。

A. 核销单　　B. 国外商业发票和装箱清单

C. 运输单据　　D. 进口货物通知书

28. 买方应按合同规定的开证时间填写开证申请书并办理开证手续，开证行对开证申请书审核无误后，收取(　　)，按开证申请书的要求开出信用证。

A. 订单　　B. 保证金　　C. 开证手续费　　D. 合同书

29. 根据《联合国国际货物销售合同公约》的规定，对发盘表示接受可以采取的方式有(　　)。

A. 书面　　B. 行为　　C. 缄默　　D. 口头

30. 进口合同如采用FOB条件，下列表述正确的有(　　)。

A. 一般由出口商办理保险事宜

B. 出口商提供的单据中应有发票

C. 发票中的货物描述应与买卖合同或信用证规定相符

D. 提单中应有“Freight payable at destination”字样

31. 我国某合资企业从韩国进口一批机器设备，该合资企业委托A进出口公司代办进口手续。A进出口公司与外商订货后，随即委托B公司具体办理货物运输事宜，同时委托上海C报关公司负责办理进口报关手续。下列出现在报关单有关栏目内的单位，填写错误的有(　　)。

A. 经营单位：A进出口公司　　B. 收货单位：我国某合资企业

C. 申报单位：B公司　　D. 收货单位：A进出口公司

32. 我国A公司向海关申报进口一批小轿车，价格术语为FOB横滨，共10 000 000日元。其中，运费为200 000日元，保险费率为5‰，消费税税率为8%。100 000日元兑换人民币买卖中间价为8 500元，小轿车的关税税率为80%。下列说明正确的有(　　)。

A. 该批小轿车的关税完税价格为871 357元人民币

B. 该批小轿车的关税完税价格为697 085.6元人民币

C. 该批小轿车的关税税额为1 704 829元人民币

D. 该批小轿车的关税税额为 697 085.6 元人民币

33. 报关基本单证包括（　　）。

A. 商业发票　　B. 贸易合同　　C. 装箱单　　D. 通关单

34. 信用证项下的汇票出票日期是议付日期，汇票的出票日期（　　）。

A. 不得晚于信用证有效期　　B. 不得晚于提单签发日后第 21 日

C. 不得早于其他单据日期　　D. 可以早于其他单据日期

35. 提单是物权凭证，持单人可凭以提货。进口人审核提单时应注意的要点有（　　）。

A. 提单应具备全套可转让提单并注明承运人的具体名称，由承运人或作为承运人的具名代理、船长或作为船长的具名代理签署

B. 提单上的文字如有更改时，应有提单签署人的签字或有签发提单的公司的签章

C. 提单的日期应迟于信用证上规定的最迟装运日期

D. 提单向指定银行提示的日期原则上不得迟于提单签发日后 21 天，信用证另有规定的从信用证规定，但无论如何不得晚于信用证的有效期

36. 使用（　　）术语时，应在信用证申请书中的保单条款前的括号打"×"。

A. CIF　　B. FOB　　C. CFR　　D. CIP

37. 在有具体唛头的情况下，保险单唛头一栏可填写（　　）。

A. 发票上的唛头　　B. As per Invoice NO. …（发票号码）

C. N/M　　D. N/N

E. M/M

38. 托收结算方式的主要当事人有（　　）。

A. REMITTING BANK　　B. PRINCIPAL

C. NEGOTIATING BANK　　D. COLLECTING BANK

E. PAYER

39. 集装箱运输的主要交接方式有（　　）。

A. 整箱/整箱（FCL/FCL）　　B. 整箱/拼箱（FCL/LCL）

C. 拼箱/整箱（LCL/FCL）　　D. 拼箱/拼箱（LCL/LCL）

E. 以上均不正确

40. 用于议付信用证项下结算的汇票可以是（　　）。

A. 即期汇票　　B. 远期汇票　　C. 商业汇票　　D. 银行汇票

E. 以上均可

三、判断题

1. 在国际贸易中，对以重量计价的商品，若没有明确规定，按惯例应以净重计价。（　　）

2. 在交易磋商过程中，发盘的是卖方，接受的是买方。（　　）

3. 投保人在投保一切险后，根据需要还可加保特殊附加险。（　　）

4. 签发国际多式联运提单的承运人只对第一程运输负责。（　　）

5.《1941 年美国对外贸易定义本》是美国法协会专门为解释 CIF 贸易条件而制定的。（　　）

6. 在 CFR 条件下，如合同未规定卖方发送"装船通知"，卖方将货物在规定时间内装上

海轮后,可以不必向买方发送“装船通知”。 ( )

7. 按照 CIF Landed 术语成交的一批货物,货物由船上卸至码头上的费用,包括舶船费、码头费,应由买方承担。 ( )

8. D/A 的英文是 Documents against Acceptance,中文翻译为承兑交单,是跟单托收的一种交单方式,指出口商的交单必须以进口商的承兑为条件。 ( )

9. 在信用证业务中,有关当事人所处理的只是单据,而不涉及单据的货物、服务或其他行为。 ( )

10. FOB、CFR 和 CIF 三种常用的贸易术语都是象征性交货。 ( )

11. 单价表述四要素是:计量单位、单价金额、计价货币和目的地。 ( )

12. 根据《托收统一规则》的规定,未经银行事先同意,货物不能直接发给银行,也不能做成以银行为收货人的记名提单。否则,由发货人自行承担货物的风险和责任。 ( )

13. 如果合同和信用证中均未规定具体唛头,货物为大宗散装货物,则发票的唛头栏可以留空不填。 ( )

14. 支票是出票人签发的,委托办理支票存款业务的银行或其他金融机构,在见票时无条件支付确定金额给收款人或持票人的票据。 ( )

15. 按我国惯例做法,若以 CFR 和 FOB 贸易术语成交,我国进口商在接到国外出口商发来的装船通知后,即应填制投保单或预约保险启运通知书,向保险公司投保。 ( )

16. 清洁提单是指提单的表面整洁、没有污点。 ( )

17. 当买方不愿负担装卸费时,在商定合同时可要求在 CIF 后加列 Liner terms、Landed 或 Ex tackle 字样。 ( )

18. 保兑行是在开证行无力付款时才履行付款责任的,所以保兑行的付款责任是第二性的。 ( )

19. 在 CIF 条件下,卖方办理保险;在 CFR 条件下,买方办理保险。因此,在货运过程中货物发生损失,前者由卖方负责,后者由买方负责。 ( )

20. 结汇时的汇票通常一式两份,第一份为正本,第二份为副本,只有正本才有法律效力。 ( )

四、简答题

1. 对于外向型企业来说,正确、及时制作出口单证对收汇具有什么作用?

2. 简述本票与汇票的区别。

3. 按 CFR 术语履行合同时,为什么卖方要特别注意及时向买方发出已装船通知?

4. 我出口公司对外报价,某产品 50.00 美元/箱 FOB 上海,后外商要求改报 CIF 汉堡价,此货物按 W/M 计费,基本运费为 60.00 美元/运费吨,燃油附加费为 10%,体积为每箱 48×25×20CMS,毛重为 27 千克/箱,保险费率为 2‰,试计算我方应报的 CIF 汉堡价。(按惯例加一成,计算过程保留六位小数,答案保留两位小数。)

5. 我某出口公司收到美国开来的信用证一份,规定:最后装船期为 2018 年 4 月 30 日,信用证有效期为 2018 年 5 月 15 日,交单期为提单日期后 15 天,但必须在信用证有效期之内。该出口公司于 4 月 10 日装船,提单日期为 2018 年 4 月 10 日。4 月 28 日,该公司将做好的全套单证送到银行议付时,遭到银行拒绝。请问:银行拒付合理吗?为什么?出口商在此情况下应如何处理?

参 考 文 献

[1] 郭晓晶,周文苑.国际商务单证实务与操作——习题与实训指导[M].北京：清华大学出版社,2012.

[2] 郭晓晶,周文苑,秦雷,张楷卉.国际贸易单证习题集[M].北京：清华大学出版社,2013.

[3] 朱春兰,佘雪峰.外贸单证实训教程[M].北京：中国人民大学出版社,2015.

[4] 余世明.国际商务单证实务练习题及分析解答[M].3版.广州：暨南大学出版社,2009.

[5] 姚大伟.国际商务单证理论与实务[M].上海：上海交通大学出版社,2010.

[6] 龚玉和,齐朝阳.外贸单证实训精讲[M].北京：中国海关出版社,2013.

[7] 全国国际商务单证考试办公室.国际商务单证理论与实务[M].北京：中国商务出版社,2013.

[8] 中国商业企业管理协会.国际商务单证教程培训与考试指导[M].北京：科学技术文献出版社,2009.

[9] 上海市对外经济贸易教育培训中心.国际商务单证应试指导[M].2版.上海：同济大学出版社,2008.

[10] 国际商会.跟单信用证统一惯例——2007年修订本[S].国际商会第600号出版物.